EXAMPLES OF TESTIMONIALS
CONCERNING THE LAST TWO DECADES
OF
DORIS HELGE, PH.D.'S WORK

"You'll get instant positive results. The techniques are well tested and easy to use. You'll use Doris' tools and information every day."
  Marsha Needham, Human Resources Director, CNN News, Atlanta, Georgia

"You will receive rapid relief from difficult problems. If you want more fulfillment and happiness at work, this book is definitely worth your time and money. Whether you work in a large organization or out of your home, your satisfaction is guaranteed!"
  Bill Uhl, Senior Instructor, OHV Training™ and winner of six gold medals for the U.S.

"This is The Bible of Workplace Happiness! So much in one volume!"
  William Richards, Managing Director, Royal Bounty, International

"Dr. Helge's work creates immediate improvements in employee satisfaction and productivity. We've hired Doris to deliver several presentations. Our employees smile a lot more. They also read Joy on the Job *over and over. Our teamwork is now the best it's ever been!"*
  Pat Hollister, Marketing Associate, Allied Systems, International

"This book is addictive. You'll read it from cover to cover, again and again. It's guaranteed to increase your happiness at work."
  Kelley Sinclair, Medical Aid Technician, Chicago, IL

"This is different! It works! Doris' comprehensive research led to remarkable insights and techniques I use every day. Doris writes in such a warm, conversational style. I feel like she's talking directly to me."
  Kenneth Baker, Regional Manager, Cost Cutter, Inc.

"Doris' work will help you master life."
  Mark Victor Hansen, Co-author, *Chicken Soup for the Soul*

"Everyone who hears Doris' message gets charged and re-charged. After attending Doris' seminar, I got a promotion I'd wanted for a long time. Now, each day at work is more exciting."
Jeanette Geiman, CPS, Office Manager, Shell Oil, Houston, Texas

"Practical . . Positive . . Powerful! What a great speaker and author!"
Joan Sherwood, Ph.D., CEO, Corporate Training Assurance, Kansas City, Missouri

"Doris offered many solutions and tools that greatly helped our employees."
Anita Orton, Manager of Human Resources, Regence BlueShield

"Excellent! Exactly what we needed. Great job!"
Kim Lindenfeld, Director of Customer Service, NFL & President, ICSA

"Doris gave so many wonderful new tools I can easily use right now!"
May Munder, Executive Assistant, Exxon Oil, Houston, Texas

"Helge spent years formulating steps you can follow to become happier and more fulfilled. Her work is a roadmap to joy and peace."
Aquarius Magazine

"Doris' work brought multiple benefits to my radio audiences."
Elizabeth Ann Wright, Host, *Ultimate Solutions*, WGUN, Atlanta, Georgia

"You brought important information to our viewers, letting them know they are not alone and helping them know how to improve their lives."
Peter Anthony Holder, Host, *CJAD Tonight*, Montreal, Quebec, Canada

"Doris' work touched and changed my life forever."
Mollie Jo Rogers, President, ABWA

"I loved it! I got tools that gave me enthusiasm and endurance during tough times."
Ana Holland, Manager, Costco

"I've tried everything. Finally! Techniques that really work! Doris' wisdom and warmth make the lights go on when other approaches fail."
Sandy O'Donnell, Corporate Trainer, Nashville, Tennessee

"Doris is a winner in life and is able to communicate her winning skills and attitudes to others.
Dr. Jack T. Cole, Professor Emeritus, New Mexico State University

"I am proud to endorse your work. You have helped me."
Sue Bailey, board member, Washington Society of Meeting Planners

"Doris' work is a must for key decision-makers who want to stay on the cutting edge of business."
Chad Boyd, Corporate Communications Manager, IntelliNet

"Thanks to Doris, I am FINALLY able to balance my personal and professional life. This book is the best bargain of this century!"
Lynn Johnson, certified athletic trainer, Seattle, Washington

"I would love to attend another of Doris' events. Her program is excellent, and the seminar was definitely worth my time. Doris has extraordinary skills in working with a diverse group."
Becky Jarvala, Washington State Farm Bureau, Olympia, Washington

"Doris is a great speaker . . . a good investment that can save you money."
Marci Russo, Assistant Vice-President, Sun Trust Bank, Atlanta, Georgia

"I'll never forget your warmth and how you touched my life."
Carol Keeffe, author, *How to Bring What You Want Into Your Life With the Money You Already Have*

JOY
ON THE
JOB

*Over 365 Ways to Create
the Joy & Fulfillment You Deserve*

by

Doris Helge, Ph.D.

Shimoda Publishing

JOY ON THE JOB
Over 365 Ways to Create the Joy and Fulfillment You Deserve

By Doris Helge, Ph.D.

Published by: Shimoda Publishing
                       c/o 1225 E. Sunset Drive., Ste. #317
                       Bellingham, WA 98226-3529
                       shimodapub@mindspring.com
                       http://www.mindspring.com/~shimodapub/
                       Also see http://www.joyonthejob.info

          Printed and bound in the United States of America
                  10 9 8 7 6 5 4 3 2 1

              Publisher's Cataloging-in-Publication
                (Provided by Quality Books, Inc.)

  Helge, Doris.
     Joy on the job : over 365 ways to create the joy &
  fulfillment you deserve / by Doris Helge.
     p. cm.
     Includes bibliographical references and index.
     LCCN 2006925943
     ISBN 1-885598-05-X

     1. Job satisfaction. 2. Happiness. 3. Self-realization.   I. Title.

  HF5549.5.J63H35 2007   650.1
                                QBI06-600140

BOOKS WRITTEN BY
DORIS HELGE, PH.D.
AND PUBLISHED BY SHIMODA PUBLISHING

JOY ON THE JOB—
Over 365 Ways to Create the Joy and Fulfillment You Deserve

TRANSFORMING PAIN INTO POWER—
Making the Most of Your Emotions
(After foreign rights were purchased, this book,
originally published in English, also became available
in Spanish, Chinese, Malay, and Turkish.)

ENJOY A POSITIVE PERFORMANCE REVIEW

SECRETS OF WORKING WITH "DIFFICULT PEOPLE"

THRIVE INSTEAD OF SURVIVE
Over 365 Ways to Triumph During Change and Chaos

Contact:

Shimoda Publishing
shimodapub@mindspring.com
http://www.mindspring.com/~shimodapub/
or
Doris@joyonthejob.info
http://www.joyonthejob.info

WARNING—DISCLAIMER

TABLE OF CONTENTS

List of Exercises xvii
Dedication xx
Acknowledgements xxi

PART ONE   THE JOY QUOTIENT   1

Chapter 1   Are You Happy at Work?   3
  ✦ Identify your "joy quotient"
  ✦ Discover what you need so you can begin
    the joy on the job journey right now

Chapter 2   What's Different About This Book? 21
  ✦ You deserve to delight in your work as much
    as a cherished vacation. Exciting new tools
    and fun insights await you.
  ✦ Benefit from wisdom gleaned during a ten-
    year quest to discover strategies you can
    use immediately

PART TWO   STAKE YOUR CLAIM TO

HAPPINESS AT WORK 45

  ✦ Avoid delight-deficiency disorder
  ✦ Discover the secrets of achieving validation,
    fulfillment, and harmony
  ✦ Use proven, practical approaches to claim
    your fair share of joy on the job

Chapter 3   Avoid Delight-Deficiency Disorder 47
Stacks of studies have proven the benefits of happy
workers. Why does the business world struggle with
delight-deficiency disorder?

Chapter 4   Delete Joyblocks 69
You can immediately identify and remove barriers
to joy on the job

Chapter 5   Is There a Recipe for Happiness at
Work? 81
✦ Explore essential ingredients identified by
employees and managers in 21 diverse
organizations and occupations across the
North American continent
✦ Identify the elements of your work over
which you have the most control so your
efforts will yield remarkable results

Chapter 6   Curiosity Creates Joy 94
✦ Curiosity creates courage and courage
crushes fear
✦ Use the peephole in your mind to vaccinate yourself against negativity at work

Chapter 7   Self-Awareness + Acceptance
= Fulfillment 98
✦ Learn splendid new strategies for valu-
ing and rewarding the one person you
can count on working with for the rest
of your career
✦ Travel *The Self-Awareness Pathway.*
It's a direct route to joy on the job.

Chapter 8   Transform Blind Spots to Freedom 105
✦ Shatter the distortions that are draining your
  dreams
✦ Discover what you offer to the world of work.
  Don't cheat the world by hiding the radiance
  of your personal light
✦ Explore sleeping giants that surround you

Chapter 9   Fulfill Yourself With Focus 112
✦ Magnify the power of your focus. You will
  instantly foster peace and fulfillment.
✦ Why savvy companies favor focus instead
  of constant multitasking

Chapter 10   Own Your Power 126
✦ Don't survive . . . Thrive! You can bloom
  in the midst of chaos and uncertainty.
✦ Use self-reliance to create validation, job
  security, and fulfillment
✦ Discover proven methods for increasing
  awareness of your value and influence

Chapter 11   Meet Your Needs Now 135
✦ How to communicate your unmet needs
  and secure the support you need so you
  can achieve personal fulfillment and peak
  performance
✦ Notice how others benefit when they assist
  you
✦ Develop an excellent support system

Chapter 12   Fully Embrace Life 141
✦ Become *experientially gifted* by taking
  steps to ensure that setbacks are seeds
  for future success

Discover the bless within a mess
Cultivate a calm mind

Chapter 13   Reframe Versus React 153
You are the sole ruler of your inner domain (your
mind). Use this miraculous tool to create inner
peace, harmony, and enthusiasm. The world will
richly reward you.

Chapter 14   Use the Power of Negative Emotions 169
Discard the happy face paint
When is a bad mood a good mood?
Use productive thinking (not "positive thinking") to elevate your confidence, ensure
faith in the process of your life, and achieve
peak performance
Discover the miracle of using neutral observation to resolve "difficult people" issues
Explore stunning new ways to transform
negative emotions into positive energy

Chapter 15   Empower Yourself With Action 183
✦ Take advantage of unlimited possibilities
that are patiently awaiting your discovery
Take healthy risks to build self esteem and
produce joy at work
Summon *your inner genius* and other sur-
prising new resources
Choose to choose
✦ Select a positive parallel reality

Chapter 16   Bust Procrastination 200
✦ Discover and combat the root causes of
procrastination
Practice being perfectly imperfect

Chapter 17 Confront Control Issues 223
✦ You always have more control than you
think
✦ Discover what you can always rule over
✦ Learn how to reduce stress and disconnect the worry wart
✦ The control paradox. Explore the hidden
power of letting go of your internal
quarterback
✦ Use your innate abilities to respond to life
in a winning way

Chapter 18 Cash In on Your Strengths 260
✦ Create a work life that feels more like play
than work. Discover the secret hiding
places of your inner genius, including untapped gifts that masquerade as flaws.
✦ Support your strengths instead of warring
against your weaknesses
✦ Develop a signature style that will help you
cash in on your unique abilities
✦ What to do if you can't express your talents
where you work

Chapter 19 It's Flow Time! 283
✦ Experience flow. It's a wonderful state of mind
in which you work for the sheer joy of doing
an activity that challenges you in a positive
way while elevating your self esteem. Time,
fear, and doubt disappear. Favorable circumstances magically appear and propel
you forward. Feel-good chemicals flood
your central nervous system.

✦ Ensure that flow-producing activities are part of your daily work life
✦ Transform routine aspects of your work into a magnificent state of flow

PART THREE   MULTISENSORY, MIND-BODY TECHNIQUES FOR A JOYFUL JOURNEY 301

✦ Special tools create a powerful *internal* support system that will ensure your happiness at work
✦ Techniques include the use of "C.W.," the *Curious Witness*, which becomes your virtual assistant. You will also create an emotional anchor, a positive resource state, and use mind maps. These techniques will feed your creativity, confidence, joy, and job satisfaction. You'll also gain *The Intuitive Edge.*

Chapter 20   Tools for a Joyful Journey 303

Would you like to avoid emotional roller coasters and expectations that are a setup for disappointment? Discover how to substitute curiosity for harsh judgments of yourself or unpleasant experiences. Explore smart new strategies you will use daily to quickly and easily access valuable intuitive hunches. Practice whole-body techniques that link the rational and emotional areas of your brain. Because your creativity will soar, problem-solving will seem almost effortless. As difficulties shift into joy, you'll relish your profound trust of the process of your life.

Chapter 21 Meet "C.W." 305

✦ Connect with a sweet inner peace that is
always present within you, even when
your thoughts or emotions are in a state
of turmoil. Allow C.W., your *Curious Witness*, to become your 24/7 virtual assistant.
C.W. will calm your internal critic and connect you to your highest abilities. C.W.
automatically unleashes a cascade of priceless insights that compel you to let go of
struggle and judgment. Bliss becomes a
new *familiar zone.*

✦ Take charge of your own life by using this
remarkable source of creative solutions to
challenges.

**Chapter 22 Create a Powerful, Positive
           Resource State** 324

Alleviate anxiety by creating an emotional anchor
and a positive resource state. With a little practice,
you will instantly evoke and use these richly rewarding inner resources. These powerful tools also
boost your confidence, enthusiasm, and creativity.

Chapter 23 Map Your Way to Joy on the Job 343

Use this easy, enjoyable technique to turn on your
creative juices, easily solve challenges, and silence
your inner critic. This brain booster will also help
you deliver flawless presentations, avoid having to
take notes in meetings, and banish thought and behavior patterns that don't serve you.

PART FOUR JOIN THE MOST POSITIVE AND POWERFUL REVOLUTION ON PLANET EARTH 355

You are now equipped with a wide variety of proven, life-changing techniques that will help you claim validation, fulfillment, and joy at work. You have proven to yourself that there are no limits to the degree to which you can experience a richly rewarding work life. You are perceiving previously invisible sources of support for your happiness. Connect with a rapidly growing community of individuals who are producing miracles every day that stretch around the globe.

Chapter 24   You are the Miracle You've Been Seeking 357

REFERENCES AND RESEARCH NOTES 372
INDEX 390
ABOUT THE AUTHOR 432
BRING DORIS HELGE, PH.D. TO YOUR ORGANIZATION 436

LIST OF EXERCISES

What's happening now? 6
Are you valued and validated? 6
Is your workload realistic and fair? 7
Are you experiencing rewarding relationships
at work? 8
Are you receiving adequate professional support? 9
Is your work enjoyable? 10
Is your personal life balanced with your professional
life? 11
Are the organization's policies and procedures
appropriate? 12
Are managers and supervisors working on your
behalf while they serve the organization? 13
Does your physical environment promote your
well being? 15
Is the organization healthy? 16
Prioritize your needs 19
What's your truth? 41
Clear your consciousness 52
Shed more myths 58
Innies and outies 66
Why wait? 70
Desires versus preferences 76
What is already creating joy at work? 85
Create more joy on the job 92
Journey into the unknown 96
Reconnect with your real self—stage one 101
Reconnect with your real self—stage two 102
Correct blind spots—stage one 106
Correct blind spots—stage two 109
Correct blind spots—stage three 110
Discover your focus 114

Prove your power 117
Foster a fulfilling focus 121
Develop focus-ability 124
Use self-responsibility to build job security and fulfillment . 129
Validate yourself with an inventory 132
Secure the support you need 137
Take a second look 145
Focus on the future 147
Cultivate a calm mind 150
Pick a perception 156
Act it out 161
Picture perfect 164
Search your memory bank 166
Notice the effects of expectations 172
Discover a different approach 174
Transform negative emotions into positive energy 177
Discover your neutral observer 180
What have you got to gain? 187
Identify your pattern 189
Choose a focus that empowers you 190
Just say "now" 193
Choose choice 195
Ready for even more joy on the job? 197
What's the root cause? 201
Say goodbye to "Someday I'll _____ " 203
Notice the difference 205
Use self-awareness to overcome perfectionism 207
Practice being perfectly imperfect 208
You can do what you've done before 213
Create instant satisfaction 215
Sense your accomplishments 217
If you're really stuck 219
Identify what you can control 225
Choose which way to run 228

Alleviate anxiety with a new focus 231
Disconnect the worrywart 234
Feed flowers, not weeds 239
Consider optimism 241
Use awareness to develop peace of mind 245
Rev up your resources 254
Promote patience 256
Who's the fairest of them all? 262
Scavenger hunt 269
Intuit it 270
Scope out your spontaneity 271
Sell yourself 272
Discover your strengths in others 274
Gain from guidance 276
Develop a signature style 280
Find your flow 289
Set the stage with management 291
Experience flow every day 294
Create your curious witness—stage one 309
Create your curious witness—stage two 311
Strengthen your partnership with C.W.—stage one 316
Strengthen your partnership with C.W.—stage two 317
Establish your emotional anchor 326
Create a positive resource state—stage one 327
Create a positive resource state—stage two 331
Create a positive resource state—stage three 332
Disassociate—stage one 337
Disassociate—stage two 339
Mind map—stage one 344
Mind map—stage two 346
Mind map—stage three 351
Way to go! . . . More to go! 359
Break Free 367
You are the Miracle 369

DEDICATION

Joy is available to all of us in quantities that are absolutely unlimited, just as soon as we realize this is possible. This book is dedicated to the millions of employees who would describe themselves in one of the following ways.

✦ Workers who yearn for happiness at work but are mired in fear that they have few viable choices (such as having an unpleasant job or no job)

✦ Employees who are experiencing some work satisfaction but want even more of the fulfillment and joy to which they are entitled by birth

Each of you has special and unique gifts to contribute to the world of work. You deserve to savor your work as much as you would delight in an exquisite five-course meal prepared by an award-winning chef.

Enjoy your journey toward work that is consistent with your talents, dreams, desires, and personality.

ACKNOWLEDGMENTS

With greatest appreciation to sweet, wise, wonderful William.

To every participant in the field-test groups and seminars. Your sincere commitment to help others achieve happiness at work and your feedback regarding the *Joy on the Job* exercises made a massive difference. Now employees around the globe can receive solutions to their most difficult challenges. We all thank you!

An immense thank you also goes to Elizabeth Hendricks, Anell Tubbs, John Beveridge, Jackie Brazil, Taylore Vance, Roi Halse, Bill Harris, Paul Scheele, Lynn Camp, Melony Vance, Paula Brown, and Jan and Marc Ellis. Thanks so much for your expertise and support. Jennifer Moore, Craig Reisch, and Larry Rexroad, your special assistance came at exactly the right time. Many thanks to cover designer, John McMahon, for your expertise.

PART ONE

THE JOY QUOTIENT

❏ Are you happy at work?

❏ Discovering your unmet needs is the first step toward joy on the job.

❏ What's different about this book?

CHAPTER 1

ARE YOU HAPPY AT WORK?

Work is love made visible. And if you cannot work with love, but only with distaste, it is better that you should leave your work and sit at the gate of the temple and take alms of those who work with joy.
Kahlil Gibran[1]

MISERY IS AN EQUAL OPPORTUNITY EMPLOYER

Rose Carlson doesn't just dread the sound of the alarm clock on Monday mornings. She winces at the thought of going to work *every* morning. Carlson dreams about the weekend from Monday morning to Friday afternoon. She doesn't think her work is valued, her workload is unrealistic, and she frequently works mandatory overtime. Carlson complains, "I have no professional support system, and most of my work is mundane or meaningless." Her family worries about her because she has low energy, even on the weekends. Carlson is moody and often snaps at those she loves.

Do you think Carlson would be happier at work if her efforts were genuinely appreciated or if she felt her work was more meaningful? Read on.

Richard Brodie was a Microsoft employee who received company-wide recognition for developing a stellar piece of software. Many other employees admitted being as jealous as a green-eyed monster. Brodie was quickly promoted to a management position. Was he ecstatic? Brodie, like Carlson, was unhappy, depressed, and exhausted. In fact, he became so miserable that he quit his job and moved across the country. His true story provides evidence that joy on the job requires more than professional recognition for valuable service.

Brodie later described his personal journey from misery to delight and a return job at Microsoft in his book, *Getting Past Okay*. He explained that he hadn't determined what he needed to be happy on the job, and he didn't know how to ask for help.

WHAT DO YOU NEED?

> Needs and desires
> are often different.

Although money cannot buy happiness, joy on the job has been associated with success, higher income, and greater productivity.[3] Clearly, happiness at work is good business. Defining your legitimate needs will be one of your major tools for achieving joy on the job.

Desires, such as "I want to make a million dollars this year," are not absolutely essential. In fact, desires often pave the road to unhappiness. Identifying what you truly require to achieve happiness at work produces very different results. Until you know just how important it is to work for an organization you respect, do tasks that have personal meaning for you, or be surrounded by coworkers who support you, you will be distracted from your genuine goals. Gaining clarity will ensure that you feed your needs instead of focusing on desires that will not bring lasting joy.

> The following will help you create a more joyful work life.
>
> ✔ Separate needs from desires.
> ✔ Identify your unmet needs.
> ✔ Take specific steps to achieve personal fulfillment at work.
> ✔ Communicate your unmet needs to management, team members, and coworkers.

IDENTIFY YOUR JOY QUOTIENT

This chapter will help you discover your current joy quotient at work. You will immediately be able to design an action agenda. Your new plan will help you create a work life that is rich with joy, meaning, and fulfillment.

The questionnaire on the following pages was developed after collecting information from employees and managers in 21 highly diverse organizations. These included small partnerships, nonprofit associations, and huge international corporations. This self-test will help you identify specific goals for change so you can claim your fair share of joy and harmony at work.

WHAT'S HAPPENING NOW?

Use the following code to answer each question.

A	=	Always
S	=	Sometimes
AN	=	Almost Never
N	=	Never

ARE YOU VALUED AND VALIDATED?

_____ Do immediate supervisors and team members regularly express sincere appreciation for your strengths and contributions?

_____ Do you receive performance reviews that are fair and focus on enhancing your strengths while you correct areas that need improvement?

_____ Are criticisms of your work delivered in a respectful and private manner?

_____ Are your ideas and opinions sought and respected?

_____ Are your requests taken seriously?

_____ Are you fairly compensated for your work?

_____ Are you confident you will receive the assignments and promotions you deserve?

IS YOUR WORKLOAD

REALISTIC AND FAIR?

_____ Is your work schedule reasonable for the time and resources you have available?

_____ Can you focus on your work without being interrupted by the needs or demands of others?

_____ Are the tasks assigned to you meaningful and consistent with your abilities?

_____ Are your assignments clear?

_____ Do you have control over how and when your work gets accomplished?

ARE YOU EXPERIENCING
REWARDING RELATIONSHIPS
AT WORK?

_____ Do you enjoy positive relationships with coworkers?

_____ Do you feel accepted and valued by coworkers?

_____ Are you treated with respect?

_____ Are you able to relax, be yourself, and confide in others when you are at work?

_____ Do you trust your coworkers?

_____ Are you confident that others care how you are feeling?

_____ Do you feel safe expressing negative as well as positive feelings and opinions?

_____ Are conflicts with others easily resolved?

ARE YOU RECEIVING ADEQUATE PROFESSIONAL SUPPORT?

_____ Are your projects supported by other employees and departments?

_____ Do you feel comfortable meeting your needs when you are at work?

_____ Is there a clear path for your career development, including opportunities for advancement and growth?

_____ Do policies and procedures reflect a sincere concern for your personal, as well as your professional, needs?

_____ When personal issues or responsibilities interfere with your productivity, are you supported by encouraging individuals and a flexible work schedule?

_____ Does the organization offer timely and confidential Employee Assistance Program (EAP) services?

_____ Do you trust the organization to enact and enforce fair policies on your behalf?

_____ Is there an ongoing feedback system designed to assist employees in meeting clear performance goals?

IS YOUR WORK ENJOYABLE?

_____ Do you look forward to going to work each day?

_____ Is your work beneficial to others as well as meaningful to you?

_____ Is your work environment fun and non-threatening?

_____ Does your job offer multiple opportunities for learning new skills?

_____ Do supervisors understand that employees are more productive when they are relaxed?

_____ Do your workdays include healthy doses of play and laughter?

_____ Does the organization provide and encourage the use of stress reduction tools such as on-site yoga, meditation, massage, exercise equipment, and humor workshops?

_____ Do you remain in your present position because it provides positive challenges you enjoy as well as opportunities to develop your professional abilities?

_____ At the end of your work day, do you feel satisfied that you put in a good day's work and your efforts were appreciated?

IS YOUR PERSONAL LIFE BALANCED WITH YOUR PROFESSIONAL LIFE?

_____ In spite of workplace tasks and pressures, are you able to sleep well and to avoid "self-medicating" (over-indulging in food or alcohol)?

_____ Are you comfortable setting reasonable boundaries regarding your time, energy, and private needs?

_____ Do you still have enough energy and time at the end of your work day to fulfill your personal responsibilities?

_____ Are you usually as energetic as you want to be?

_____ Do you have time to do the things that matter to you, including spending time with family and friends?

ARE THE ORGANIZATION'S POLICIES AND PROCEDURES APPROPRIATE?

_____ Are workers asked to redesign tasks and organizational structure so they can do their jobs in the most productive and enjoyable manner?

_____ Are employee needs considered when new policies and procedures are designed?

_____ Are all employees equally valued?

_____ Are workers involved in making decisions concerning how and when they accomplish their tasks?

_____ Are employees consulted before the organization implements changes?

_____ Does the organization support and train employees who must enact changes?

_____ Are workers encouraged to meet urgent personal needs during work hours?

_____ Are employees encouraged to leave work tasks, cell phones, and e-mail behind during vacations, weekends, and holidays so they can enjoy leisure activities, regenerate, and nourish personal relationships?

ARE MANAGERS AND SUPERVISORS WORKING ON YOUR BEHALF WHILE THEY SERVE THE ORGANIZATION?

_____ Are you encouraged to provide feedback to supervisors and managers regarding their effectiveness?

_____ Is management supportive and respectful of every employee?

_____ Are the instructions you are given consistent with your assigned priorities?

_____ Is communication clear and consistent?

_____ Are required meetings meaningful and productive?

_____ Do you trust your supervisor?

_____ Does management understand that teamwork is not effective when the needs of individual employees are not met?

_____ Does management understand what truly motivates employees?

continued on the next page . . .

_____ Do the people in charge know what they are doing and understand what is required to accomplish your job?

_____ Are employees encouraged to express their true feelings and opinions?

_____ Is it effective for you to discuss your problems with management?

_____ Are decisions that affect you and your work openly discussed?

_____ Do managers and supervisors establish trust with their employees and lead by example and persuasion rather than by control or fear?

_____ Is your supervisor's management style consistent with how you prefer to work?

_____ Do managers and supervisors prohibit favoritism, power plays, and other abuses of power?

DOES YOUR PHYSICAL ENVIRONMENT PROMOTE YOUR WELL BEING?

_____ Does your work area have natural lighting?

_____ Does the organization protect you from electromagnetic frequencies (EMFs) and toxic radiation emanating from fluorescent lights, computer monitors, and other sources of toxins?

_____ Does your work area have fresh air or use quality air filters?

_____ Is your work area arranged in ways that facilitate your work?

_____ Are your office equipment and working space ergonomically designed?

_____ Does your work setting provide the privacy and quiet you need in order to do your best work?

_____ Are you shielded from any workers or clients who would try to intimidate or bully you or who are chronically negative?

IS THE ORGANIZATION HEALTHY?

If you work in a department that has a different culture than the larger organization, answer the following questions for your work group.

_____ If other job opportunities were available to them, would most employees choose to stay in their present positions?

_____ Is staff morale high?

_____ Does the organization have a strong commitment to receive and consider honest feedback from all employees?

_____ Do you agree with the direction the organization is taking?

_____ Can you depend on the organization to stick with its stated priorities and avoid secrecy, which creates distrust?

_____ Does the organization actively empower you to change things for the better?

_____ Does top management have a clear sense of how to make the organization success-ful and the competency to achieve this goal?

Use the following chart to tally your answers.

Category	Times marked	X	Value of category	=	Total
A		X	4	=	
S		X	3	=	
AN		X	2	=	
N		X	1	=	

Your total score = _____

If your total score is:

300 – 324 Congratulations! Your work setting is practically perfect. Are you happy at work?

230 – 299 Your work environment has a number of strengths. More often than not, you feel valued and your needs are met. This book can assist you in gaining *even more* fulfillment on the job.

continued on the next page . . .

181 – 229   You frequently feel overworked or under-valued. You may be dissatisfied with your work resonsibilities or have inadequate resources to do your job. You may also have difficulty balancing your personal life with your professional life. This can create unnecessary fatigue and impair your health. The tools in this book will definitely be of assistance to you.

80 – 180   Your work is providing serious challenges. It appears you are undervalued. You may not be adequately rewarded for your contributions, in spite of heavy responsibilities. Professional support is insufficient. It is not surprising that you often feel exhausted and are having difficulty balancing your personal and pro-fessional life. Read this book!

PRIORITIZE

The next step is to determine your greatest concerns so you can design specific goals for positive change. Rank ordering your needs will make the messages and exercises in this book even more useful to you. It will only take a minute or two to rate your requirements. Just look at the list below and arrange the items on a scale from one to ten. Number one represents your greatest concern. Number ten represents the area you are least worried about at this time.

Employees from the twenty-one organizations that originally used this instrument found their first responses valid, so don't spend a great deal of time analyzing the list or the order in which you rate each item.

PRIORITIZE YOUR NEEDS

At this time, my greatest needs at work are as follows.

_____ Be valued and validated, from verbal appreciation to monetary compensation

_____ Have a realistic and fair workload

_____ Experience rewarding relationships with others at work

_____ Receive adequate professional support

_____ Do work I enjoy. This includes experiencing challenges that are related to my interests and appropriate for my abilities.

_____ Balance my personal and professional life

_____ Make sure the organization's policies and procedures are appropriate

_____ Make sure managers and supervisors are working on my behalf at the same time they serve the organization

_____ Have a physical work environment that promotes my well-being

_____ Make sure the organization is healthy

Note the items you marked as your top three priorities. Write down one to three goals that will help you experience more joy on the job. Keep this initial list in mind as you read this book.

Be sure to refer to your priorities and goals as you read each chapter. You will gain new insights, confidence, and enthusiasm. This will help you refine your desires and move forward more rapidly than you may have thought possible.

FEED YOUR NEEDS

You have now taken the first step in an exciting new adventure! You will immediately be able to use the unique and powerful approaches in this book to claim your fair share of joy and harmony at work.

If you want the sun to shine on you,
should you wait for the dawn
or chase the sunset?

If you opt to chase the sunset . . .
an endless journey . . .
you will see the world
in its most beautiful light

Rick Jackson

CHAPTER 2

WHAT'S DIFFERENT ABOUT THIS BOOK?

When I look at the future,
it's so bright, it burns my eyes.
Oprah Winfrey

THE PAIN DRAIN

Work is the single greatest avenue for most people to fully express their special talents and experience personal growth while contributing to society. More people than ever feel they have a right to happiness at work, but studies indicate that most of today's employees are unhappy in their present positions.[1]

Global marketplaces, new management practices, and technological advances have charged the world of work with more tension than ever before. "Wired and tired" managers and employees complain about fuzzy markers between their personal and professional lives. The pace of work has accelerated as productivity demands have escalated. "Digital assembly lines" often discourage creativity and independent thought. Electronic surveillance has become widespread.

Change and insecurity appear to be constant corporate companions. Four generations of workers now compete for the same jobs. Experienced elders are often taught new programs by tech-savvy youth. Chronic complaints regarding gender communication barriers are often overshadowed by clashes between individuals of diverse cultures and those who speak different languages.

As a result, job satisfaction has reached a record low in many countries.[2] The most important developments in the future world of work might not be new technologies but ways to lift the human spirit.

Fortunately, only a few significant insights stand between your current situation and one in which you usually feel contented and fulfilled at work. Begin by considering the perspectives below. They were gleaned from a ten-year quest to discover and share solutions from across the world.

DOWN WITH BLAME

Many workplace policies blame employees for their unhappiness at work. They advocate a shape-up approach that admonishes workers to change their attitude or even quit their jobs so they can discover their right livelihood. Books often blast ill-tempered bosses and corporate culture while providing tips for getting along with difficult people. Because such approaches generally dwell on *symptoms* rather than *causes* of the problem, they offer a meager menu of possible responses.

> Notice why and how
> blame disempowers you.

✦ Change is an inside job. It is rare that one individual can force another to modify his or her behavior on a long-term basis. Of course, you can never coerce someone to adopt a certain attitude or belief. Because most people want to be accepted just as they are, attempts to alter them initiate a resistance to change. It is a basic law of physics that force creates counterforce. More effective ways to influence the behavior of others will be discussed throughout this book.

✦ Since it is virtually impossible for a lone employee to single-handedly change an entire organization, blaming your dissatisfaction on a toxic corporate culture promotes the belief that you are powerless. It also maintains a focus on problems rather than on options for resolving your challenges.

> The premise for blaming individual employees and managers for today's unhappy work scenario is also invalid. It is based on the assumption that someone is deficient or wrong and needs to be corrected. Consider another perspective.

Regardless of their positions, the vast majority of today's workers simply want to go to work, have a nice day, do a good job, and know they have earned their pay. There are very few truly heartless, incompetent, or anti-social people. Most of the corporate executives in today's global, pressure-cooker environment feel as vulnerable as do their employees.

This book is based on the
following assumption.

I'm OK.
You're OK.
However, there really is a problem.
The problem is specific unmet needs
of employees.

You have already identified your unmet needs. Now you will be provided specific solutions for coping with workplace hurdles. This material will help you alter perceptions that impede your ability to resolve challenges and reframe negative situations to your advantage. You will avoid being mired in *the blame game,* a hopeless melodrama that inevitably results in a no-win situation.

WORK IS NOT ABOUT WORK

Work is a way to make a living, but it is also a major component of the School of Life. Those who adopt the point of view that work is more about learning and growing as a person than about the surface issues of products and pay feel richly blessed by the continuous flow of challenges they experience. Meaning becomes a magnificent motivator. Concerns about job status, compensation, perks, and power pale. Then, as if by magic, those aspects of their jobs take care of themselves.

Happy employees are as curious as an enthusiastic preschooler about what they will learn next. Because they don't resist challenges, new dilemmas unfold in a gentle manner. Each produces more joy than the last. Eventually, there is little separation between work and play.

HAPPINESS IS A CHOICE

You would be powerless if happiness at work were caused by any external event, person, or circumstance. Understanding that happiness is a conscious choice, rather than an automatic response to external stimuli, provides you with tremendous freedom. You become confident that you have the ability to create joy at work each and every day.

Happiness is a state of mind. Mastering the content of your inner life is much easier than you may have thought. You, and you alone, have the ability to control your thoughts and attitudes. Your workplace joy will be directly related to the degree to which you do the following.

> ✦ Experience meaning and fulfillment on the job.
> ✦ Accept responsibility for creating and maintaining a peaceful and contented state of mind.
> ✦ Refuse to blame anyone or anything for the circumstances of your work life.

Once you determine what does and does not make you happy at work, you can always place yourself in the driver's seat. This book is helping you accomplish the following.

✦ Learn to achieve joy on the job by seeking meaning at work instead of chasing after the elusive butterfly of happiness.

✦ Discover the incredible freedom that arises from accepting personal responsibility for a-chieving peace and contentment.

✦ Gain new sources of autonomy, even if you previously felt you had no control over your work life.

✦ Divorce yourself from the social programming that work is the opposite of play.

✦ Practice an abundance of proven techniques for creating joy and fulfillment on the job. These include developing a signature style, sharing your special talents, redefining problems in ways that serve you, and creating magic moments.

POWERLESSNESS DOES NOT CAUSE UNHAPPINESS AT WORK

Pause for a moment and reflect on the last time you were unhappy at work because you felt you had no control over an unpleasant situation. Do you think those who are placed in higher-level positions have the authority to change situations or direct the efforts of others in ways you do not?

Most employees think someone is powerful at work if they have the ability to manipulate others or force them to do what they would not choose to do on their own. *In truth, those who feel empowered do not seek to control the actions of others. Only those who feel powerless do so.*

Genuinely powerful people, such as Mahatma Ghandi, who led an entire country to victory, align themselves not with forceful actions but with causes that serve all concerned. They seek win-win solutions instead of using force because they know that coercion creates counterforce.

Recognizing and effectively using your personal power is a major key to creating happiness on the job. Unfortunately, personal power is one of the most misunderstood concepts in the workplace.

Perhaps the greatest addiction in our society is the addiction to the *illusion* of being powerless. *Most people unconsciously fear their personal power.* Why? Once they acknowledge how capable they truly are, they can no longer consciously blame others for their circumstances or feelings. Instead, they leap out of a familiar zone. They leave their known reality, which is not serving them, and enter a level of personal freedom they never dreamed possible.

This document is helping you accomplish the following.

✦ Uncover any hidden resistance to acknowedging and activating your full capabilities.
✦ Let go of fear of change. Lose an old identity of "powerlessness."

JUDGMENT IS A SELF-CREATED PRISON

A key principle of this book is that all experiences, including those that are the most unpleasant, are opportunities. A story is often told concerning how Oprah Winfrey learned that negative experiences are gifts in disguise. According to the legend, young Winfrey was sobbing during an airplane flight because she had just been told she wasn't talented enough to host a radio show. After expressing empathy regarding Oprah's disappointment, her wise seatmate remarked, "Honey, there's something much better waiting for you. You'll find out what it is, and you'll be so glad this radio opportunity didn't work out."

After Oprah was told by numerous media executives that she lacked the "right stuff" to hold the attention of audiences, she stopped trying to function in the image-conscious, negatively-oriented media she did not agree with. Then, magic unfolded. One building block after another steadily fell into place until Oprah formed her own network. She created an organization consistent with her own goals and beliefs, a media giant focused on empowering her audiences.

When frustrated, all of us sometimes blame unpleasant events or the actions of other people for our unhappiness. When we do so, we cause ourselves additional problems.

+ We give away our power.
+ We forfeit the freedom to create the peaceful state we desire.
+ We stifle our personal growth.

We handcuff ourselves each time we ask, "Why me?" "Why this?" or "Why now?" during an event that feels unpleasant. As we focus on negative judgments concerning a situation, a domino effect occurs. We reinforce the idea that we are victims. We feed our fears and false beliefs. In reality, we are simply having a life experience which offers a particular opportunity for growth. When we whine and pine, we delay our next step forward because we miss clues for positive change that are patiently awaiting our discovery.

We become liberated when we stop judging workplace experiences in negative ways. Without negative judgments, it is impossible to blame anything or anyone for our challenges. This frees us to perceive obstacles as learning experiences that empower us. That point of view paves the road to joy on the job.

The exercises in this book are helping you achieve the following.

✦ Prove to yourself that negative workplace experiences are gifts in disguise.
✦ Transform related emotions from negative to positive.

SECURITY IS A TRAP

Helen Keller believed, "Life should be a daring adventure or nothing." Consider the enormous contributions to the world made by this courageous deaf and blind woman who traveled the world. The more risks she took, the more her gifts and talents multiplied, and the more she inspired everyone in her presence. She opened many doors for those who have disabilities, and her life's story challenges all of us to meet our full potential. How do her contributions compare with those made by we who chain ourselves to a limited potential by striving to maintain economic or job security in a world where neither exist?

Security is a dangerous illusion that cheats far too many people out of the opportunity to fully experience life. Humans are hardwired to thrive as a result of realistic challenges—not stagnant conditions. In fact, we are quickly bored when we are not challenged.

So-called comfort zones are actually *familiar zones.* We allow fears, misperceptions, and old habits to cloud our vision and thwart healthy risk-taking. We swim in a sea of repetitive thoughts and perform automatic, robotic behaviors like a school of fish that stays in its known reality instead of exploring a giant ocean filled with infinite possibilities.

Unlike fish, the human brain craves new discoveries. Change is an essential ingredient for human survival and growth. It is also required for consistent joy on the job.

Self-confidence often declines when we are cozy and content, but it escalates when we muster the courage to meet intense challenges. Only when we flee the well-lit prisons of safety and security do we discover that we thrive in dark, scary circumstances that can only be illuminated by our inner light. In the darkness, we explore and eventually accept our shadows. These are characteristics that are unfavorable, but part of the human condition. Examples include cowardice, rage, greed, and jealousy. In dim and gloomy circumstances, we realize our innate resiliency.

Security fails to result from routine, predictable actions, but it bursts forth as a spontaneous blessing for those who explore the adventurous simply because they crave wisdom, meaning, and personal growth.

Illuminate your work life internally because nothing can dim the light that shines within you.

Tiptoeing around to avoid making an error may help you dodge some mistakes, but you will sacrifice joy on the job.

This document is empowering you to accomplish the following.

+ Determine when a desire for security conflicts with your needs for autonomy, independence, and personal freedom.
+ Access and follow the wisdom of your intuition.
+ Identify and take healthy risks rather than clinging to the illusion of security.
+ Develop the true source of safety and stability—peace of mind.
+ Explore your full potential so you can use your work as a way to accomplish your life purpose.

> Gain fulfillment
> by leaving the
> comfortable and
> convenient behind
> so you can follow
> your heart's desire.

Happy employees take healthy risks. Because they shun the "safe" path of habitual, meaningless, and unproductive behavior that compromises self-discovery, their work lives are a consistent source of personal growth. They experience a great deal of joy at work because they are constantly in touch with a rich array of inner resources that help them resolve challenges.

NEGATIVE EMOTIONS ARE FRIENDS IN DISGUISE

Instead of perceiving anger as inherently destructive, this book recognizes the true nature of angst and ire.

✦ Anger is a normal human emotion.

✦ Annoyances are often essential ingredients for improving your life.

✦ Irritation is a symptom of unmet needs.

✦ Anger is often a mask used to disguise deeper, more uncomfortable feelings. It is easier for many people to become enraged than to experience hurt, fear, shame, or the fear of rejection.

✦ Ill feelings are usually surrounded by positive attributes. These can be employed for the advantage of everyone concerned. Anger is almost always evidence of passion for positive change. Intense displeasure also indicates a state of heightened awareness and focus.

Anger and fear are packed with power. You can use these potent forces to create positive changes at work. You only have to learn to experience negative emotions in constructive ways that benefit everyone concerned. Attempts to deny or repress anger cause it to fester and erupt, usually at inappropriate or inconvenient times. You are reading material that will help you channel anger in ways that produce the results you truly desire.

In the end, you will discover how to use all emotions, including those you once judged to be negative, as fuel for creating fulfillment and happiness at work.

THE CRITIC IS NOT YOUR ENEMY

The internal voice chattering that you are not capable or that you lack the advantages you need to achieve happiness or success at work is often so infuriating that you want to chop out its larynx. Forget that you've been advised to banish the critic!

✦ It has served you since you were a small child.
✦ You can befriend this guardian in disguise and redirect its powerful voice to help you achieve your dreams.

Secrets for transforming the internal critic are spread throughout this book. Your critic is already a loyal employee, even though it is sometimes off-track. You can transform it into your personal virtual assistant.

ACCEPTING WHAT EXISTS IS THE KEY TO POSITIVE CHANGE

Reliable and rapid ways to create *misery* at work include the following.

✦ Negatively judging yourself, your circumstances, or your emotions
✦ Resisting, instead of accepting, your present situation

Of course, it is necessary to recognize and address problems at work. It is also essential to take appropriate actions concerning aspects of your own performance that you desire to improve. However, your ability to accomplish these goals will be severely limited if you are consumed with negative judgments, resentment, bitterness, or unnecessary stress.

> Typically, we do not accept situations we don't like because we fear they will never change if we honor their existence. The irony is that the very act of accepting what exists initiates positive change!

This book is helping you achieve the following.

✦ Discover the magical balance between attempting to change what you don't like and accepting things as they are.

✦ Accept situations that can't be changed so you will focus your energy on efforts that produce joy at work.

✦ Learn how acceptance of what you judge to be off-track spontaneously alters an unpleasant situation to your advantage.

✦ Prove to yourself that the process of your work life is always unfolding to your advantage.

Contrary to what you have been taught, there is absolutely nothing wrong with your current circumstances. Life is a journey, and you are always where you are supposed to be at any particular time. When you understand that, you stop struggling and your path becomes much easier.

Even if your present situation feels uncomfortable, it is the perfect way for you to learn more about yourself so your next adventure can naturally unfold. Your stresses are essential to the process of positive change. They are the ideal steppingstones for you to achieve self-actualization. The tools presented herein provide clarity and reduce your resistance to life's experiences so you can fully gain the value available from them. This is why individuals who used the methods in this book *spontaneously* alleviated situations in their work lives that felt painful.

DON'T TRY TO CHANGE YOURSELF

A young prince once searched for years to find the perfect blossom to present to his bride-to-be. As he traveled through each division of his father's kingdom, he was shown hundreds of varieties of flowers. He carefully analyzed the size, scent, and beauty of every bloom, comparing each with the memory of all he had previously assessed.

The prince awoke one day with a startling realization. He could spend his entire life searching for the perfect blossom, or he could acknowledge that every flower is a masterpiece and return to the love of his life.

You have similar choices. One option is to expend all of your energy attempting to be perfect and trying to bend and mold your work life to fit your image of perfection. Life will respond with such a sly and endless resistance that another option is worth considering.

Perfectionism is a frustrating full-time job that produces a pitiful rate of pay. Since the end results of perfectionism include being perfectly miserable, perfectionism is inconsistent with joy on the job and is not advocated in this document. There are far easier ways to create positive change.

You can realize that both you and your life are already in perfect harmony. You can trust the process of life and fully embrace it just as it is. Then you will benefit from every morsel of learning available, and you will avoid unnecessarily repeating difficult challenges.

Although you will naturally change some of your life patterns or habits as a result of reading this book, the objective of the manuscript is not to create change. *The intent is to increase your awareness of existing behaviors, patterns, and attitudes because self-awareness spontaneously creates change.*

Change occurs naturally. *Trying to* alter behaviors or attitudes is evidence of resisting what exists. Since force creates counterforce, resistance inhibits change. When you simply *notice* your current behaviors and attitudes without judging them, they spontaneously shift as needed.

When you acknowledge your shadow side without judgment or resistance, it has no control over your behavior. In fact, once you observe *any* behavior pattern, it no longer has power over you. It may hang around a little while as a test so you can prove you will no longer unconsciously feed it, but it will eventually disappear.

A RICH RELATIONSHIP WITH YOURSELF IS THE ULTIMATE SHIELD AGAINST WORKPLACE NEGATIVITY

Although most business courses emphasize skills for relating to coworkers, managers, or customers, the easiest and quickest way to develop more enjoyable workplace relationships is to consciously cultivate a rich relationship with yourself.

Self-respect is the most powerful and dependable support system you can cultivate. The external world of work mirrors your relationship with yourself back to you—usually, in a magnified manner. This powerful reflection enables you to see yourself clearly. Then you can choose to function in ways that are consistent with your true potential.

As an example, when you perceive that those around you are not owning their power, you may decide it is time for you to stand up for yourself or engage in additional training that will help you demonstrate your true potential. After doing so, you will be rewarded with a mirror of more contented and empowered coworkers.

This document is helping you do the following.

+ Identify "human mirrors" at work so you can see yourself more clearly.
+ Recognize benchmarks so you can measure your recent progress.
+ Get to know and accept your shadow side because self-awareness, without judgment, creates spontaneous positive changes.
+ Identify your strengths so you can capitalize on them.

BRING YOUR BODY TO WORK

You have often been told to focus on using your mental abilities and technical skills while maintaining a positive attitude. Although these attributes are essential to your success, consider the following perspective.

> You will not access your full potential or achieve lasting happiness at work until you know how to fully engage your body, mind, *and* spirit while you conduct work tasks.

Since scientists have proven that the mind and body are one, this book provides a multitude of ways you can accomplish the following.

✦ Engage the full array of your sensory abilities. This will relax you while stimulating your full mental potential.

✦ Signal your nervous system to reach a state of emotional balance during intense mental challenges.

✦ Reduce stress by engaging your body in your work even when you are sedentary.

✦ Consciously use physical movements, your posture, and your breath to fight fatigue and elevate your confidence, mood, and mental abilities.

DOWN WITH DIFFICULT PEOPLE

While it is popular to label others as emotional vampires or toxic bosses, this strategy is doomed to fail. It also postpones joy and fulfillment on the job.

> When we label someone else "difficult," we give away our power.

Although one individual cannot change another, when we modify our own interactions or perceptions, the behaviors of so-called difficult people usually spontaneously change. Our actions elicit different behaviors in them as *human mirrors.*

Blaming discourages collaborative problem-solving, and conflicts are seldom one-sided. In addition, labeling others as difficult does not help them learn what they need to learn.

The universe operates like a giant boomerang. As soon as we label someone else as difficult, the favor is sure to be returned. Even small conflicts escalate.

In other people, as well as within ourselves, negative behaviors and attitudes are actually symptoms of unmet needs. Understanding this empowers us to take positive actions.

Because those labeled difficult are often merely different, the difficult people syndrome contradicts the reality that we all need to work with individuals from other cultures and belief systems.

If we really want to meet our full potential at work, we will fully engage with the exotic buffet of growth opportunities provided by those we label difficult. Although we often do not fully appreciate our teachers, we learn to communicate better not by talking with those who read our minds but by interacting with those who cannot comprehend our wisdom or motives. We become more tolerant by observing others being intolerant. We increase our patience by engaging with those who test our patience.

> Difficult people
> are presents
> camouflaged
> as problems.

When you adopt the new paradigm described in this book, you will be able to do the following.

+ Quickly detect and reframe misperceptions about others.
+ Discover how your style of interacting affects others so you can make small adjustments that achieve remarkable results.
+ Use your innate wellspring of creativity. This natural resource can help you easily diminish defenses and build bridges when confronted by challenging situations with other individuals.

TRUTH AND CONSEQUENCES

If you would be a real seeker after truth, it is
necessary that at least once in your life you
doubt, as far as possible, all things.
René Descartes

In the previous chapter, you identified your unmet needs and determined your priorities for positive change. In this chapter, you explored some of the ways that social conditioning has twisted the truth and stifled your ability to create a more enjoyable work environment.

Illusions become harmful when they are unconscious, so your increased awareness will liberate you to determine your own truth. If you are open to the possibility of new understanding, test the ideas in this chapter. You will easily create opportunities to do so. Anything you cannot prove to yourself is not your truth at this time. Just consider it as a possibility until a later date.

WHAT'S YOUR TRUTH?

1. Describe some of the distortions you have been taught about happiness at work.

2. Since you are now aware of these illusions, you can establish your own truth and believe in your own perceptions. How will your new awareness help you create a more fulfilling work environment?

BENEFIT FROM PROVEN PRACTICAL APPROACHES

If you have yearned for happiness at work but have been mired in fear that there are only two choices in your work life—an unpleasant job or no job—know you don't have to relinquish the sweet dream that you can find personal fulfillment at work.

This book is packed with over 365 practical, no-cost strategies that are already in use by employees around the world. The approaches will prepare you to directly resolve your challenges without waiting for the organization where you work or another individual to change. In fact, you will be able to increase your enjoyment at work immediately. Use the questions, exercises, and sidebars in each chapter to achieve the following.

+ Identify, communicate, and fulfill your unmet needs.
+ Develop a healthy awareness of your personal power.
+ Ensure support and positive feedback within the organization, including during performance reviews.
+ Create emotional anchors and positive resource states that will support you during testy situations.
+ Shield yourself from workplace negativity.
+ Bring humor and fun to work on a daily basis.
+ Claim your fair share of joy, validation, and fulfillment.
+ Create a work environment consistent with your talents, dreams, and personality.

Over time, the social programming that work is *work* will fall away. Don't be surprised when your job becomes more and more fun and the ever-expanding mystery that is you unfolds.

It's always fun to do the impossible.
Walt Disney

PART TWO

STAKE YOUR CLAIM TO HAPPINESS AT WORK

❑ Avoid delight-deficiency disorder

❑ Discover the keys to workplace happiness so you can claim your fair share of joy, validation, and fulfillment

❑ Use proven, practical approaches to create happiness and fulfillment at work

CHAPTER 3

AVOID DELIGHT-
DEFICIENCY DISORDER

You know what happens in the beehive?
They kill the drones.
William Poage

HAPPINESS AT WORK IS NOT AN OXYMORON

Study after study has validated the productivity, financial, and other benefits of happy workers.[1] Since the jury has made its decision, why does most of the business world continue to struggle with delight-deficiency disorder?

❑ Work and Fun are Viewed as Opposites

This myth persists in spite of stacks of studies showing that most of the happiest people on this planet receive joy and personal fulfillment by expressing themselves and their abilities at work. Many career training programs promote the point of view that work is *a necessary evil.* Employment counselors often help clients match their skills to available jobs while neglecting their long-term vocational desires and passions.

In reality, many employees are so passionate about their work that they have to be coaxed to take vacations. To them, work is play, so they often combine vacations and work.

❑ The Thank God It's Friday Syndrome

This affliction is perpetuated by both employees and managers. Supervisors who have never created a work arrangement that generated peace and contentment think it is impossible to experience a continuous flow of joy on the job. Most managers are trained in almost every topic relevant to increasing productivity except methods of fostering joy on the job.

❑ Corporate Tunnel Vision

Too frequently, companies don't perceive the competitive advantages of an organization filled with smiling employees. Satisfied employees produce satisfied customers. Organizations that focus on employee fulfillment reap handsome benefits in productivity as well as in more subtle discretionary efforts of workers. Happy employees are more creative and loyal than their disgruntled peers. Gratified workers are committed to positive outcomes of their teams. They are more apt to help others who need their assistance.

Employee-centered workplaces also achieve significant savings. Lawsuits diminish. Absenteeism decreases. The cost of health insurance and disability claims declines. Employee turnover and tardiness are remarkably reduced.[2]

❑ Joy Alarms

As illustrated on the next page, organizations are not solely to blame for delight-deficiency syndrome.

Olly: Work . . . work . . . work! Morning until
        night . . . morning until night!

Molly: You poor guy! How long have you
        been at your job?

Olly: I start tomorrow.

The majority of workers think joy on the job is available in limited quantities. Most of us set an internal *joy alarm* to ensure that we do not experience more than our quota of bliss at a given time. Happiness is so poorly understood that joyful people are often viewed as abnormal. In an article in the *Journal of Medical Ethics,* Richard Bentall, a Liverpool University psychologist, jokingly classified happiness as a psychiatric disorder. His reasoning? "Happy people are dangerous because they can be unpredictable."[3]

❏ Happiness and Pleasure are Often Confused

Pleasures occur in the present moment. They are often transient. These good feelings are often experienced through readily available, temporary gratifications such as good food, sex, movies, and other amusements. Unfortunately, most people are starved for the bliss that travels hand-in-hand with meaning and fulfillment on the job.

The media often portray laborers gathered at the local bar after work as the most guilty of confusing pleasure and happiness. However, this myth was shattered three decades ago by a groundbreaking book, *Working,* written by Studs Turkel.

Mr. Turkel revealed discussions with laborers in jobs such as gravediggers, skycaps, and hospital aides. Even in chats with laborers who performed the lowliest jobs, conversations that began with mundane details concerning their work rapidly moved into the realm of the existential. Employees conducting all types of jobs search each day at work for daily meaning, not just for daily bread. Savvy workers nourish themselves on the job with a steady diet of long-lasting nutrients like peace, contentment, and joy. Short-term pleasures are embraced as occasional, nonessential desserts.

> *Pleasure without joy*
> *is as hollow as passion*
> *without tenderness.*
> Alan Jay Lerner

❑ Unconscious Addictions

Most of us are addicted to unhappiness and fear of the future, even if just at a slight level. Even though it is often subtle, the social programming during the current age of anxiety is intense and pervasive. If you wonder if unhappiness is a comfort zone for you, remember the last time you engaged in any of the following.

✦ Didn't feel at ease with your joy because those around you weren't happy

✦ Felt devastated by another person's negative comments instead of considering their state of mind

✦ Didn't reward yourself for a job well done because, "*There is so much more I need to accomplish*"

✦ Blocked your success by not taking advantage of an opportunity

✦ Received what you wanted but still felt dissatisfied

✦ Were unhappy in spite of the fact that nature's beauty or other free sources of joy surrounded you

✦ Dragged the past into the present. Have you ever woken up *expecting* to have a bad day at work? If you commute to work during rush-hour traffic, notice how often you grimace as soon as you slide into your vehicle.

❑ "Selfish Software"

Many people have been programmed to think it is narcissistic to seek more fun at work.

Newsbreak:

Being happy is altruistic!

You're more helpful and compassionate when you genuinely sing a happy tune on the job. You're also more productive, more creative, and a better team worker. As explained earlier, you save your organization money. This indirectly increases the profits available to pay all employees.

Joy creates an open state of mind so you can build lasting, positive relationships with coworkers. Because you view others as individuals instead of members of racial or other groups, you connect with other people more easily. Since rapport with others is often noted as a key source of meaning and joy at work, a beautiful cycle unfolds.

You're also more resilient to potential stressors when you enjoy your work. You bounce back from setbacks more quickly and easily. Happiness at work may even save lives! Did you know the most common time of death for working adults is at 9:00 on Monday mornings?[4]

CLEAR YOUR CONSCIOUSNESS

Answering the following questions will help you shed any "selfish software" lurking in your unconscious.

1. Describe how your increased happiness at work can benefit the organization where you work as well as your team, co-workers, or customers.
2. How will your ability to bounce back from setbacks lower your stress, enhance your health, and increase the quality of time you spend with loved ones?

CONDITIONS THAT WILL NOT CREATE HAPPINESS

Advertising and other social programming constantly pound your consciousness with misconceptions concerning how to create happiness. You can make more money. You can look better or smell better. You can buy things to enhance your status.

The first step toward happiness is to dismantle the slick packaging you have been sold. Your ability to experience bliss at work is not based on any of the factors described in the following section. Your happiness is not dependent on *anything* external to you.

❑ The State of the Job Market or Economy . . . The Degree of Organizational Toxicity

It may be easier to sing a happy tune when the economy is booming than when unemployment lines are long. Smiles may be spontaneous when employers are tripping over each other trying to seduce you with the highest pay and the most outrageous perks but scarce when organizations are downsizing. However, millions of employees achieve bliss at work despite some pretty dire working conditions. This isn't because they put on a happy face or persuade themselves to think positively. These employees know how to maintain inner piece when pink slips are rampant. They are contented even when their jobs don't match their competencies. When loud machinery runs nonstop, they hum a pleasant song. When chaos triumphs over reason, they watch for an opportunity to help push the pendulum the other direction.

❑ The Actions of Other People

Millions of happy employees are surrounded by potential bullies, loud-mouthed grumps, and workers who just won't carry their fair share of the workload. In spite of difficult conditions, contented employees exude tranquility. How do they do it?

✦ They trust the process of life. They understand that every challenge is an opportunity to learn and grow.

✦ These resilient individuals expect and embrace constant change.

✦ They are aware that no one but themselves can create a smile on their face.

✦ They understand that depending on others for approval is a perfect recipe for unhappiness. Those we expect to validate us are compelled to mirror our neediness back to us by disapproving of who we are or our actions. This "gift in prickly wrapping paper" eventually teaches us to rely on internal, instead of external, approval.

❑ Job Status or Rate of Compensation

You have met blue-collar workers who have higher job satisfaction than CEOs. How many wealthy attorneys do you know who are bored with jobs in which they shuffle mounds of paperwork but can't convince themselves to engage in a lower-paying job? Physicians are increasingly dissatisfied because they lack autonomy over their work and feel they can't effectively serve their patients.

During the last fifty years, a variety of researchers have clearly established that money is not related to job satisfaction. Money is such a poor motivator that, even in lean times, salary ranks well behind factors such as doing an interesting job and working with enjoyable people. Rank and title tend to be more important than pay in determining how respected employees feel, but, in job satisfaction polls, both are dwarfed by purposeful work, a flexible schedule, and other aspects of a positive corporate culture.[5]

Although money can't buy happiness, joy on the job can definitely escalate the wealth of your inner life. A desire for status or money may compel you to ignore your vocational passion and accept a job you won't enjoy. While fame and fortune can be tempting, they can't produce enduring happiness because they cannot fulfill your psychological or spiritual needs. No wonder Mark Twain frequently advised people to "work like you don't need the money."

❑ Perks and Possessions

Neither perks nor the possessions that one's salary can buy create happiness. Employees who own the most possessions are only as likely to be happy as those who own the least.

However, those who value what they have are twice as likely to be happy as those who actually own the most possessions.[6] People who appreciate what they have and don't worry about how it compares to what others have tend to be the happiest. They value what they have far more than they worry about what they don't have or can't afford.[7] In fact, happy people waste very little time or energy making social comparisons. When they do, they rapidly recoup from disappointments.

❏ Your Dream Job

Most social scientists agree that we have a genetic *setpoint* for happiness. Some of us have focused on our deficits and the ways life has disappointed us since we were small children. Others consistently find the sunny side that is available in even the most dismal circumstances.

After obtaining their dream job, a person with a setpoint oriented toward unhappiness will fairly quickly discover that someone else has a more prestigious job or a larger office. Pretty soon, the individual whose glass is always half-empty is as disgruntled as they were before achieving their goal.

A person with a setpoint oriented toward happiness operates with a different style. Far from a Pollyanna, this individual feels momentary disappointment after being passed over for a higher-level position. However, he or she quickly regains a hopeful attitude and identifies potential advantages.

> A fulfilling life
> doesn't create
> a happy person.
> A happy person
> has created
> a fulfilling life.

When happy people are disappointed, their balanced perspective and trust of the process of life produce comments such as, "It must not yet have been time for me to get this promotion. I'll find a substitute goal for now. Then I'll be even more prepared when the time is right for me to advance. In the meantime, I'll use this opportunity to develop new skills and enjoy my loved ones more."

Happy people have high hopes that are also realistic. They expect life to be meaningful, and they design opportunities for enjoyment.

Although we all have emotional addictions that are reflected in our neural networks, our brains are pliable. A tendency to interpret life situations in dysfunctional ways can change with awareness, intention, and willpower, and the tools in this book will prepare you to do this.

❑ A Reason to be Happy

Smiling children are amazed when adults ask them, "Why are you so happy?" Kids know they don't need a reason to be happy. Employees who easily ride the ups and downs at work have a similar outlook. They choose balance and tranquility rather than basing their moods on external circumstances. Individuals who can jump for joy—without a reason—haven't forgotten that our natural state is bliss.

❑ Rowing Your Boat Without Concern for What Your Oars Touch

The discoveries of physicists such as David Bohm and Rupert Sheldrake[8] have confirmed that everything in the universe is connected with everything else. Their experiments also validated the old saying, "What goes around comes around." Because we are all linked, our decisions and behaviors affect other people. It is essential for us to be aware of how our motivations and actions fold back in upon themselves. When our decisions and behaviors are supported by the intention to promote the good of all concerned, we simultaneously create the potential for personal happiness.

❑ The Ability to Force Others to Accept Your Point of View or Follow Your Instructions

David Hawkins, M.D., author of *Power vs. Force,* conducted thousands of experiments to determine what thoughts, beliefs, desires, and motivations would weaken subjects' bodies and which would strengthen them. Hawkins' results overwhelmingly indicated that aligning one's self with integrity, excellence, love, compassion, and forgiveness was empowering. Aligning with revenge and negative judgments, on the other hand, was disempowering. Such negative beliefs, thoughts, and desires weakened the bodies of subjects involved in the experiments.[9]

People who feel empowered have no desire to control or manipulate others, and they would not feel joyful or fulfilled if they did so. They understand that some individuals feel a temporary sense of satisfaction when using force against others, but they are not personally motivated by this short-term point of view. They gain peace and long-term satisfaction by living their truth and aligning themselves with positive approaches that solve problems.

IDENTIFY ILLUSIONS

Most of us unconsciously suffer from illusions regarding what will and will not create joy on the job. Distortions are supported every day by the media as well as by individual workers and managers, but you can gain clarity that will produce peace of mind. The next exercise will help you continue to discover and shed myths.

SHED MORE MYTHS

Make a checkmark by any of the following factors you previously thought were related to your happiness at work.

_____ The behavior of other people

_____ The state of the job market

_____ The degree of toxicity in your organization's culture

_____ The economy

_____ Job status

_____ Salary

_____ Level of recognition

_____ Perks

_____ Job duties

_____ The degree to which others agree with your point of view

_____ Your ability to force others to follow your instructions

> Acknowledge your ability
> to create your happiness

HEROIN HIGHS . . . OR INNER PEACE?

Nan and Drew are sales representatives at Busy-R-Us, Inc. Even though they both go to the same sales training events, their work styles and results are dramatically different.

Drew favors the fast track. His focus is rigid. He is consistently attuned to winning sales competitions. At home, Drew's wife, Terri, worries when Drew is gloomy or preoccupied as he sits in an easy chair staring at the mantle. "What's wrong, Honey?" she reaches out. "You look so tired, and you seem so restless."

Drew's answer is always the same. "Oh nothing, I guess. I'll just be so happy if I can win the next sales competition."

Terri sighs as she glances at a mantle and wall filled with years of awards. She often wonders if Drew's entire career will pass by, and his kids' childhoods, while the family waits for Drew to be happy. With each award, he enters the house beaming, "I'm pumped! I just got the sales award again!" The family celebrates a bit, but within a short time, Drew is sullen and focused on the next competition.

Terri, a mental health professional, sums it up. "Drew's searching for something none of us and no medal can give him. His highs are like that of a heroin addict. He goes on and on about how great he feels in the moment he wins, but after a brief bubble of ecstasy, he's down in the dumps waiting for another shot of something to make him smile."

While Drew continues to promise himself that another victory will produce happiness, Nan views happiness as a "side effect." She doesn't concern herself with competing, and she takes pride in living a balanced life. If you're wondering if Nan is a slacker, a gander at her office wall demonstrates she has also won more than an average share of sales competitions.

What is Nan's secret to success? Her words follow.

Because I'm very in the moment, I don't miss the journey. While many other people focus on and worry about competitions, I live the entire adventure.

Whether it's exciting or ho-hum, I stay centered and trust my vibes. If I get a hunch to call a potential client I've never called before, I do it. If it feels like I'm wasting my time pitching to a client who's supposed to be a sure thing, I go another direction.

I'm at work one-half of my waking hours, so my job's got to bring me joy. I figure as long as the company is selling valuable products—and it does—I'll use the job as a tool for personal growth. That perspective peaks my interest, which maintains my enthusiasm, so everyone wins.

People come and go. Challenges come and go. Awards come and go. The only things that will remain no matter what my job may be are my personal goals to stay balanced in spite of anything that happens and to have fun every chance I get. I don't wait for a company award to make my day.

Instead of waiting for a reason to be happy, Nan structures her work life in ways that ensure a state of balance. These include the following.

✦ Being guided by her intuition
✦ Consciously experiencing each moment
✦ Focusing on what she can learn

SHORT BLIPS VERSUS CONTENTMENT

Nothing outside of yourself can make you happy. This includes promotions, pay raises, key assignments, or words of praise, although any of these can produce a temporary exuberance. As illustrated by the true stories of Microsoft employee Richard Brodie in chapter one and Drew in this chapter, feeling on top of the world can produce surprising, unpleasant effects.

✦ A sensational high often triggers a deep longing to clear up related, unresolved issues.
✦ The experience often initiates a craving for additional moments of ecstasy.

Momentary highs are a fun part of being human, but they feel almost trivial once you have developed the ongoing tranquility and balance the tools in this book can help you achieve. A deep-seated peacefulness is the key for transcending every challenge that emerges. A calm and curious spirit ensures your ability to spontaneously access your intuition.

Inner peace provides you the keen judgment and the certainty of a sailor who braves storm after storm, knowing that the depths of the ocean remain serene underneath surface turmoil.

True happiness is not a quick fix of pleasure or fun, but the bliss that results from emotional balance. This condition is unfamiliar to the majority of the population. Most people have been chasing rainbows for a very long time because they have been unable to identify what they truly crave.

> *Happiness is not in our circumstances,*
> *but in ourselves. It is not something we see,*
> *like a rainbow, or feel, like the heat of a fire.*
> *Happiness is something we* are.
>   John B. Sheerin

We never discover peace or happiness outside of ourselves because bliss is rooted deep within our core, in a rich inner life and in the present moment.

Most people compare each minute to a time in the past they have labeled as a standard to re-create. The sad irony is that moment wasn't valued when it existed. In fact, it was lost. Instead of delighting in the glorious sensations it offered, they were too busy to experience it. Their minds were consumed with comparing it with a potential positive event in the future.

A series of enjoyable, permanent changes unfold when you truly attain a state of emotional balance.

+ This condition becomes a benchmark by which you gauge your other emotional states.
+ You return to it time and again, with less effort.
+ You don't allow external circumstances to diminish your capacity for joy.

While you are the only person who can define what happiness feels like for you, it is important to identify the difference between short bursts of ecstasy when you think something outside of yourself makes you happy and deep, continuous feelings of peace and balance. True contentment emerges when your work feels meaningful and you are personally fulfilled on the job. The chart on the next page illustrates the difference.

RACE FOR THE GOLD	DISCOVER THE GOLD WITHIN
✦ Something external, such as a compliment, promotion, or recognition, triggers a short burst of joy.	✦ You are confident you are doing good work.
	✦ You know you are making a meaningful contribution.
	✦ Your work is appropriately challenging, so you are always expanding your abilities.
	✦ The work itself feels meaningful to you.
	✦ Because you feel fulfilled, your job is a source of satisfaction and personal growth.

The next chart describes why *the race* may produce only temporary pleasure, while the discovery process feeds emotional balance and long-term peace of mind. Pursuing pleasure can be like chasing a gorgeous kite in a hurricane wind. When we madly pursue a source of transient elation, we lose the ability to create long-term happiness. Genuine happiness is free. Bogus joy is like counterfeit cash. When the fraud is eventually unveiled, we feel emptiness and loss.

RACE FOR THE GOLD	DISCOVER THE GOLD WITHIN
✦ Your self-esteem is related to external circumstances that are out of your control. Therefore, it is unlikely that "winning the race experiences" contribute to life mastery. You may be unable to repeat a particular positive experience. Your joy will likely disappear or decrease when the event or the original excitement about the external recognition subsides. Then you will hunger for an additional boost.	✦ Your self-esteem is related to who you are (your values and intentions) instead of being based on specific actions, such as what you produce. Since you are the master of your emotions, you have control over how long your joy lasts. Because your ability to experience joy is not dependent on an external situation, you regenerate positive feelings at will. You create meaning in each moment.
✦ Your transient elation is an adrenaline high like that experienced by a racer who wins one event but then must wait for another victory	✦ An ongoing state of bliss emerges from being conscious in each moment, fully embracing every challenge life brings you without neg-

continued on the next page . . .

before experiencing any additional delight. ative judgments, and trusting that each experence will provide insights and wisdom. Every obstacle in your life educates, entertains, or enlightens you.

Some individuals are naturally competitive. If you are such an individual, it is easy to determine whether an adrenaline rush benefits you in the long-term. Simply consider your responses to the following questions.

✦ Do you feel more capable or worthwhile when you win and someone else loses?
✦ Can you internally validate your achievements or do you feel dependent on another person or something else that is external to you?
✦ Are you satisfied and contented between competitive achievements, or do you feel restless, anxious, or unsatisfied?
✦ Is it necessary for one person to lose in order for someone else to win?

Consider the possibility that you will achieve lasting, rather than temporary, joy when you find ways to contribute to the happiness of others. We make a living by what we get, but we build a wealthy life by what we give.

The next exercise will help you clarify short and long-term sources of joy on the job.

INNIES AND OUTIES

1. During the next week, identify internal and external
   sources of satisfaction at work. Examples include
   the following.

External	Internal
✦ You win an award.	✦ *You* recognize you are doing a good job.
✦ Your work is praised.	✦ You notice your work has value or meaning for yourself or others.
✦ You receive a promotion or a raise. You are told others gain value from your efforts.	✦ Your work challenges you to learn or grow. For example, you discover how to make repetiteve tasks meaningful. You decide they are a good way to learn to be more patient or to develop greater compassion for others. You create a signature style of completing a routine job. You take pride in the quality of your work.

continued on the next page . . .

2. At the end of the week, read what you wrote concerning internal and external sources of joy on the job. Recall the feelings you experienced during the actual events. Which sources provided you the most job satisfaction—internal or external?

3. Which column has the most entries?

4. Which sources of job satisfaction produced a greater awareness of your abiities? Genuine confidence cannot be taken away from you!

5. Do you have more control over external or internal sources of joy and fulfillment?

6. Which column contributes to your long-term bliss and a state of balance?

Enjoy the pleasure afforded by the short-term bursts of joy that come your way. Keep the positive evaluations and letters you receive in your desk drawer so you can pull them out for review when times are tough. At the same time, be very conscious of the long-lasting effects of internal sources of satisfaction.

DISCOVER LASTING SOURCES OF JOY ON THE JOB

> *If an Arab in the desert were suddenly to dis-*
> *cover a spring in his tent, and so would always be*
> *able to have water in abundance, how fortunate he*
> *would consider himself. So too, when a man who . . .*
> *is always turned toward the outside, thinking that his*
> *happiness lies outside him, finally turns inward and*
> *discovers that the source is within him.*
>
> Søren Kierkegaard

The world of work is packed with people who trample others and sacrifice their values in a futile search for happiness from external sources. Most of these individuals never comprehend that the only lasting sources of happiness lie within themselves. They never discover the vast wealth of inner contentment that is always available to them.

The power to change yourself is the power to change the world around you. The next chapter will explain how you can avoid the most common barriers to joy on the job.

CHAPTER 4

DELETE JOYBLOCKS

Is there anything that men take more pains about than to render themselves unhappy?
Benjamin Franklin

Willy: At my last job, I waited for my employer to make me happy. That never happened, but it created a strong determination to find happiness at my current job.
Lilly: Have you?
Willy: I'm still trying to jump over hurdles.
Lilly: Check for joyblocks.

We personally erect the major roadblocks to our happiness at work. These barriers include the following.

✦ Waiting for reasons to be happy
✦ The seekers syndrome
✦ Missing the meaning
✦ Judging or resisting what exists

WAITING FOR REASONS TO BE HAPPY

As illustrated in the next exercise, when we delay feeling joyful until we have a reason to be happy, we give away our personal power.

WHY WAIT?

Get some paper and a pen and be ready to write with your nondominant hand. If you are right-handed, your nondominant hand is your left hand. If you are left-handed, it is your right hand. Using your nondominant hand activates different areas of your brain than writing with your dominant hand. This provides new sources of information for resolving challenges.[1]

1. Complete the following sentence stems by writing as rapidly as possible. Record the first thoughts that come into your mind. Don't edit. If no thoughts occur, just scribble on your page until insights come to you because the act of scribbling will build feedback loops in your brain. Continue writing until you have recorded all of your thoughts.

    ✦ I'll be happy at work when _____.
    ✦ I'm waiting until _____.

2. Review your answers.

continued on the next page . . .

3. Are you waiting for something outside of yourself to signal that it's time to experience happiness at work?

4. Which of the circumstances you are waiting on are under your control?

5. Which situations are not?

Happiness is a choice, not a condition. Joy on the job will not emerge as a result of a certain event. Are you aware that you can produce your own signals to tell your nervous system to feel contented, relaxed, or blissful? Exercises throughout this document will help you do this.

✦ You can give yourself permission to be contented now, rather than waiting for a certain event or outcome to occur.
✦ You can achieve happiness and own your power by positively influencing the situations that you can affect.
✦ You can signal your nervous system to create a state of emotional balance.

THE SEEKER'S SYNDROME

Happiness at work means different things to different people. Betty thrives on high-stress challenges. Bryan enjoys what he calls "mindless, repetitive work" because it allows him to think about the novel he's writing at night.

There are many ways to push workplace joy away. A highly effective method is to engage in a scavenger hunt for happiness because joy is similar to a beautiful butterfly. Both are very difficult to catch if you chase them. However, when you sit quietly, the butterfly eventually lights within perfect view and happiness warms your heart.

> Even though happiness is a choice, you will never be happy as long as you want to be or try to be.

Although setting goals is important, goals can limit your achievements, particularly regarding your enjoyment of life. This is because most goals are based on desires. "I want . . . " usually originates either from the belief that you lack something you need or the fear that a situation you dread will occur. In either case, you are empowering doubt and feelings of neediness or fear. You are focusing on what you don't want instead of on what you want.

This is truly a cultural obsession. We are blasted with hundreds of advertisements each day that strive to convince us that we are unhappy, others are happier than we are, and we need certain products or a certain lifestyle to be contented. Our tears and fears are usually equal to our desires.

The most magnificent aspect of the fact that no one else can make you happy is that you are totally in control of the degree to which you are delighted, peaceful, or contented.

> Happiness at work is an inside job.

MISSING THE MEANING

Good or excellent working conditions do not ensure joy at work any more than difficult environments guarantee unhappiness. A dramatic illustration was reported to the Monks of New Skete, authors of *In the Spirit of Happiness,* by a Nazi concentration camp prisoner who had dug ditches with Victor Frankl. When the fellow prisoner complained about his fate to Frankl (who later wrote *Man's Search for Meaning*),[2] Frankl explained, "This is where you've got to find your happiness—right here in this trench, in this camp."[3] Frankl helped countless individuals during and after the war understand that it is possible to be just as happy in a horrific concentration camp as when experiencing life's more enjoyable environments.

As discussed earlier, it is impossible for you to make yourself happy at work by fishing for joy. Frankl didn't search for happiness. He made a decision to consciously experience each moment of his life. Unlike most of us when experiencing trauma, instead of trying to overcome his pain, Frankl probed his daily life in a constant quest to discover meaning. Knowing that wisdom is derived from experience, he allowed all aspects of life to touch him—those that made his gut retch, as well as those that were pleasant. His only expectation was that the meaning of each event would be unveiled to him at some time.

You won't always be in a blissful state of flow of work, but you can always follow Frankl's example and discover meaning in every challenge. This book provides the tools you need so you can do the following.

✦ Stop chasing the elusive butterfly of happiness and commune with it.

✦ Experience the contentment that spontaneously emerges when you consciously and fully experience each workday.

JUDGING OR RESISTING WHAT EXISTS

We all desire to improve certain aspects of our work lives, but we delay our progress when we feel a desperate *longing* for something different.

> Struggling with what exists stifles positive change. When you feel an urgent need to modify something about yourself or your life, you are a prisoner of what you want to change. This is because you are operating within a framework of lack and desire. This causes emotional turmoil because your attention is consumed with a focus on what you don't want. Whether it is wanted or unwanted, whatever you give your attention to will expand.

Additional quick and easy ways to cheat yourself out of workplace happiness by resisting what exists are covered in other chapters. Anxiety-producing techniques include comparing yourself to others and attempting to deny or suppress negative emotions.

You cannot walk north and south at the same time, so decide which of the following scenarios to empower. One choice is to worry about or hone in on a specific desire. Your feeling that you don't or can't have what you want will create a more intense craving for what you don't have. You will identify with the statement, "I don't have what I want," and you will be distracted from your true goals.

Understand that your subconscious mind is your obedient servant. The subconscious ensures that what you say, do, feel, and possess is consistent with the images it receives from your conscious mind. Your loyal subconscious accepts the instructions you give it, without question. Most of us unconsciously program our subconscious with fear-based thoughts. Then we wonder why we experience an unpleasant reality.

It is important to monitor your thoughts. Rather than creating internal resistance by trying to change thoughts and beliefs, just observe them. Simple awareness initiates a spontaneous change progress. Notice that your thoughts are emotions (joy, sadness, fear, etc.) that are rooted in so deeply that they have produced new seed.

When you are consumed with ideas such as, "I need this assignment," "I wish I felt supported by others," or "I must have this promotion," you are programming a work life that emphasizes lack. You are also feeding worry and other sources of disharmony. A second, more effective scenario entails the following.

✦ Identify your needs and preferences as you did at the end of chapter one.

✦ Recognize that you deserve to receive your preferences.

✦ Trust the process of your life.

Employees who adopt this approach identify with the statement, "My preferences—or something even better—will emerge in my life at the perfect time." The true path to peace is paved by trusting the unknown while avoiding negative judgments concerning life's unpleasant experiences. Techniques for walking this path are discussed throughout this document.

In this second scenario, instead of being consumed with struggle and unhappiness, your energy is fully available to you in each moment. You perceive every clue you need concerning your best next steps at precisely the right time.

These signals are always available to you. You simply need to allow yourself to receive them. When you select option two, you spontaneously take actions that demonstrate your special abilities and your sense of accountability to a positive future.

This more neutral stance is not based on anger concerning what exists or fears about the future. Because you are not functioning from a sense of lack, your preferences become reality faster and easier.

DESIRES VERSUS PREFERENCES

Craving a specific situation, such as meaning and fulfillment at work, keeps it beyond your reach. This exercise illustrates how the desire for happiness can create unhappiness.

1. Identify an area in your work setting in which you feel an urgent need for change. Feel related sensations in your body, particularly in your throat, chest, or gut.

2. Imagine that you no longer have a desire for the situation to be different—that you do not feel a yearning to be happy at work. Instead, assume for just a moment that you feel perfectly okay with every aspect of your current situation. Think of yourself as if you are a beautiful calm lake located in the heart of your work environment.

continued on the next page . . .

3. Notice the difference in how your body feels. Do you feel happier just because you temporarily relinquished your desire to be happy?

> You can more easily achieve happiness by focusing on your internal state of mind than on aspects of your work environment that you cannot control.

4. Experiment with the approach you practiced in steps 1-3 during the next few days. Notice that when you stop thinking about something, your desire for it disappears.

Most of our so-called needs are based on a distorted desire to achieve the illusion of security. Since inner peace is the only true tool for feeling secure, once we obtain what we thought we wanted, our insatiable ego screams that we must achieve something else. Throughout history, sages have been grateful for their current circumstances and trusted that all of their needs would be met, and the universe responded accordingly.

Numerous exercises in this book, such as the Emergency Mind-Calming Technique, will help you quiet your mind and accept life on its own terms. Intuitive insights will be more readily available and propel you toward harmony and fulfillment.

Just recognize that you will not lose anything if you let go of a perceived need for things to change. In fact, your fondest dreams will most likely manifest when you let go of the desire for something different. The key will be a shift in your attention. It is that simple! You begin to notice what you already have and what is working for you. An attitude of gratitude emerges. Since what you focus on expands, you spontaneously create more of what brings you joy.[5]

When you are no longer preoccupied with thoughts of what you think you must have, you have relinquished your attachment to a certain outcome. As if by a miracle, what you said you wanted becomes available. In other words, you don't have to let go of the preferences you identified in chapter one. Continue to be aware of them. At the same time, be willing to release feelings and thoughts related to neediness or lack.

ADDICTIONS TO UNHAPPINESS

Because we have been so programmed to expect and allow only a certain degree of joy in our lives and have ridden so many emotional roller coasters, most of us initially question our judgment when we step away from the melodrama of a frenzied world. Ongoing tranquility feels strange. It lacks drama, so our internal critic clamors for attention. It screeches like a wild monkey in captivity that desperately longs for a more entertaining

world, "This is boring. Where's the challenge?" The latter question really means, "Where's the struggle?" Unfortunately, most
of us then fling ourselves back into our familiar zone. We fret
about problems that are nonexistent, initiate an argument, or
engage in other self-sabotage.

When you quiet the critic and allow peace to reign, you eventually comprehend that most of us have been unconsciously
choosing to be unhappy. We have traded one concern or problem for the next because negative thinking has been our known
reality. We know how to function when we are dissatisfied, so
this known reality is comfortably uncomfortable. We know what
to expect, and we are unwilling to change.

The first time I realized just how unconsciously addicted
I was to focusing on problems and feeling distraught while I
dragged past dilemmas into the present, I was horrified. I had
been enabling a vicious cycle composed of steps like the following.

+ "This situation is so unfair. I just hate it! It re-
  minds me of past circumstances that also hurt."
+ "I'll handle this problem somehow."
+ "Whew! I'm sure glad that issue is resolved."
+ "Oh no! Here's another stinking problem to re-
  solve! This reminds me of another negative
  thing that happened to me in the past."
+ Endless repetition of the cycle (ad nauseum).

It requires courage to swim against the social current and
allow yourself to experience more and more joy on a continuous basis. Of course, the rewards are amazing. You will radiate
an inner light that most people never seek, much less obtain.
You will be a happy, fulfilled individual whose mere presence
inspires others to choose joy instead of fear and discover their
full potential.

STAKE YOUR CLAIM TO HARMONY AT WORK

Genuine joy is similar to the Biblical phrase, "the peace that passeth understanding," because it is almost easier to experience than to explain. It includes such a profound sense of harmony and contentment that no external chaos or vile circumstances can cheat you out of your happiness. You are fully present in each moment. Because you observe your work world without expectations or judgment, nothing and no one can rob you of your tranquility.

Life is short.
It's up to you
to make it sweet.
Sarah Louise Delaney

CHAPTER 5

IS THERE A RECIPE
FOR HAPPINESS AT WORK?

*Happiness must be cultivated.
It is like character.
It is not a thing to be safely
let alone for a moment
or it will run to weeds.*
Elizabeth Stuart Phelps

The idea to write this book originated after I delivered a keynote address to a very distraught audience. The participants were members of a national organization concerned with organizational and employee wellness. They were employed by a wide variety of industries, large and small, across North America. I had first addressed the group two years earlier, and a number of the participants had corresponded during the two-year lapse. During the first few months, their spirits were high as they related how they were using the techniques they had learned at the convention in their daily work lives. Then one after another experienced major changes on the job. These changes tested their courage, their trust in the process of life, and their stress reduction skills.

In preparation for the second keynote, I conducted a follow-up survey with the entire group. Over half of the original participants had been downsized. Many had moved to new locations so they could find other jobs and provide for their families. Others had been directed to take on the duties of colleagues who had been let go, but they were still performing most of their previous assignments.

Participants whose organizations had not restructured or downsized were also experiencing the effects of organizational stress. Over three-quarters of the group felt drained by increased performance demands and other pressures that had piggybacked on the installation of new technologies. The most distressing response from the questionnaire was that the vast majority of the participants feared the worst was yet to come.

I poured my heart into preparing for the event and conducted telephone interviews with a representative group of participants. I also searched for the keys that were helping some employees remain peaceful and enthusiastic during a tumultuous upheaval in organizations across America. A research assistant and I reviewed U. S. Bureau of Labor Statistics data and poured over hundreds of studies concerning employee satisfaction and job fulfillment.

My goal was to pack as many proven ideas as possible into the forty-five minute presentation and to remain available afterward to share more ideas with individuals who wanted to chat. The audience was so hungry for information that I ended up staying an extra day to work with informal groups of convention attendees.

One thing led to another as participants corresponded after the event, providing feedback concerning what ideas and strategies worked for them when they reached their home offices. As I branched out to work with additional groups, it became quite clear that there is an overwhelming need for the information in this document. During the next few years, many groups and individuals volunteered to field-test specific segments of the material.

Over time, a book seemed like the logical way to share the information on a widespread basis. I will never forget what a relief it was to have the original draft available when a seatmate on an airplane flight asked, "Isn't happiness at work something that only exists in a fairy tale?"

WHERE IS THAT RECIPE?

> *Happiness, that grand mistress of all the*
> *ceremonies in the dance of life, impels us*
> *through all its mazes and meanderings,*
> *but leads none of us by the same route.*
> Charles Caleb Colton

Why is there no magical formula for workplace joy? Happiness is self-created. It is an internal state of mind that people experience and describe in unique ways. We are all individuals with distinct needs and preferences, and there are thousands of workplace contexts. To add to the complexity, what you need and prefer today will probably change at another point in your life. Betty may eventually tire of the high-profile, high-stress job challenges that thrill her today. When Bryan completes the novel he is working on at night, he may become bored with the repetitive tasks he now prefers during his day job.

ARE THERE ESSENTIAL INGREDIENTS?

The ideas in these pages are based on the foundation that is described below.

> There are unlimited possibilities concerning how to experience delight while earning a living. Happiness is always available. It patiently awaits your discovery.
>
> Employees do have some common needs, preferences, and values. According to the workers in 21 diverse organizations, joy on the job is more likely when even one of the criteria described on the next two pages exists.

In order to blur the line between work and play, you need to know what is already providing you satisfaction. Even if your job seems like drudgery, there are areas where your work is already like play. It will benefit you immensely to identify current sources of satisfaction so you can build on the foundation your past choices have established. As you work through this book, you will identify how you want to use your job as a flame to light your soul and achieve your purpose in life. After all, work is not really a way to make a living. It's a way to create a more joyful life.

WHAT IS ALREADY CREATING JOY AT WORK?

The conditions described below are related to joy on the job. Place a checkmark by each situation that you currently experience. Then allow the material in this book to help you create even more frequent episodes of happiness at work.

_____ You believe that your work is meaningful and can benefit others.

_____ You are engaged in appropriate levels of challenge. This stimulates new ideas and you develop new skills.

_____ You know how to gain support, positive feedback, and coaching from supervisors and team members.

_____ You can take advantage of growth and advancement opportunities.

_____ Your work is consistent with your personal needs, values, and goals.

continued on the next page . . .

_____ Your work nurtures you as a holistic individual composed of a body, mind, and spirit.

_____ Your imagination and curiosity are stimulated by your work responsibilities.

_____ You know how to grow from mandated changes.

_____ You possess the skills to meet challenges posed by "difficult people."

_____ You know how to develop a relationship with time that empowers you to accomplish your goals without undue stress.

_____ You balance your personal and professional life.

_____ You know how to reduce stress.

_____ You transform your internal critic into a valuable resource.

_____ You create a sense of autonomy even when you have no control over some aspects of your work environment.

_____ You take advantage of every opportunity to bring fun to work.

Happiness is not a destination. It is a method of traveling. Joy on the job is not a product. It is a byproduct of seeking the meaning of your professional and personal life. Because happiness is a choice, you can select particular ways of navigating through life that will most likely result in joy and contentment. You can trust the process of life. You can be more curious than judgmental. You can laugh and love more while embracing all of the stages of your work life.

IS THIS THE RIGHT STUFF?

Criteria for the inclusion of the topics covered in this book included the following.

✦ Participants across the North American continent indicated that the issues were their most significant concerns.

✦ The topics concern the elements of your work over which you have the most control. Thus, they are the areas in which focused effort will yield the most remarkable results.

You have the ability to discover, create, and master every single characteristic associated with joy on the job.

Happiness is a matter of owning our personal power. Bliss belongs to those who choose to develop a rich inner life and experience tranquility as frequently as possible.

CHARACTERISTICS TO CULTIVATE

As the project that produced the content in this book unfolded and suggested strategies were used by employees in a variety of occupations, socioeconomic groups, and cultures, it became apparent that no specific job circumstances are required for workplace happiness. However, certain behaviors, beliefs, and characteristics can facilitate joy on the job. This section briefly outlines those qualities. Subsequent chapters provide more descriptive material as well as exercises that will help you integrate the strategies into your daily work life.

☆ Develop a Rich Relationship With Yourself

This is absolutely the most important ingredient in a joy on the job stew. Future chapters include exercises that will help you live your values, befriend your inner critic, and stop wasting energy comparing yourself to others. You can be praised, raised, and recognized without compromising your personal life or values.

☆ Be Aware of Your Strengths and Passions

When you are aware of your unique talents, life purpose, and passions, you dramatically increase your ability to be well-compensated while you make a unique contribution to the world. Recognizing your abilities enables you to generate your own sources of happiness. You identify and use all of your choices, and you feel comfortable asking for the assistance you deserve and need. You can also change some of the aspects of organizational culture that cause unnecessary frustration or stress.

☆ Practice Acceptance

Although one of the first steps toward joy on the job is to identify your needs and preferences, it is equally important to accept the current conditions of your work life. Labeling circumstances you cannot control "negative" paves the pathway to pain. Your resistance—your focus—invites more of what you don't want. You encourage your inner critic to babble. The opposite happens when you are at peace regarding what exists. Your sense of harmony helps you graduate yourself to a new and better stage of your life because you perceive hidden opportunities available in your current situation.

☆ Choose to Experience Rather Than Judge

Make a commitment to steer clear of judging yourself, life, emotions, and other people. When you consciously experience every aspect of your work environment without judgment, you leave yourself wide open for positive change. Because you are fully present, instead of wishing you were living in a more enjoyable future or past, you learn the lessons available in all events of life. Each moment contains every clue you need to graduate yourself into the next phase of your existence.

Happiness is a side effect that results when you engage with all aspects of life. This includes those you have declared to be unfavorable and those you have labeled pleasant.

☆ Develop Emotional Strength

When you safely and constructively experience all of your emotions without judgment, negative emotions such as anger, fear, and sadness lead you to their counterparts: peace, self-confidence, and joy. Instead of assuming that frustration and anger are inherently negative, learn to use the raw power of negative emotions so you can channel them into positive endeavors. Discover how to use the whole-body approaches in this book to link your emotional and rational brain. Then a peaceful state and intuitive nudges will help you create more joy at work. Use the strategies in this book to create emotional anchors and positive resource states that will support you during testy situations.

☆ Acknowledge Your Personal Power

Own your personal power instead of buying into the social addiction of powerlessness or waiting for something outside of yourself to make you happy. So that you can prove to yourself just how rewarding self-responsibility is, this book will help you do the following.

✦ Enjoy rewarding connections with other people, including those you've labeled "difficult."

✦ Structure positive feedback in your work environment, including during performance reviews.

✦ Nurture yourself with self-care, an excellent support system, and stress management practices.

✦ Bring fun to work so laughter and play can boost your immune system while elevating your creativity, job satisfaction, and performance.

☆ Cherish Change, Challenge, and Uncertainty

Have a love affair with change, challenge, and uncertainty because happiness is a byproduct of putting our complete self into the pursuit of the meaning of life. Humans crave challenges. We become bored and unhappy without them, even though we require a balanced life that includes periods of rest and recuperation. The challenges we judge the most harshly usually provide our greatest insights and growth. Since uncertainty drives us to self-actualize, change is truly the zest of life. Frustration and confusion are essential to learning. Practice the exercises within these pages. They will help you trust the process of your life.

Cultivate your curiosity because a hunger for knowledge is a gold mine in disguise.

✦ An inquisitive mind keeps you from engaging in judgment. Because you avoid negative feelings, you are much more likely to focus on your preferred outcome instead of empowering what you don't want by maintaining a negative focus.

✦ Curiosity protects you from unnecessary pain. A sincere desire to understand the unknown helps you thrive during periods of uncertainty and change.

✦ Wondering what you can learn when you face adversity ensures that you will quickly bounce back from setbacks.

✦ Craving new knowledge contributes excitement to your life.

CREATE MORE JOY ON THE JOB

You have the ability to expand your happiness at work, whether your current position includes several or only a few of the essential ingredients identified by the employees of the 21 organizations surveyed. Which of the characteristics below have you already mastered? Which do you want to enhance?

Characteristics	Have Mastered	Will Enhance
Enjoy a rich relationship with yourself	_____	_____

continued on the next page . .

	Have Mastered	Will Enhance
Be aware of your strengths as well as your passions	_____	_____
Accept, instead of resist	_____	_____
Experience, rather than judge	_____	_____
Develop emotional strength	_____	_____
Own your personal power	_____	_____
Cherish change, challenge, and uncertainty	_____	_____

To attain happiness in another world,
we need only to believe something,
to secure it in this world,
we must do something.
Charlotte Perkins Gilman

CHAPTER 6

CURIOSITY CREATES JOY

I have no special gift.
I am only passionately curious.
Albert Einstein

Happy employees don't have time or energy to groan about the obstacles they face. This isn't because their workload is too demanding. It is because they have an insatiable curiosity. They feel compelled to fully engage with each moment of their lives.

For a frame of reference, consider the difference between a puppy and its owner when they go for a walk. The dog smells a snakeskin and rushes toward it. While the caretaker shrieks, "Don't touch that, Fido! It's dead!," puppies are as inquisitive as a two-year old. They wag their tails furiously while picking up the skin and investigating every fiber they can sniff and paw. Then they chew on the skin to gain the full flavor of the new experience. When Fido feels complete, the caretaker walks away disgusted, but the dog dances with glee. He has had an extraordinary adventure learning about something new.

Like Fido, happy people focus on what they can learn by embracing new experiences. When problems arise, they label them "challenges" and eagerly resolve them.

Thomas Edison is a perfect example of Fido in the world of work. Edison failed thousands of times during his struggles to invent an incandescent light source. His persistence and eventual success were fueled by unquenchable curiosity. Once, upon signing a guest book that had a column for "Interested in _____ ____" after the attendee's name, Edison wrote, "Everything."[1]

Even the observers who belittled Edison's efforts and chided his dedication noticed the joyful atmosphere surrounding his work. Curiosity vaccinated Edison against negativity and self-judgment. His inquisitive nature spontaneously transformed the ingredients for despair into an exciting adventure.

> Curiosity
> spontaneously
> creates courage.
>
> Courage
> crushes fear.

Most people function within a relatively small *familiar zone.* The limits of the zone have been defined by fear and misperceptions regarding their personal limitations and external barriers to change. Those who confine themselves in this way are occasionally willing to take tiny steps outside of their known reality. However, very few dare to fully expand their awareness of their capabilities and choices.

The critics don't realize that even when we stumble and fall during our first attempts to leap forward, we gain the satisfaction that is born when we dare to do something different. We also gain precious feedback that we use to enhance our self-image and fuel our courage for future endeavors. Rather than feeling stagnant and fretting about potentially negative outcomes, we fill our lives with meaning and joy. Our dreams grow more vibrant each day.

JOURNEY INTO THE UNKNOWN

During the next few days, observe social programming in your environment that encourages fear, dependence, and unhappiness. Pay attention to advertisements and comments made by coworkers, bosses, and friends. Notice your personal behavior patterns. Identify your *familiar zones*. When is fear of the unknown an automatic response that curiosity can curtail? Do you ever resist getting off the emotional roller coaster because drama makes you feel alive or tranquility feels unusual?

The next time you wish you could wave a magic wand and make an unpleasant situation disappear, remember the dramatic role model provided by Viktor Frankl. His determination to discover meaning even while forced to perform slave labor helped him achieve peace of mind. Since self-awareness can produce peace and joy, ask yourself, "I wonder what I'm learning by experiencing this situation?"

Practice being excited.
Bill Foster

The universe constantly challenges us to be creative because learning and growth are the sparks that ignite happiness. Notice that you gain insights when you shift your focus from judging an experience as bad, which is a fear-based response, to nurturing your curiosity and enthusiasm for learning. The hidden gifts inherent in every unpleasant situation become apparent. Even more exciting, since you achieve personal growth, you stop re-creating similar challenges over and over.

Emotional balance is far superior to the emotional roller coaster, and the first step to reach this state is to become aware of your existing patterns. All you have to do is notice them. Trying to change behavior patterns feeds internal resistance to change. Simply being mindful of your current pattern, without judging it, produces a more desirable result. You initiate a gradual and permanent change process.

> Celebrate! You are
> already moving closer
> to joy on the job
> as a new Familiar Zone.

NEXT, PLEASE

Because curiosity and creativity are so important, each subsequent chapter includes concepts and exercises that tickle your imagination and awaken your inner genius.

CHAPTER 7

SELF-AWARENESS
+ ACCEPTANCE
= FULFILLMENT

It is not easy to find happiness in ourselves,
and it is impossible to find it elsewhere.
Agnes Repplier

Happy employees know a lot about themselves. They are aware of their strengths, preferences, and what areas they need to improve. They have identified their core needs and values regarding the world of work. Happy workers know what feeds their souls, and they focus on how they can make a positive contribution.

When consulting with Able Manufacturing, I noticed how Trina Williams, an administrative assistant, worded her request for an expensive new computer system, "I'd like to have this update because it will help me produce higher quality reports for the entire engineering department. Making the engineers' lives easier will also make my work more meaningful."

When I complimented Trina on her approach, she grinned and explained, "I'm not an engineer and I don't understand a lot of their graphics. Since I'm a *people person*, I have to relate to the human aspect of a job in order to feel good about what I do. When I ask for resources, I'm always clear about how the request relates to my desire to make a positive contribution. That way, we all win." It's not surprising that Trina's requests for resources are routinely approved.

REMOVE THE MASK

Trina's true story provides an excellent illustration of combining self-awareness and the need to achieve fulfillment on the job with one's ability to make a beneficial contribution. There are many reasons discovering more about yourself feeds joy on the job.

✦ You are the one person you can count on working with for the rest of your career.
✦ Self-awareness fosters self-acceptance.
✦ It's never who you are that holds you back. It's who you think you are.
✦ You are happier when you connect with your true self.

Each of us possesses a *True Self* and a *False Self*. Your True Self is the essence of who you are, no matter what other people have told you about yourself. Unfortunately, your True Self is often overshadowed by your False Self. This self-image includes erroneous negative perceptions and self-judgments.

You can easily tell the difference between the two. Since your True Self is the real you, when you are living that reality, you are more likely to experience the following.

✦ You feel confident.
✦ You think clearly.
✦ You feel peaceful, contented, or joyful.

When your False Self is in control, you are more likely to experience the reality described below.

✦ Judge yourself harshly.

✦ Feel separate from others.

✦ Compare yourself unfavorably to others, or vice-versa.

✦ Feel that you must be superior to others in order to feel secure or self-confident.

✦ Insist you are right and devalue other points of view.

✦ Have a negative outlook on life.

Your False Self thrives by being out of sync with the present moment and the infinite possibilities available to you. It plays old movies that vividly portray a wide variety of unpleasant events from your past. Sinister soundtracks screech and hiss. Your *False Self Theatre* also specializes in graphic, detailed horror movies regarding potential, but very unlikely, future events. When False Self runs the show, it is as if you invited the most critical commentator you could find to shadow you 24/7 and deliver a devilish documentary detailing evidence that you are capable of making mistakes. (Who isn't?) The dreadful dialogue ends with the forecast that your life will never improve.

The next time you notice that your False Self is running the show, make a decision to create inner peace by spending a few minutes reconnecting with the real you. The exercise on the next page can produce surprisingly rapid results. The procedure uses a multisensory process because self-awareness develops through our senses.

Exhalations are emphasized because the process of exhaling opens our mind to mental imagery. It expands our consciousness so we can perceive and use multisensory input. The closed-eye process expands awareness of sensations. The exercise has a meditative quality because meditation also develops self-awareness.

RECONNECT WITH YOUR REAL SELF

STAGE ONE

1. Find a quiet place where you won't be disturbed while doing the exercise.

2. Relax and close your eyes. Breathe five long, deep breaths. Concentrate on your exhalations. When you think you have totally exhaled, exhale more . . . and then a little more. Notice tense areas in your body and release muscular tension with each exhalation.

3. Continue to breathe slowly and deeply. Count to five after each inhalation and each exhalation.

4. When you are relaxed, anchor the pleasant sensation by imagining the smell of one of your favorite aromas, such as vanilla or chocolate, wafting through the air. Pretend to breathe this scent deeply into your lungs. This action creates a positive neural connection in your brain that will help you avoid unnecessary stress.

5. Pause to enjoy the positive sensations and feelings before going about your day.

As time progresses, notice that you are more compassionate toward yourself and others, less frustrated, and more hopeful. Since your cells and your external reality respond to how you feel about yourself and life, this new level of acceptance will provide a sturdy foundation for spontaneously creating additional job satisfaction. Because we are holistic beings (body, mind, and spirit), pleasant feelings and sensations are much more powerful tools for creating beneficial changes than merely using positive thoughts or words.

RECONNECT WITH YOUR REAL SELF

STAGE TWO

Now that you have set the perfect stage within your mind and body, you will make decisions that fuel inner peace. Get paper and a pen and use your nondominant hand to answer the following sentence stem. If no thoughts emerge, just keep your pen moving on the page until they do. Continue to write until you receive insights that clarify your next steps.

I can achieve more fulfillment at work and make a positive contribution at the same time by doing the following.

1. _____
2. _____
3. _____

USE SELF-AWARENESS AS A STEPPINGSTONE TO JOY ON THE JOB

Self-awareness is an absolutely essential tool for enhancing joy on the job. Since giving is receiving, self-knowledge will help you define ways to enhance your job satisfaction by contributing to your work environment.

Self-awareness and self-acceptance will also help you avoid unnecessary roadblocks to happiness at work. You are constantly creating situations that reflect your core beliefs and values, even when you are unaware of them or do not want to acknowledge them. People who accept themselves treat failures as isolated incidents that don't reflect their capabilities. People who lack self-acceptance concentrate on their defeats. They inflate the importance of every mistake. Because they adopt defeat as a self-image, a multiplier effect is born. Eventually, a past failure predicts the outcome of future life events.[1]

Employees who accept themselves make conscious efforts to stay connected with their Real Selves. When a false self-image such as "I'm not good enough" rears its head, they reconnect with their True Self and view themselves more objectively. As Pat Duncan, author of *Go For It,* says, "I'm no longer the kid who was afraid to speak in class."

Self-acceptance is liberating. When we decide we are worthy just as we are, a lovely chain of events unfolds. We spontaneously accept other people, we no longer feel isolated at work, and our jobs are much more fun.

> When you make friends
> with yourself,
> you're never alone.

You will be fulfilled and successful when you do what is right for you. As the following true stories indicate, self-awareness will help you discover your best course of action.

When contemplating her son's future, Pablo Picasso's mother forecast, "If you become a soldier, you will become a general. If you become a monk, you will become the pope." Picasso decided not to become a soldier, a general, a monk, or the pope. Instead, he decided to paint. He became Picasso.

Botanist George Washington Carver was a religious person, but he often said he was once disappointed by God. When, as a young lad, Carver prayed for the mystery of the universe to be revealed to him, he was told that such knowledge was reserved for the Almighty. After reflection, Carver asked a different question, "God, tell me the mystery of the peanut." Carver said the next response he heard was, "Well, George, that's more nearly your size." Carver became a world-renowned agricultural chemist and educator. He made massive contributions to humanity by developing hundreds of uses for the peanut, soybean, and sweet potato.

The secret of happiness in this world
is not only to be useful,
but to be forever elevating one's uses.
Sarah Orne Jewett

CHAPTER 8

TRANSFORM BLIND SPOTS
TO FREEDOM

We do not see things as they are.
We see them as we are.
Anaïs Nin

Happy workers are aware of the power of their perceptions, and they welcome opportunities to correct inaccurate impressions. They know they unconsciously create illusions as a result of their thoughts, beliefs, and preferences.

If you stand on a railroad track, the two parallel lines of the rails seem to merge in the distance. In truth, the tracks never even come close to a point of union.

Why do we go out of our way to enjoy a beautiful sunrise or sunset? The sun only rises or sets in our belief systems! The next example of an illusion illustrates how correcting a blind spot can provide peace of mind at work.

Be cautious when you think someone is judging you harshly or intends to harm you. They are often too absorbed in their own issues to notice you or your actions.

Use the following exercise to identify the power of your misperceptions.

CORRECT BLIND SPOTS

STAGE ONE

There are two dots on the next page. Place your hand over your left eye as you focus on the dot on the left while holding the page about eight inches from your nose. Slowly move the page away and then back toward you until the dot on the right disappears. (This will only happen for a moment, so move the page slowly.) When the dot disappears, stop moving the book.

You have just identified the blind spot in your right eye. This is the spot where the nerve attaches to the back of your eye and there are no rods or cones to receive the light. To identify the blind spot in your left eye, repeat the exercise by covering your right instead of your left eye and focusing on the dot on the right.

Now, gaze around your environment. Notice there are no black holes in your vision, even though it just seemed as if there is a spot in each of your eyes where you literally see nothing. There are no empty spots because your mind is programmed to make sense of things, so it completes gaps for your comfort. Your mind simply fills in the blank spaces with whatever shapes and colors exist in your surroundings.[1]

This process isn't limited to your visual perceptions. When there is a conflict between what exists and what you believe should exist, your mind will dutifully report to you what "should be." For better or worse, our rational minds shelter us from a great deal of information that does not match our beliefs. This ensures the survival of our existing assumptions and convictions. Most of us will only consider responding to our environment in ways that support our belief systems.

It is as if we are trying to train for an Olympic swimming competition by paddling around in a kiddie pool. We self-sabotage by allowing our known reality—our current knowledge and experience—to define and limit our understanding of life.

Most of our beliefs are unconscious. The vast majority of our convictions and assumptions were thrust into our minds by authority figures, friends, and relatives like a brain implant injected into an unsuspecting character in a science fiction movie. Most of these individuals had never even examined the validity of the beliefs they bestowed upon us. Why? Because when they were children, an avalanche of nonsensical notions and dogma were dumped on them by other people. We are all functioning with unexamined presumptions. We thoughtlessly swim in repetitive circles in a sea of misinformation and act as if illusions are true.

THE IMPACT OF EMOTIONS AND ENTHUSIASM

Happy employees understand the power of feelings, including enthusiasm. Einstein consistently said that imagination is mightier than logic. Whatever we believe, *when combined with emotion,* becomes our reality. Our minds then block contradictory information from our consciousness. Our senses also create perceptions and misunderstandings.

The olfactory system provides a good example of how our brains develop habitual, unconscious neural networks that are stimulated on a daily basis. The olfactory system is the quickest and most effective sensory link to our emotions. The smell of fresh chocolate chip cookies may stimulate unconscious memories of being nurtured as a child. The smell of disinfectant may remind you of unpleasant chores. If these facts are true, you will accept bad news on the job more easily when you are offered a warm chocolate delight than when you are standing next to a freshly cleaned floor that reeks of ammonia.

CORRECT BLIND SPOTS

STAGE TWO

Use the following thoughts and exercise to prove to yourself that your perceptions are not real. They are merely reflections of your beliefs, including your prejudices and insecurities.

1. Think of an individual who believes they are incompetent or powerless, even though it is obvious to you that they are highly capable. Sometimes, this person is yourself.

2. When four eyewitnesses to an accident are interviewed, they provide four different versions of what happened. Each individual has a different emotional response to the incident. Therefore, each person assigns a different meaning and value to the objects and people involved.

USE A SELF-CORRECTING LENS

Why are personal blind spots important to you when you plan your strategies for achieving greater happiness at work? The following is just one example. Companies and bosses are perceived as having all of the power on their side. Yet, companies can't function without people and employee shortages have been forecast for decades to come, even during economic recessions.[2]

CORRECT BLIND SPOTS

STAGE THREE

Blind spots can be as dangerous as driving a car without rear- and side-view mirrors. The following will help you overcome barriers to happiness at work.

1. Identify your blind spots.   Do you sometimes undervalue your skills, strengths, or contributions?

2. Identify blind spots in your organization that affect you.

3. What steps can you take to correct these blind spots? As an example, how can you increase awareness of your value and let people know when you need additional professional support?

TRUTH IS TRUTH

Truth is tough. It will not break
like a bubble at a touch.
Nay, you may kick it about
all day like a football,
and it will be round
and full at evening.
Oliver Wendell Holmes, Sr.

You live in a world of unlimited possibilities. Inaccurate perceptions can restrict your dreams, as well as your joy on the job. Discover who you are and what you offer to the world of work. During tough times, this truth will serve you like a torch that gleams through dense fog. There is always a market for the truth, and there is always a market for who you really are. Don't cheat the world by hiding the radiance of your personal light.

CHAPTER 9

FULFILL YOURSELF WITH FOCUS

We become what we think about.
Marcus Aurelius

THE POWER OF YOUR FOCUS

Happy employees focus on what will foster their peace and contentment, while unhappy employees focus on limitations and on what displeases them. A similar distinction exists between successful individuals and those who are unsuccessful. High achievers are aware of problems and take steps to minimize distractions and obstacles, but they focus on what helps them meet their objectives. Viktor Frankl discovered how to concentrate on joyful memories and the book he wanted to write instead of focusing on the horror of daily life in Auschwitz.

Creatures of nature provide wonderful role models of spotlighting objectives and ignoring alleged limitations. Observe how intently focused a bumblebee is when flying here and there.

The bee is totally unaware that scientists have determined that it is aerodynamically impossible for it to fly. When a salamander's leg is severed, it grows another because it doesn't know that it is "impossible" to do so.

Discontented employees compare themselves and their achievements to others. Contented workers compete only with themselves. In the rare instances when satisfied workers compare themselves with others, they compare downward. Instead of complaining, "Mary Ann sure has an easy job," they notice, "Joe's having a tough time."

The benefits of this style of thinking are enormous. Upward comparisons such as, "Juan gets the best assignments," feed feelings of envy and inferiority. Downward comparisons such as, "Joe's having a tough time," stimulate well-being and empathy ("I'm going to encourage Joe"). Compassionate thoughts and actions feed self esteem and foster happiness. In the above instance, happy employees are aware and take action if their own workload is inappropriate, but they do not waste their precious energy steaming about someone else's light workload.

Because satisfied workers compete with themselves instead of against others, they are careful when comparing their current achievements to those in their past. Instead of groaning, "I wish I were as successful now as I was before the economic recession," they ask themselves, "Have I learned more about myself or the process of life since the recession? How can I use that knowledge?" Since failures and mistakes help us learn and grow, such questions ensure that contented employees avoid the trap of judging themselves or their achievements as inadequate.

I find my joy of living in the fierce
and ruthless battles of life, and my pleasure
comes from learning something.
August Strindberg

DISCOVER YOUR FOCUS

1.   During the next week, observe the focus of your thoughts. Are they dominated by limitations and what displeases you or by your strengths and what you are learning about yourself and life?

2.   Notice your upward and downward comparisons.

WHO IS IN CHARGE OF YOUR DESTINY AT WORK?

Your work life is a canvas, and you are the artist. When you think a situation is dreary or gray, it can be easy to forget that you hold an entire palette of colors in your talented hands. You can shade a given scenario with grim tones or you can select vibrant and hopeful hues. You are even more powerful. If you don't like the first results you achieve, you can continue to tinker with your artwork until you are immensely satisfied.

Physicists and social scientists have proven over and over that there is very little absolute reality in your life. Instead, there are infinite possibilities. What unfolds in your life is influenced by your thoughts, attitudes, emotions, and beliefs. Your reality is even affected by the way you carry your body. You proved all of this to yourself when you completed the blind spots exercise.

When discussing the field of infinite possibilities, physicists speak of multiple data streams. They remind us that an eyewitness affects the outcome of an experiment. Whether a particle is a particle or a wave depends on the observer. In a similar manner, different potential realities simultaneously exist in your work life.

You hold many more playing cards in your hand than you may think. Physicists have proven that you can choose between parallel realities.[1] You can choose to engage in a pleasant or unpleasant scenario at work, just as an artist can create a canvas portraying hope or despair.

Thoughts and words are Day Planners™. Experiments have consistently demonstrated just how powerful the actions are that go on behind the locked door of your subconscious mind. In "priming experiments," subjects were told that their task was to unscramble sentence fragments. They spent just five minutes working with phrases such as the following.

✦ Sunlight makes temperature wrinkle raisins
✦ Should now withdraw forgetful we
✦ Shoes give replace old the
✦ From are Florida oranges temperature

Although the subjects had been told they were taking a language quiz, psychologist John Bargh was actually investigating their behaviors as they walked to and from the exam. The sentences they unscrambled were heavily peppered with words like Florida, old, bingo, lonely, gray, wrinkle, and worried. The study was designed to stimulate the participants' adaptive unconscious to think about a negative state of being old.

The participants actually walked slower after leaving the experiment than on the way to the exam. In later tests, participants were primed to be rude, patient, or confident. Words and thoughts are so powerful that all of these effects occurred after spending only five minutes unscrambling sentences![2]

Japanese researcher, Masuru Emoto, has traveled the world investigating the positive and negative impact of words and thoughts on water. Because our bodies are composed of approximately 80 percent water, his initial work stimulated other scientists to investigate the effects of positive and negative thoughts and words on the human body. Dr. Emoto and those who followed his lead proved that emotions such as enthusiasm and appreciation are powerful sources of designing a plan for your future.[3]

Even if your thoughts are being *un*consciously programmed by print media, peers, or television, words and ideas are conditioning your body and mind. If your focus is filled with thoughts about what you don't want or like, your life experience will reflect that negative focus. This book provides tools to deal with unnecessary fears because worry possesses magical powers. Unfortunately, the sorcery that accompanies worry is much more like voodoo than the sweet magic spread by Tinker Bell. When you worry, you unconsciously use your imagination to create what you don't want.

Your subconscious mind does not judge one experience as good and another as bad. It just follows the directions it receives from your conscious mind. No matter what your focus may be, your subconscious mind *automatically* creates a tapestry that reflects it.

The subconscious is as single-focused and systematic as Santa Claus on Christmas Eve. It is constantly arranging and rearranging the details of our lives to correspond with our thoughts, assumptions, motives, and opinions. The situations in our lives are visible records of our thought processes.

Even when we are unaware of the power of our subconscious, it remains a mighty force. Clearly, we endanger our sense of well being by allowing unconscious thoughts to become unintentional suggestions. The good news? All we have to do is be aware of our thoughts and manage or shift our focus.

When we concentrate on what we don't like about ourselves or our lives, the master weaver within us has to take a back seat. When we choose a positively directed path, we create a much more enjoyable result.

PROVE YOUR POWER

It is essential that you comprehend your innate ability to create agony, neutrality, or happiness. Then you will consistently shine the light on what's right.

1. Choose a time when you won't be disturbed. Think of a circumstance at work that doesn't trigger positive or negative emotions because the situation doesn't directly affect you. An example would be noticing the arrival of mail to another department in your building. If you feel neutral about this activity, it has little or no effect on your body or your work life.

2. Assume for a moment that something about the situation you selected is inadequate, inappropriate, or wrong. Mentally pick the scene apart. Write notes criticizing everything that is not perfect about the people, procedures, policies, timing, or equipment involved. What should be different?

3. Jot down notes about your emotions. How did they affect your body? Did anger make your heart palpitate or elevate your blood pressure? Is your gut uncomfortable? Is your jaw tight?

. . . continued on the next page

4.   Take a few deep breaths. Let go of the imaginary angst you have created so you can move on to the next step of this exercise.

5.   In this step, imagine that the situation you selected is excellent. In fact, everything about it is absolutely perfect. Focus on what works. What's good about *the exact same* people, procedure, policies, timing, or equipment involved?

6.   Make notes about the pleasant emotions you experience when considering this point of view. How do these positive emotions affect your body?

7.   Notice the difference in the results—for you—when you hold a focus on what is wrong and when you concentrate on what works.

> You have just acknowledged your power! Even when there are very valid reasons to be concerned about a situation that must be corrected, you can create a more enjoyable reality for yourself. Simply adopt a non-judgmental observational stance. This will foster objectivity for problem-solving. You will also conserve your energy so you can initiate productive corrective actions.

I am *not* advocating that you limit your experiences by rigidly attempting to program your reality. Life is poised to offer you a vast and rich panorama of experiences that will test your courage and help you develop splendid character. Trying to create your future by extrapolating a wish list based on what you already know exists would dramatically restrict the wealth and scope of your tomorrow.

Bullheaded attempts to predetermine your experiences are based on feelings of desperation. You don't trust the process of your life, and you are afraid that your needs won't be met. In a short-sighted attempt to produce safety and security, you toss away some pretty incredible opportunities for growth and wisdom. Who wants to spin around and around a creaky old wheel as if they are a hamster trapped in a poorly maintained cage? It's boring and frustrating.

FILL THE SPACE OF YOUR FOCUS

Select another alternative from your personal choice toolbox. Since you are always consciously or unconsciously creating the situations in your life, decide to do so in a thoughtful manner. Choosing your attitude provides a sense of control over your life.

As soon as you take responsibility for your thoughts, you discover that you are a powerful alchemist. It becomes impossible to blame anyone outside of yourself for your circumstances because you are aware that you personally orchestrated each and every event.

Make a commitment to take healthy risks and trust the process of your life. Decide to become more aware of the effects of your thoughts and attitudes on your daily life. Because the object of your focus expands, an attitude of gratitude reaps rich rewards. When you concentrate on what pleases you and what is working, the experiences you enjoy multiply.

Henry Ford often said he was so busy thinking about what he wanted to achieve that there was no room for considering the possibility of what he didn't want. Although it is important to acknowledge negative thoughts and emotions, it is absolutely essential to identify what is working in your life and to discover the vast potential for even greater success and joy on the job.

It is extremely difficult to focus on two opposing emotions or thoughts at the same time. Most of us can't love someone if we think we hate them. We can't simultaneously feel peaceful and furious.

Therefore, all you have to do is honor the negative when it exists—without indulging it. Then shift your focus to the *feeling* of the situation you prefer.

> Like a boomerang, we attract into our lives what we radiate out. Observe your thoughts. Acknowledge your personal power by understanding that every thought serves as a prayer regarding the future content of your life. Do not initiate an internal battle (resistance to change) by judging your negative thoughts or trying to change them. Simple awareness initiates positive change, so be patient with yourself.

Patience doesn't mean being stuck in the slow lane. In fact, it usually elevates us into the fast lane! Patient people achieve what they want because they exude a calm, serene energy that attracts spontaneous assistance and unexpected blessings.

FOSTER A FULFILLING FOCUS

Decide how you can concentrate on what helps you meet your objectives while minimizing distractions and obstacles.

1. When you notice a negative point made by your inner critic, pose a counterpoint, without resisting the original banter. Address thoughts like, "There's no way I'll get the promotion I want" with "*Someone* will get the promotion. I can take one step and then another to become more qualified. That will help me in the broader job market, no matter how this particular potential opportunity turns out."

2. Challenge yourself to think and talk about the focus you would like to empower for 24 hours. Instead of judging, resisting, or trying to change negative thoughts, just observe your inner dialogue. Without indulging the dysfunctional thoughts, notice if you are focusing on—empowering—what you don't want. Accept this part of yourself because it is part of the human condition.

3. Become more aware of what is occurring within your subconscious mind. Close your eyes and

. . . *continued on the next page*

envision symbols that represent your preferences at work. How far do they seem to be from the context of your current life? If you want funding for additional training, does an email stating that your goal will be supported appear to be a remote possibility . . . or an event in your current reality? If you want a more spacious office, can you actually feel yourself within the new space . . . or has your unconscious mind been picturing someone else there? If achieving your goal seems distant, notice how you feel when you imagine that the representative symbol exists within your daily work life.

4. Your brain is pliable and your thoughts and neural networks can be shaped by external influences. Choose to interact with happy, thriving employees. Read biographies of successful people. Listen to inspirational audio programs. The more you know, the more you grow.

5. Notice what happens during the times you feel grateful for what is working and you sincerely trust that something positive is about to occur. According to the laws of physics, these thoughts and feelings attract additional favorable experiences.

CAN YOU FOCUS WHEN YOU MULTITASK?

Employees in the Industrial Revolution were often bored while performing the same task over and over with few work breaks. Today's high tech employees often groan about being expected to soothe an angry customer on the telephone under strict time constraints while interacting with a complex computer program.

Multitasking is much more interesting than picking up a widget and placing it in a tray on a conveyor belt all day long, but it can actually slow your progress. While you are achieving one task, your brain is partly occupied with the next activity. The human brain needs transition time when shifting from one set of cognitive rules to another. One study indicated that the I.Q. of employees decreased when they were multitasking.[4]

Even though we all have an innate, undeveloped genius capacity, most of us haven't fully developed it. Therefore, there is a limit to how much attention we can spread across several activities and a limit to how effectively concurrent tasks can be performed.

Focus has a different effect. It builds confidence as well as competence. You enhance your problem-solving abilities when you broaden the depth of your experiences. You also achieve a stronger emotional connection with teamworkers and customers when you pay 100 percent attention to the matter at hand instead of pondering your next activity. Focus is essential to reaching an enjoyable state of flow.

Because unnecessary mistakes create stress and unsuccessfully executed activities have to be redone, many savvy companies have begun to advocate "go slow to go fast." Stay tuned for widespread social change as cultural creatives clash with corporate clones. The creatives are arming themselves with briefcases of data proving that a single focus produces positive results that promote profits.

DEVELOP *FOCUS-ABILITY*

1. Do what you can to minimize interruptions. The average employee is interrupted by noise, visual distractions, and talkative visitors 16 times a day (21 times a day when work-related distractions are included). Since most workers require 2.9 minutes to recover their concentration, most employees spend about an hour a day trying to refocus on their work. This is in addition to the time involved in the actual distraction![5]

2. Studies have concluded that peppermint or cinnamon essential oil can help you stay focused on your true goals and increase your performance.[6]

3. You can also train your mind to stay in the moment by regularly practicing meditation, qi gong, tai chi, yoga, or breathing exercises. Your new ability to focus will carry over to activities at work.

4. When you are in the middle of an activity and your attention wanders to your next task, instead of struggling to remember your thoughts, jot a note to yourself. Then return to the task at hand.

. . . continued on the next page

5. Stay organized. Keep your work environment as uncluttered as possible. Set and maintain time limits for projects, meetings, and telephone calls. To block distracting thoughts and conversation, tell other participants at the beginning of a meeting or phone call how long you can be available. When the time limit is up, take a process break. Whether you decide to continue with the task at hand or move to the next activity, do so with full focus.

Focus feeds success and feelings of well-being. Consciously use your focus and will to create joy on the job.

CHOOSE WISELY

If I hadn't started painting,
I would have raised chickens.
Grandma Moses

You may not get to choose how or when you die, but you can definitely determine the focus on your attention. Choices eventually control the chooser. You become what you decide to do and you become what you choose to think about. You hold the key to your destiny.

CHAPTER 10

OWN YOUR POWER

Indeed, man wishes to be happy
even when he so lives
as to make happiness impossible.
St. Augustine

Because happiness is a choice and does not depend on external circumstances, you are responsible for your satisfaction at work. This fact liberates and empowers you because you are the ultimate authority concerning what will bring you fulfillment. The first step is to sincerely care about your workplace joy.

Start with the basics. Even during the toughest economic climate, no one else can choose your occupation or where you work. Only you can listen to your inner voice. You are the sole individual who can monitor your gut feelings to ensure that required activities and company values are consistent with your personal values and goals. You alone decide whether or not your job is meaningful.

> Our work lives do not happen *to us*.
>
> They happen *from us*.

Happy employees have overcome their fear of their personal power, which is fear of change (anxiety about losing an old identity of *powerlessness*). Joyful workers refuse to engage in games in which they play victim or blame others for their circumstances or choices. They accept responsibility for their thoughts, feelings, and the course of their lives because they know this is the most dependable source of inner peace. They welcome input that helps them identify limiting belief systems and behavior patterns. Open-minded and curious, they are more interested in achieving positive results than in endlessly defending their point of view. When they identify joyblocks, they transform negative habits and beliefs into positive patterns.

CALLING ALL EMPLOYEES

Ecstasy is the accurate term
for the intensity of consciousness
that occurs in the creative act.
Rollo May

Workers across the world are challenged by downsizing, constant reorganization, lack of job security, and the struggle to achieve balance in their personal and professional lives. Because entire industries are in chaos as corporate boundaries and hierarchies dissolve, even a fortuneteller can't foresee which career paths will blossom and which will wilt on the vine.

In the new economy, most employees will change jobs every two years and careers every two years or less.[1] It is clear that both organizations and employees must reinvent themselves in the information age.

Your key to sanity and success is to take control of your own professional life. Then you will thrive in an age in which long-term loyalty between employer and employee is virtually non-existent. When you view yourself as a freelance worker, even if you remain in your current position for the rest of your career, you find joy while constantly updating your skills and strategically planning your career moves.

Assume you will partner with a specific manager or organization as long as it is mutually beneficial and consistent with your work ethics. Many organizations today view their relationships with employees as task specific. When particular jobs are completed, working arrangements are either terminated or updated.

Because it will be clear to you that you are in charge of your own life and happiness, you will avoid feelings of betrayal or bitterness when an organization's agenda changes. You will thrive in the midst of corporate chaos and uncertainty, and you will be filled with the highest level of self-respect.

BECOME A ONE-PERSON BUSINESS

How do you journey toward this peak? Think of yourself as the CEO of your own single-employee organization. Even when we are working for someone else, each of us is the CEO of our own corporation. We are constantly making decisions and engaging in negotiations and other actions that affect our livelihood and the degree to which we are happy at work. Whether actively or unconsciously, we are consistently reshaping our goals, evaluating our progress, developing desires for additional training, and determining how to transform lemons into lemonade. The next exercise will help you make these efforts more rewarding.

USE SELF-RESPONSIBILITY
TO BUILD JOB SECURITY
AND FULFILLMENT

Assume you are the CEO of your own single-employee service organization. Read the examples below. Then list actions you can take to enhance your mobility and job fulfillment.

WHAT ORGANIZATIONS DO	WHAT YOU CAN DO
Develop short-term and long-term goals.	Develop long-term goals. Break them into short-term, measurable objectives with timelines for completion. Review your goals regularly. Modify them as needed.
Research trends in the industry or field. Conduct internal research.	Be aware of industry trends. Read. Attend conferences and seminars. Participate in local trade associations and other professional groups that enhance your knowledge and networks.

continued on the next page . . .

WHAT ORGANIZATIONS DO	WHAT YOU CAN DO
Evaluate progress of the organization and employees.	Develop a professional support system. Partner with someone you trust so the two of you can periodically evaluate each other's marketability.
Shift priorities and strategies based on industry trends and quarterly reports	Shift goals and game plans after considering external feedback, your own analyses, and intuitive messages.
Downsize and reorganize	Turn setbacks into steppingstones. Build job security with your sense of self-responsibility. Develop a career ladder for yourself.
Train employees on an as-needed basis	Ensure that the most important employee in your organization (you) receives the best training possible. Constantly develop new skills.

> Empowering yourself by perceiving yourself as a CEO will not decrease your loyalty to your current employer. It will increase your value to the organization and help you highlight your achievements.

INVEST IN YOUR FUTURE

Accept responsibility for your marketability by seeking opportunities to learn and use new skills. Work with a mentor or mastermind group. Ask the human resources or training department in your organization about additional educational opportunities. Learn by tutoring or by volunteering to lead a project.

Enjoy self-education. Discover how many new skills you can learn with only a few weeks of concentrated effort, whether through self-education or enrollment in an Internet or community college course. Watch your self-confidence soar as your marketability increases.

DISCOVER THE JOY OF SELF-RELIANCE

Rather than assuming that your long-term interests are identical to those of your employer, establish some stability by developing a safety net with some funds for emergencies. Stash funds that are equivalent to a couple of months of your salary in an easily accessible place, such as a money market fund. Plan and manage your own pension fund.

Knowing you have choices will cause you to radiate self-confidence that will ensure you cannot be threatened. You will be amazed at the degree to which people will compete for your services—inside and outside of your current organization.

BE AWARE OF YOUR VALUE AND INFLUENCE

You know something that too many anxious employees don't know. The Bureau of Labor Statistics has forecast a tight labor market for decades to come, regardless of periodic economic downturns.[2] Since you understand that you are an absolute treasure to your current and potential employers, act accordingly. The following exercise will help you begin.

VALIDATE YOURSELF
WITH AN INVENTORY

☆ Make a list of your strengths and skills, and keep it handy.

☆ Compile a *kudo folder* in which you keep cards, letters, and other papers that document your skills. Review these materials next time you feel unsuccessful, incompetent, or powerless.

continued on the next page . .

☆ Recognize the areas where you have control over how enjoyable your work activities are.

☆ Note how many of your skills you use and how engaged you become in some tasks but not in others. Take steps to ensure that you more often use the skills that produce fulfillment at work.

☆ List your greatest spheres of influence. These might include your expertise, knowledge, reputation for honesty, skills of persuasion, charisma, control of resources, open mind, compassion, or your genuine concern for the bigger picture instead of being consumed by self-interest.

☆ How can you more effectively use your sources of influence to shape your work environment?

☆ Begin to think about how you can structure opportunities for positive feedback.

☆ How can you raise awareness of the importance of your tasks?

☆ Monitor your own performance to ensure that you feel good about yourself and your productivity.

Farmers know they can't plow a field by turning it over in their mind. Forward movement is also required if you are to ensure happiness at work. Review your answers to the above, determine your first step, and spring into action now.

THE FREEDOM OF SELF-RESPONSIBILITY

Self-responsibility is
the forgotten side of freedom.
Viktor Frankl

Self-responsibility is the most overlooked and the most exciting element of professional freedom. In the interviews that led to the publication of this book, it was evident that happy employees accept personal responsibility for their lives, including their level of joy on the job.

Use the exercises in this chapter to acknowledge your capabilities and employ self-responsibility so you can create personal security and fulfillment. Employees who are not afraid to own their personal power radiate self-confidence. They are inherently influential. A positive cycle ensues in which their inner and external resources boost their joy on the job.

CHAPTER 11

MEET YOUR NEEDS

Unquestionably, it is possible
to do without happiness;
it is done involuntarily by
nineteen-twentieths of mankind.
John Stuart Mill

Satisfied employees have a conscious intention to experience joy on the job. They understand that humans possess two needs that occasionally clash—the desire to grow and the longing for safety and security. Joyful workers make sure their basic needs are met. Then they focus on an innate yearning to discover meaning in their professional and personal lives.

They identify their unique strengths and talents because they know it feeds their souls to express themselves at work while making a special contribution to the world. They know which work activities make them feel the most alive. They identify the legacy they want to leave behind when they depart from a particular work position, and they focus their efforts accordingly.

✦ Happy workers nurture themselves. They communicate what they need in order to achieve personal fulfillment while delivering their best performance. They know they deserve assistance, and they ask for help when they need it.

✦ Contented employees cultivate an excellent professional support system.

COMMUNICATE YOUR UNMET NEEDS

In chapter one, you identified your unmet needs and determined your highest priorities for positive change. Do you know how to communicate your needs to management and team members in ways that serve you?

A client whom I will call Connie felt overworked and underpaid. She only enjoyed a few of the tasks she was assigned, but she lacked the authority to delegate or outsource her work. She was so unhappy that she considered hiring on with another company for less pay.

I persuaded Connie to identify her key strengths and to clearly outline what would bring her joy at work. Because this process shifted her attention from her complaints to what she wanted to achieve, she stopped empowering what she didn't want with an intense focus. In the next step of our work together, we role played the win-win communication strategy described below.

✦ **Put the organization's needs first.** Connie addressed potential benefits the organization would receive if her job was restructured so that most of her activities focused on the use of her unique skills.

✦ **Sell yourself and your idea by promising accountability.** Connie was very clear regarding what she was willing to do to achieve her goals. She promised specific results (accountability) in exchange for a raise.

At first, Connie was nervous about expressing her needs, but she allayed her fears by doing a self-check to confirm that her work was more than adequate. She knew she had far more to gain than to lose. She decided she could accept the worst possible outcome if necessary. In her case, this would mean hearing an answer like, "No way!"

The reality turned out to be quite different. Because Connie had done her homework so well, her boss agreed to outsource her other tasks on a six-month trial basis. At the end of the six-month trial period, the results were so dramatic that Connie was awarded an additional raise, even though the economy was slow. She was given full support to continue her new job responsibilities.

SECURE THE SUPPORT YOU NEED

Do you feel that asking for or accepting help is a sign of weakness? An admission that you are overextended or unqualified? If so, your self-worth may be linked with achievement, even if the demands imposed on you are unreasonable. The following exercise will help you clear this hurdle.

1. Get a pen and paper and spend a minimum of five minutes completing each of the following unfinished sentences, which are related to your

continued on the next page . . .

ability to ask for assistance and meet your basic needs. It is important to keep your pen moving on your paper, so write whatever comes into your mind. If you have no thoughts, just scribble on the page until your thoughts become clear.

✦ "I'm waiting until . . . "

✦ "I'll ask for help when . . . "

2. Now, review your answers, without judging them as right or wrong. How does waiting keep you from meeting your own needs?

3. Record at least one reason that receiving what you need will benefit your organization or co-workers.

3. Write down the next action you will take so you can secure more professional support and become happier at work. What do you need to request? How and when will you do so?

4. Anticipate any potential resistance to your request, and identify your response to possible challenges.

5. Practice presenting your idea as a win-win approach that will benefit all concerned.

DON'T CHEAT THE OTHERS

Our society works best when everyone contributes
their unique talents and skills. If you don't
let others contribute to you, you mess up
the system—mostly for yourself.

Alan Cohen

Stacks of studies have indicated that others feel good when you ask for help and allow them to assist you. Your request boosts their self-esteem.

> Consider the following myth-busting facts regarding meeting your needs at work.

✦ **Meeting your needs at work is not selfish.** Needs such as, "My work has to be meaningful" or "I need to get along with my coworkers," are different than desires like "I want to make over a million dollars this year." When your needs are met, you are more effective.

✦ **You are ultimately responsible for identifying and meeting your needs.** Your employer or team members may never perceive your needs, partly because your needs may be very different than theirs. You are the ideal spokesperson for yourself. No one else will ever understand you as well as you do.

✦ **You must take responsibility for communicating your unmet needs in ways that ensure you will be understood by others.** If you don't communicate your needs, they will probably continue to be unfulfilled. When you do meet your needs, emotional turmoil will transform into contentment.

✦ **It is not a sign of weakness to ask others for help.** It is a sign of inner strength and high self-esteem. ("I deserve assistance.") When you request support, you honor the strengths of others.

✦ **You do not lose respect when you ask for assistance.** You connect with the core humanity of others. None of us has the time or is capable of doing everything that needs to be done, and we all sometimes need assistance. Whether they are aware of it or not, other people help themselves when they lend you a hand.

BECOME THE KEY PLAYER

Rather than stand on the sidelines wishing your needs were fulfilled, become an active participant in the great game of giving and receiving. Tell others how meeting your needs will serve the organization. Contribute to the lives of others by allowing yourself to receive the support you deserve.

Happiness does not lie in happiness,
but in the achievement of it.
Fyodor Dostoyevsky

CHAPTER 12

FULLY EMBRACE LIFE

Learn to wish that everything
should come to pass
exactly as it does.
Epictetus

Flowers must go through a lot of dirt before they can bloom. Their secret is keeping the light deep in their roots while experiencing the darkness. Contented workers know how to do this.

They don't expect ecstasy to follow them around 24 hours a day. Instead, they understand and cherish the polarities of life, such as day/night, pain/pleasure, and fear/self-confidence. They have watched enough movies to know it is impossible to have a happy ending without first experiencing a challenge that needs to be resolved. Hang around happy workers and you will hear cheerful banter such as, "Light follows darkness" or "Struggle is the first step to a breakthrough."

Because these individuals understand the value in the entire range of human experiences and emotions, they laugh at media advertising and other social hype that touts messages like the following.

✦ People should always be happy. If you aren't, there is something wrong with you. You should purchase our product!

✦ It is always better to be happy than to be sad, angry, unsure of yourself, or fearful.

This does not mean that those who fully embrace life expect their jobs to be difficult or view work as drudgery. Even though they recognize that unpleasant events are essential because they are nutrients for the creation of enjoyable experiences, the process of their lives does not resemble a graph with wild gyrations between peaks and low points.

A diagram symbolizing their work lives is more like the steady, smooth flow of tides in a peaceful ocean. Like ocean waves, growth-producing insights consistently drift through their consciousness before the results of their work flow back into their environment. Both the workers and the world benefit from this balanced process.

As in the sea, there are occasional storms in these workers' lives, but contented employees accept—and even embrace—turmoil. They know from experience that a tumultuous tide deposits interesting treasures to comb through. They eagerly explore the new material without judgment. After gaining clarity, they keep what is useful and let go of what they don't need.

Out-of-the-box thinking helps them embrace instability. As world history has proven time and again, turbulence is both disturbing and creative. Progressive ideas are usually only adopted when old stagnant systems have been so thoroughly jolted that they lose dominance. Broken eggs make delicious omelets.

Happy employees also maintain tranquility by thriving on failures, which they define as feedback. They know there is no such thing as a failure because, even if they don't achieve their original goal, they always obtain a result.

These resilient individuals bounce back very quickly when disappointed by life or their own performance because they regard mistakes as one of their best learning tools. They transform pain into purpose by placing personal anguish in perspective. They trust they will always learn from a disagreeable situation. They reframe the incident instead of judging it, which is a vital tool for gaining meaning from unpleasant events. Because they do not waste time or energy judging their experiences as unfortunate, contentment governs their lives. On the flip side, they savor every nugget of joy that comes their way without wondering when someone will drop a hammer on their toes.

When these workers discuss Aldous Huxley's book, *Brave New World*,[1] they chuckle about the fact that workers were given "happy pills" so they would complete their tasks. To the contented employee, work itself is the happy pill. As one wise employee commented, "In what other arena of life am I paid to learn more about my strengths, life purpose, and passions?"

You will also enjoy a more tranquil work environment if you have the intention to fully embrace each gift life presents to you, even if you find some of the wrapping paper distasteful. Since there are so many aspects of life that we cannot control, accepting life on its own terms will provide you with profound personal freedom.

When you, like Viktor Frankl, trust that everything is purposeful, you are sure that the value of unpleasant experiences will eventually become clear. You only need to be fully conscious in each moment and make an effort not to judge harsh experiences. Then you stop missing the clues and miracles that life continuously provides.

> *There is some shadow of delight and delicacy*
> *which smiles upon and flatters us*
> *even in the very lap of melancholy.*
> Montaigne

DISCOVER THE LIGHT IN THE DARKNESS

A robust seed of opportunity is planted in the heart of every hardship. When life at work disappoints you, rather than presuming that you must search for or invent a more pleasant possibility, assume that it already exists. Then be conscious enough to hear it knock on your door.

Grace and Walter Lantz almost missed an amazing opportunity because they first judged its messenger as annoying. After trying to shoo away a woodpecker pecking at the roof of their quiet honeymoon cottage, they decided to view the bird as a positive possibility rather than as a pest. The couple decided to make the redhead they named Woody Woodpecker into a cartoon character. Over time, millions of people enjoyed chuckling at Woody's antics. The Lantzes made a fortune because they befriended, rather than continuing to judge, what first appeared to be an obstacle to bliss.

Of course, the greatest opportunity in each adversity is the chance to get to know yourself better. Mastering challenges escalates your self-esteem, confidence, and optimism. Each of these internal states leads to joy on the job.

TAKE A SECOND LOOK

1. During the next week, jot down the following.
   ✦ Circumstances that challenge you
   ✦ Events you judge to be unpleasant or unfortunate
   ✦ Situations you label as hidden opportununities or lessons to be learned

2. Review your list and identify the following.
   ✦ What thinking patterns and emotions empower you
   ✦ Which drain your energy

3. Hold the intention to capitalize on new opportunities that are inherent in disappointments.

IF YOU ARE STANDING BAREFOOT ON A CACTUS, REACH FOR THE STARS

The brilliant Greek philosopher Epictetus was quoted at the first of this chapter as saying that we should trust that everything that happens is perfect just as it is. He believed we should address events in life as we would approach food at a banquet, taking a portion of everything offered even if we think we will dislike the taste.

Epictetus' words were based on experience. He limped to Rome in a slave caravan because his knee had been shattered by repetitive beatings and then left untreated. Even as a slave, Epictetus shaped the actions of powerful individuals, including Roman emperor Marcus Aurelius. Although Epictetus' life banquet included servings of some pretty thorny cacti, he was eventually surrounded by passionate students. His insights have helped shape the lives of thousands of thoughtful, happy, and successful employees. One soldier who became a Hanoi prisoner of war kept himself sane during five years in a small, dirty Hanoi prison cell by practicing Epictitus' wisdom.[2]

Whether you have been stabbed by a prickly pear cactus or your computer crashes while you are working on a tight deadline, you will lose if you argue with what exists. Choose a different approach.

> Give thanks for what frustrates you because you can use it as a stairstep to climb to something more enjoyable. Make a commitment to invite and embrace problems. Seek to grow as a result of troubles instead of trying to eliminate them because challenges make you stronger, more fulfilled, and more successful. Consider yourself *experientially gifted* each time you take steps to ensure that setbacks feed new growth and understanding.

CHOOSE A FORWARD FOCUS

The most direct route to happiness is the path of surrendering to life. When you accept what exists, all of your energy and awareness are available to respond intelligently to any situation you encounter. You avoid automatic knee-jerk reactions. You never feel like a victim.

FOCUS ON THE FUTURE

Your power emerges from your attitude and your focus when you are faced with disagreeable circumstances.

✦ Decide to discover the bless in the mess. Hold the intention to identify and explore the hidden opportunities for learning and growth that lie within every difficulty.

✦ Explore how you co-created the unpleasant situation. Which of your outdated belief systems contributed? If this is difficult to determine, identify the belief systems that are associated with the results you have achieved. Examples: Consistent self-sabotage, procrastination, and perfectionism can indicate fear of failure and feelings of unworthiness. Avoiding opportunities to share your inner light more broadly with the world can be based on the assumption that the world is not a safe place for you or that your truth won't be accepted.

continued on the next page . . .

✦   Don't waste energy or delay your progress by feeling ashamed that you have
beliefs that don't serve you.   We all
have them.   Most of our assumptions
were *unconsciously* shaped by childhood experiences in which we tried to
feel safe by   adopting certain beliefs.
Most people spend their entire lives *automatically* operating with unconscious
convictions concerning themselves and
the world. Become aware of your outdated beliefs so you can *consciously* choose
how to live your life.

✦   Focus forward. Own your power to create
a positive future.   Concentrate on solutions. Give yourself a massive boost forward by refusing to judge yourself, your
circumstances, or other people.   Avoid
blame and victim games. Substitute the
discovery game. Develop immense curiosity regarding what you can learn in a
troublesome predicament.

✦   Develop a clear, multisensory vision regarding what you want. Hear, feel, sense,
and taste the experience of meeting your
goals.   Savor these feelings so you can
recall them at will.

continued on the next page . . .

✦   Identify what works and do more of it. Cultivate an attitude of gratitude so that even more enjoyable things can emerge in your life.

✦   Nurture your willingness to receive what you say you want. Notice, without judgment, any ways you feel undeserving. Then watch dysfunctional beliefs transform.

✦   Experience the sweetness of surrendering to life. When you trust each moment and live consciously in the present, you easily notice clues regarding your next steps.

PRACTICE PREVENTIVE MAINTAINENCE

Develop your ability to meet challenges before they arise. Cultivate inner peace and maintain a strong body by practicing meditation, deep breathing, qi gong, tai chi, or other reflective exercises. Nourish yourself with healthy food, fresh air, regular aerobic activity, adequate hydration, and deep sleep.

Enjoy meaningful connections with other people. Nurture your personal and professional support systems. People who engage in satisfying social relationships are healthier, happier, and more productive.

Journal writing about your feelings can help you stay in the present moment. It can also ease tension so you can gain the restful sleep you need in order to fully embrace your life each day.

CULTIVATE A CALM MIND

This very simple exercise produces rapid re-sults. Although it is highly effective when done as you sit in a quiet location, you can use it to gain inner peace at any time, even when you are in a meeting or taking a walk. The multisensory aspect of step one enhances the benefits of the exercise. It engages diverse parts of your brain and connects the emotional center of the brain (the amygdala) with the rational prefrontal cor-tex.

Step one can be omitted when you are in a hurry or need to focus on the events around you as you do the exercise. Use step one over time when doing the exercise to help you reprogram your neurology. The goal is to develop new neu-ral networks associated with a calm response to situations that would previously have felt stress-ful.

1. Breathe deeply and slowly. Notice the ar-eas of your body that are tense. Envision stress and tension as red paint dripping from your body. Imagine that the red paint is hot and thick. Smell the fragrance of the

continued on the next page . . .

red paint as puddles form on the ground and then disappear. Then imagine a cool, refreshing mint fragrance emanating from a sparkling lime green essence that fills the newly cleansed areas of your body.

2. Inhale to the count of four while you continue to breathe deeply and slowly and mentally say, "Accept."

3. Exhale, continuing to breathe deeply and slowly, to the count of eight while mentally saying, "Trust."

4. Continue the exercise until you feel calm. Notice that you have more energy to meet your challenge.

EMBRACE DARKNESS TO ILLUMINATE THE LIGHT

Fully experience your work life instead of trying to avoid unhappiness or chasing after pleasure. Since the object of your focus expands, a dogged determination to sidestep misery is destined to create unhappiness. Seeking pleasure can only result in temporary amusement. Genuine happiness results when you let go of your judgments and accept yourself, others, and your life, warts and all.

When you accept what exists, you never feel like a victim. In fact, you own your power to create joy by responding, rather than reacting, to difficulties in intelligent ways that yield the results you desire. Since your life will always be in a state of flux, acceptance, including self-acceptance, will vaccinate you against unnecessary stress.

When disagreeable events arise, remind yourself that every obstacle is an opportunity to create more joy. It's not a form of punishment! Be grateful for challenges. Resist the temptation to self-sabotage by setting conditions or demands for happiness.

Use exercises such as Cultivate a Calm Mind to achieve the internal balance that prepares you to meet challenges. When you flow with life, joy emerges in the most surprising ways and places.

Stop worrying about the potholes
in the road and enjoy the journey.
Barbara Hoffman

CHAPTER 13

REFRAME VERSUS REACT

There is no reality except the one contained within us.
That is why so many people live such an unreal life.
They take the images outside them for reality
and never allow the world within to assert itself.
Hermann Hesse

MASTER THE KINGDOM WITHIN

Because of his experiences climbing from poverty to emerge as a financial giant and philanthropist, W. Clement Stone firmly believed that challenges enrich our lives by stimulating us to become stronger and more self-confident. When colleagues and employees approached him with, "I have a problem," he smiled and exclaimed, "Congratulations!" This feedback usually stunned Stone's associates, so they protested, "But it's a tough problem!" Stone's second response was even more enthusiastic, "Then, double congratulations!"

Employees who are peaceful and fulfilled recognize that most challenges can be resolved by shifting our perceptions. The following wisdom is ingrained in their brains.

It is impossible for any situation to trouble us. This is true whether we are demoted, lose a job, or face an impending death. Only our *opinions* of circumstances cause despair, anger, and agony. Inner turmoil is never caused by what exists. It is brought about by the desire for something different. Pain is created by resistance to what exists.

The mind is our private inner sanctuary of freedom and peace. Because the mind is capable of creating a lifetime of joy and tranquility, contented employees identify fear-based thoughts and upgrade them to thoughts that serve them.

They refuse to be reactive. Instead, they acknowledge the power of their assumptions and perceptions. They know their life story is the sum total of all of the choices they have made. Since they know they are the sole ruler of their inner domain (their mind), they use this miraculous tool to create inner peace, harmony, and enthusiasm for problem-solving. Like Clement Stone, they reframe unpleasant situations as opportunities to learn and grow. When they change their perceptions, the world around them rewards them with a very different reality.

HOW IS THIS POSSIBLE?

❏ Most Assumptions and Perceptions Are Automatic, Unconscious, and Untrue

We have an arsenal of assumptions about work, life, ourselves, and other people. The majority of our beliefs are unconscious. We may think our assumptions are based on facts, but this is usually not true. Most of our passionate convictions were passed onto us by family members and other significant individuals who unconsciously accepted the notions of others. Even though we cannot visually perceive the pressure of public opinion, American diplomat James Russell Lowell believed it is similar to the pressure of the atmosphere.[1] When the equivalent of sixteen pounds per square inch consistently presses on our consciousness, it packs a powerful punch.

We also choose our perceptions, although this process is usually automatic and unconscious. Perceptions are also seldom based on facts. For better or worse, our perceptions are directly related to our beliefs. Unexamined beliefs, such as "I'm not good enough," significantly retard our progress. We cheat ourselves and everyone around us when we live an unexamined life.

The man who never alters his opinion
is like standing water
and breeds reptiles of the mind.
William Blake

PICK A PERCEPTION

1. Use a coin or another round object similar in size to draw a circle on a white piece of paper. Totally fill in the circle so that it is a dark round object on a white background.

2. Look at your drawing and focus on the circle. Consider the following possibilities and then write as many ideas as you can regarding what your drawing might be.

   ✦ A black marble placed on top of clean white paper
   ✦ A chocolate cookie on top of fresh snow
   ✦ A bowling ball without a thumbhole

3. Shift your focus. Instead of concentrating on the dark round object, focus on the area outside of it. Now your drawing could be your view of a vast dark sky as you peer from a peephole!

4. The interpretation in step three emerged after you shifted your focus. You opened your perception to an entirely different view of your world.

❏ You Can Reframe Frames

Since perceptions and assumptions are the foundation of your version of reality, *you can transform your reality by altering your perceptions and assumptions.* This shift not only modifies your thoughts and emotions, it affects your neural circuitry. When you change your physiology, you modify the next chapters of your life. This book contains many multisensory exercises that will empower you to consciously reframe events and circumstances that don't serve you.

Mental structures, *not facts,* determine how you view the world

↓

Your assumptions and perceptions affect your thoughts and emotions

↓

Your thoughts and emotions affect your physiology

↓

Your physiology affects your neural circuitry

↓

Your neural circuitry changes the next chapters of your life

Your brain is more powerful than a supercomputer, but it strives to simplify complexity to achieve efficiency. This is a very useful, adaptive mechanism. You don't have to relearn how to open the office door each time you want to enter. You can focus your senses only on what you need to perceive when you are in a hurry to catch an airplane flight. Unfortunately, the brain's simplifying tendencies can make us simpletons. We sometimes think inside of an empty box we should be tossing into the recycling pile.

When someone introduces a different point of view, we often assume that the message bearer is clueless. We can't grasp the fact that our own senses are also shut down. Consider the experience of two employees named Dr. Jekyll and Mr. Hyde. Their employer asked them to sketch the layout of an innovative training room at a conference they had just attended. Jekyll and Hyde disagreed about virtually every detail of the layout, and the situation grew nasty. A frustrated but polite Hyde pleaded, "I beg to disagree with you, Dr. Jekyll. It is *my* picture that is the training room." Jekyll was incensed and swore, "You idiot! *My* picture is the training room, not yours." The ugly situation continued until Jekyll threatened Hyde with his life.

Neither could perceive the truth—*neither* of their pictures was the training room. Both pictures were only pictures. Only the training room could be the training room.

Like Jekyll and Hyde, the mental structures that determine how we view the world are usually not based on facts. They are composed of frames, which are symbolic representations of our version of reality. These images are encoded in our brains, similar to the way songs are burned onto a CD.

Like a CD-RW, data in our neurology can be erased and updated. We can consciously exchange one frame for another. Exercises throughout this book provide examples of how we can use simple stories and multisensory experiences associated with positive insights and emotions to reframe our mental frames. Instead of continuing to overlook or reject facts that don't match our existing picture of life, we can update and improve our reality.

> You can make a decision to exchange a mental frame that is not serving you for one that will. When you do so with enthusiasm (emotion and passion), new neural circuits form that change your life in positive ways.
>
> Since our behaviors change when we shift our mental frames, we create more joy on the job. We stop limiting ourselves. We take what exists and give it our best. We discover true contentment on the job—the power of gaining every possible benefit from any situation. We remember that our minds always offer the freedom to choose contentment and joy. We discover inner peace, and we retain it even when the world is reeling in chaos.

The quality of life at work is directly related to: (1) how we communicate with ourselves concerning events that occur and (2) our ability to thrive when we are challenged. When we fall flat on our backs, we can moan that we will be down-and-out forever. This is a "thought-prayer" for being stuck or miserable because our minds use our thoughts and feelings to create our future.

There is another choice. We can acknowledge our pain and have compassion for ourselves, while considering babies as a role model. Babies fall down a lot when they learn to walk. They cry a bit, but scrapes do not deter them from meeting their objective of moving forward.

Psychologists call this strategy situational optimism. This is very different from telling someone, "Just think positive!" Many of us are not innately optimistic. *Dispositional optimists* are people who *always* wake up on the right side of the bed. Situational optimism is perfect for the rest of us. *Situational optimism is a valuable tool that can be learned.* Fortunately, it is not necessary for you to change your personality to acquire this trait. You only need to do the following.

✦ Be aware of your predominant pattern.
✦ Consciously choose to use *realistic* positive thinking for specific immediate challenges.

In the best possible way, our brains are much more like plastic milk jugs than hard rocks. They are infinitely changeable. Simple behavior modifications create new neural networks! People who consistently practice situational optimism can become dispositional optimists.

Since situational optimism strengthens your immune system, it will also help you cope with stress. Humor is a wonderful strategy to combine with situational optimism. When contented workers fall flat on their backs, they often make a comment such as, "Well, now there's no where to go but up!"

The next exercise combines a playful approach with rich mental imagery. The technique will strengthen neural networks in your brain that are associated with your ability to consistently transform roadblocks into steppingstones that lead to more joy on the job.

ACT IT OUT

This exercise can be done alone or with others. Make three chairs available. Label chair one, *Despair Chair*, chair two, *Happy Chair*, and the last chair, *Inspirational Chair.*

One person at a time, or you alone, will sit in each chair while telling a true story related to the topic of that chair. When sitting in chair one, the storyteller talks about a time in their working life in which they experienced sadness, fear, or despair. When sitting in chair two, the individual shares a story regarding an enjoyable experience at work.

Upon moving to chair three, the storyteller must reframe the "despair story" to inspire an audience of employees. If this is difficult for you, assume that you are sharing your story with a group of immigrants who have just arrived in this country. You have been hired to empower them with your knowledge concerning how people grow personally through challenges at work. At the end of your presentation, you want them to feel they can succeed in this country. Inspire them with your honesty, sincerity, and best wishes for their happiness on the job.

continued on the next page . . .

Your stories should include comments regarding the following.

✦   What your despair experience taught you about yourself, work, and life
✦   What strengths you gained from challenges. Examples include compassion, humility, determination, awareness of your unique talents, belief in your abilities, and feelings of worthiness.
✦   How you developed the courage to meet other trials
✦   Why challenges at work can be viewed positively as well as negatively

Audiotape your presentation so you can listen to it later. After hearing the recording, jot down new insights concerning the following.

✦   Your inner strengths
✦   The value of reframing unpleasant experiences
✦   Your next steps toward creating a more joyful work environment

Although you can do this exercise without moving from one chair to the next (you can simply write or tell a story), please resist any impulse to do so. Shifting seats stimulates different areas of your brain. You create a rich multisensory experience, and this produces a wealth of insights.

continued on the next page . . .

The story you tell in chair three incorporates the proven principle that tutors gain at least as much as their students.

If you lack an audience when telling your stories, imagine that one exists. Become totally involved in giving your presentation instead of evaluating every word you utter. The more engaged you become, the more you will benefit from this experience. Participants who audiotape themselves sharing their experiences with an audience gain additional appreciation for their capabilities when they listen to the tape at a later time.

When doing the Act It Out exercise, many participants have discovered that their despair experiences paved the road to some of their happiest work experiences. They created a much more fulfilling work experience after being downsized or required to change duties, work location, or software. Even though they were reluctant to do so, their jobs eventually became more enjoyable.

What positive results have occurred in your work life after going through experiences you originally judged to be negative?

PICTURE PERFECT

Since happiness is a conscious decision instead of an automatic response, we can choose joy. We can also select what shade of happiness to experience. If you were an artist, what color would you paint your work today? The peaceful rosey hue of the dawn? A brilliant red-orange like the flaming sun at dusk?

You always have the power to choose a different color (to reframe) any events that might otherwise disrupt a peaceful workday. What hue of paint will you sprinkle on events at work that might otherwise disrupt your day? How can a new tone or theme totally change your interpretation of an experience?

Our thinking patterns are actually similar to the act of painting a community mural. Our perceptions and opinions are never truly complete because we can choose to endlessly revise them.

How can you do this when an old identity screams for you to maintain a narrow perception that will limit your thinking, your behavior, and ultimately, your potential to achieve joy on the job? The next exercise will help you achieve a fresh approach to problem solving. You will link your conscious search for an answer with nonconscious associations. (At present, you are unaware of these neural networks in your brain.)

Why is this important? When we are faced with challenges, we usually forget that most of the answers we frantically search for are patiently waiting our *re*-discovery. We just have to retrieve them from our vast arsenal of unconscious memories. According to memory experts, the ratio of our conscious and nonconscious awareness can be understood by comparing 15 inches to 11 miles. According to MRI scans, conscious perceptions and thoughts are represented by a span of 15 inches. A distance of 11 miles symbolizes material that is not conscious.[2]

No matter how baffling a puzzle that faces us or how unique a particular dilemma appears to be, we have either solved a similar challenge in the past or we have observed or read about someone else having done so. Since we often don't pay attention to experiences that don't have obvious personal relevance, it is no wonder that the solution we seek is not on the tip of our tongue.

It can be. All we have to do is trigger an associative link in our nonconscious mind that will help us remember what we already know. The following exercise uses what Albert Einstein called combinatory play.[3] Most ideas emerge when we synthesize a unique concept with existing neural associations in the brain. This is why discovering relationships between two vastly different items like a pencil and a car stimulate imaginative thinking that assists with problem solving. It is also why asking absurd questions like, "What if we paid customers to buy our product?" have yielded creative and phenomenally successful results. (People often buy a specific product because they can obtain a rebate.)

The technique used by the exercise on the next two pages causes participants to relax and creatively find easy ways to resolve a challenge. Creativity makes anxiety run for cover; and, as Einstein often said, imagination is more important than knowledge when we seek solutions to dilemmas. The exercise is a fun example of how you can reframe challenges instead of negatively judging or hastily reacting to them.

SEARCH YOUR MEMORY BANK

Although this exercise can be done by a single individual using a tape recorder, I recommend that you work with a group or partner who has a common desire to address a specific challenge.

1. As a group, all participants will gaze at a variety of objects in the environment until their attention is drawn to a single item that attracts their focus. Most of the time, each person will spontaneously select a different object, but there may be some overlap.

2. Each group of two participants should then take turns with first one partner and then the other being: (a) the person talking and (b) the individual who listens and records the other person's responses. When a participant is talking, he or she should close their eyes and speak out loud, in the present tense, while answering the questions on the next page. The speaking partner should continue to talk out loud, especially if they find themselves rambling, because that is usually when groundbreaking ideas surface. The listening partner's job is not to talk or react to what the other person says. The listener's job is to pay attention to the content stated in a nonjudgmental manner and record major trends of the speaking partner's conversation.

As needed, listening partners will remind speaking partners of the questions they are to answer so speakers can keep their eyes closed and concentrate on the stream of information rapidly flowing through their consciousness. If no thoughts occur to a speaker, their partner should encourage the individual to ramble out loud instead of not talking or searching their mind for thoughts. It is usually helpful to say, "Tell me more."

3. After each partner has been both a listener and a speaker, the group will hear each recorder's notes and discover an innovative solution.

> Here are the questions
> for each participant to answer.

✦ The object I picked is _____ .
✦ The characteristics of this object are ____
  _____ .
✦ These characteristics are related to solving our problem in the following ways____
  _____
✦ This is how this experience changed my perspective about solving this problem __
  _____ .

REINVENT YOUR WORK LIFE

Often, we don't choose our first thought concerning a situation we don't like. It is usually an automatic response based on an emotional trigger associated with an unpleasant past experience. We can always choose our next thoughts! Assume that for everything in your work life you don't like, there is an opposite condition you will cherish. Allow it to be revealed to you.

Take excellent care of yourself so that your full capabilities will be available to make the best long-term choices. Remember the HALT adage. Don't make assumptions or major decisions when you are **h**ungry, **a**ngry, **l**onely, or **t**ired.

Nourish your mind, body, and spirit. When you feel fatigued or a solution to a perplexing problem seems out of your grasp, enjoy exploring a rich array of creativity-boosting strategies, such as the one used in the last exercise. A playful approach will invite fresh new perspectives and ideas.

Develop an excellent support system. Listen to others with an open mind, but don't expect those who have abandoned their life dreams to support yours.

If you really want to be happy,
no one can stop you.
Sandy O'Malley

CHAPTER 14

USE THE POWER
OF NEGATIVE EMOTIONS

Those who don't know how to weep
with their whole heart
don't know how to laugh enther.
Golda Meir

DON'T PUT ON A HAPPY FACE

Happiness at work is a choice. This doesn't mean you should ignore problems, particularly those you can solve. Trying to ignore negative situations disconnects you from reality. If a supervisor hands you an impossible project with a due date of yesterday, it won't serve either of you if you smile and say, "Of course, I can do this!"

Don't reach for a jar of happy-face paint when you are disgruntled. Negative feelings provide value. You are authentic and grounded in your current reality. Constructively experienced negative emotions are stairsteps that lead to higher levels of positive feelings.

> Unhappiness is sometimes
>
> a shortcut to happiness.

THE VALUE OF NEGATIVE THINKING

Because there is wisdom in every piece of life, negative thinking can be very productive as long as it is not so continuous that you lose sight of opportunities or feel hopeless. Be honest with yourself about your feelings. Resisting what exists saps your energy and creates unnecessary stress. Buried feelings never die. In fact, they rise from the grave when you let down your guard, usually at a time when it is inconvenient to deal with unresolved issues from the past.

Most people try to squelch fear, anger, sorrow, shame, and other negative emotions because they fear they will be overwhelmed by uncontrollable discomfort. Negative emotions just need to be acknowledged. Then, all of your energy is available to you, so you can take charge of your life instead of being ruled by your environment or the internal critic.

There is no such thing as a bad feeling. Moods and emotions such as guilt, jealousy, anger, hatred, laziness, depression, greed, lust, shame, and confusion may be unpleasant, but they are all part of the human experience. Feelings don't take action. *You* do.

Negative emotions are part of an essential cleansing process that enables you to create a more enjoyable life. Clean, fresh-smelling clothes can only emerge from a washing machine after soiled material is churned around so dirt and debris can be released. A similar process occurs with negative emotions. The closer you or your team are to reaching a major goal, the more likely it is that submerged fears, self-doubt, and other insecurities will rise to the surface. The agitation provides an opportunity to identify and clear emotional debris.

WHEN BAD MOODS ARE GOOD MOODS

In an interview in the February 1996 issue of *Elle* magazine, tennis pro Steven Turner, acknowledged the power of negative thinking. Turner swam against the popular current of "just think positive" by stressing the importance of embracing one's shadow side. Turner advocated harnessing the energy of our negative attributes by bringing our shadows into the light and looking them squarely in the eye. Most people assume that essential energy exists only in our favorable characteristics, but it also resides in our doubts, cynicism, and faults. People who accept their negative energy accept themselves. They are more whole. Turner discovered that embracing shadow material was a key ingredient in producing his winning record.

> When we acknowledge
> our unfavorable characteristics
> and negative behavior patterns,
> they have no control over us.

Everyone sometimes feels insecure, guilty, incompetent, or even unethical. All of us are sometimes unmotivated, greedy, envious, or uncompassionate. Because we lack total awareness, we are sometimes dishonest, especially with ourselves, concerning our motivations and characteristics. Denial and defensiveness concerning human weaknesses create resistance to change. Owning our faults unlocks the door that leads to positive change.

Acknowledging our negative characteristics in a matter of fact manner is evidence of self-love and self-responsibility. Instead of thwarting positive change by judging ourselves as inferior, we acknowledge that we are part of the human race. We feel connected to the whole of humanity because we are no longer afraid someone will discover and expose our dark side. When we accept ourselves, warts and all, supportive individuals emerge in our lives. Our negative characteristics transform more quickly.

POSITIVE THINKING . . . OR PRODUCTIVE THINKING?

The fastest way to change how you feel (which you often cannot control) is to change how you think (which you can always control). Positive thoughts create feel-good endorphins. What you focus on multiplies, so people who expect the best usually receive just that.

Realistic optimism is best. Perceive the world as accurately as you can while you focus on achieving the outcome you desire.

NOTICE THE EFFECTS OF EXPECTATIONS

Unhappy people develop tunnel vision and continue to validate their negative expectations. You can prove this to yourself. Notice what happens when you expect others not to approve of you, your work, or your ideas. Also observe what happens when you are absolutely certain that you will be warmly received by others. From people to pay, from products to parking spots, things generally fall into place when you are in a positive mood, you know you are taking your next step, and you trust the course of your life.

You can adopt a productive attitude even when you are upset. This disposition will emerge from realistic thinking that reflects the following.

✦ Believing in yourself
✦ Awareness of your existing strengths
✦ Confidence in your ability to learn and grow
✦ Faith in the process of life

This is very different from putting on a happy face and mouthing empty affirmations designed to cover up feelings of inadequacy or fears of the future.

People who deny reality or ignore negative clues forfeit opportunities to prevent problems. Those who play Pollyanna focus on the future to the extent that they miss present-moment messages regarding how to upgrade their situation. You have observed misguided people riding in a leaky vessel who have sabotaged themselves and wasted time they needed to solve a problem. As they smiled and affirmed, "Everything in my life is fantastic," their boat sank into a putrid pond.

Save your rose-colored glasses for a masquerade party, but make a choice to recognize and experience all sources of joy on the job. Life provides a profound abundance of raw material, and we are alchemists.

DISCOVER A DIFFERENT APPROACH

You probably can't force yourself to think happy thoughts when you are fuming or frightened. Instead of trying to drown tears, fears, or anger with denial or fake optimism, take a different approach.

✦ Remember that everyone feels negative at times.
✦ Trust the process of your life. A thunderstorm can only hide the sunshine for a limited time. Feelings also have a limited lifespan, so accept them, knowing they will fade over time unless you do something to restimulate them.
✦ Acknowledge your emotions without indulging them. You are not your emotions. You are the result of your *actions*, so observe your feelings without attachment or judgment.
✦ Learn to use the raw energy that is available in every emotion, whether it is positively or negatively charged.

Be true to yourself instead of cheating yourself out of the richness of life's emotions. Every emotion and every experience serve a purpose. When humans truly experience their sadness, a chemical is released that converts sorrow to sweetness. Other chemical reactions cause safely expressed anger to melt and become peace of mind. Fear that is rationally dealt with transforms into self-confidence.

DISCOVER THE TRUTH ABOUT YOUR EMOTIONS

Emotions are physical sensations in your body. When we accept them as "just energy" and experience all emotions safely and constructively, we can use even the most negative thoughts to boost our success and joy. The following example illustrates how to use negative thinking and negative emotions to your advantage.

A few years ago, I supported a client whom I'll call Sean. He was being unfairly evicted from his office suite after his landlord was unexpectedly called into military service and left his son, Ted, to manage his property. Ted lived out of the area and viewed his new responsibility as an unnecessary burden. Ted's solution to his dilemma was to evict Sean without following proper legal procedures.

Sean and I felt confident that a judge would rule in Sean's favor. As we sat in a courtroom waiting for the arrival of the justice, we noticed Ted sitting a few rows away. His anxious, furrowed brow was saturated with perspiration. Sean and I were relieved to be relaxed in a judicial setting.

All of a sudden, chills ran down my spine and Sean's face faded from olive to ash-colored. I was baffled that our calm demeanor had been interrupted, so I turned around to discover the cause. Thirteen unshaven men wearing bright orange jumpsuits were being coerced into the room by guards armed with pistols. The unpleasant smell of fear was pervasive, and I would have sworn that the temperature in the room had soared by ten degrees. A glance at the shackles and handcuffs on the prisoners confirmed that the fear belonged to the inmates.

Research by scientist Candace Pert, author of *Molecules of Emotion*, has proven that emotions are molecules (neuropeptides) that circulate throughout the body.[1] Understanding emotions in this way helps us understand how we sense other people's fear, experience gut reactions, and read the emotions present in a room.

As I told Sean, there were several reasons we could use the fear we had perceived in a positive way.

✦ We were sensing other people's anxiety. The proof was that before the entrance of the prisoners, we felt relaxed and self-confident.

✦ Since only human judgments define emotions as positive or negative, we could choose to perceive the sensations as *just energy* rather than experiencing them as fear.

✦ Emotions travel in pairs (polarities), so the way to feel calm and peaceful when you're afraid is to allow yourself to feel the fear without labeling it as bad.

Although it was very unpleasant for Sean and I to feel the knots in our stomachs and the jittery energy circulating through our bodies without trying to repress the sensations, the strategy proved to be successful. Within only a couple of minutes, our jagged nerves shifted into a sweet peacefulness.

We both smiled, and Sean whispered, "Wow! Now, I have a lot more energy to work with! I feel much stronger!" Our new emotional state felt much higher because our previous calm had been recharged by additional energy.

You can guess the end of this true story. The judge ruled in Sean's favor, and we left the courtroom feeling energized.

IDENTIFY THE STARS IN THE DARKNESS

The sun and stars are always present. We just don't always perceive their presence. The co-existence of negative and positive emotions is similar. As Sean's story indicates, emotions are experienced in polarities—pairs of feelings that we usually label as negative and positive. Examples are fear/self-confidence, anger/peace, and sadness/joy. This is why Sean quickly discovered that the feelings he yearned for were readily available. You can benefit from Sean's insight.

Usually, when an inmate tries to escape from prison, the result is a longer sentence. A similar process occurs when people try to run from unpleasant emotions. Their focus on what they want to avoid feeds what they are resisting.

People who experience life and acknowledge all feelings in a safe and constructive way and without judgment have a very different adventure. *Their negative feelings conclude in a brisk manner. This simultaneously activates a new cycle of positive feelings.*

TRANFORM NEGATIVE EMOTIONS INTO POSITIVE ENERGY

Use the following proven strategies for converting negative emotions into positive energy.

✦ Experience each moment consciously, feeling emotions that you might otherwise judge as unpleasant or negative.
✦ Think of your emotions as molecules of energy. Allow them to flow freely so you can develop new layers of personal power, as Sean did.

When we experience negative feelings without judgment, they create a perfect path to positive feelings.

After you work with the above technique for a while, you will spontaneously prevent the emergence of many negative feelings because you will experience life with curiosity instead of judging situations, yourself, or others.

EMOTIONAL RELEASE—THE GOOD, THE BAD, AND THE UGLY

Venting anger and other intense emotions can ease tension and raise our spirits as long as we accept total personal responsibility for our actions. Sometimes anger is the missing piece that is essential to the completion of a peace puzzle. An internal explosion can create transformative energy for our next step.

There is, however, a serious downside to repetitive cathartic releases that are self-indulgent. The temporary sense of relief that follows a fiery emotional outburst can be more enjoyable than the thoughtful give and take that is required to solve problems in a mature manner.

Because patterns and neural networks are developed and reinforced by intense emotions and passion, a nasty habit can develop. Individuals who feel entitled to spew angry explosions into the world engage in chronic temper tantrums. They develop tunnel vision. They refuse to take responsibility for their actions. Since their energy is consumed with building and releasing frustrations, they fail to understand how they co-create problems and could cooperatively resolve them. Relationships sour. Negative expectations regarding the behavior of *the two-year-old employee* contribute to a self-perpetuating cycle of tantrums. Joy on the job seems like a lost dream.

TRYING TO CONTROL YOUR FEELINGS IS ALSO INEFFECTIVE

We can always control our behavior and change the focus of our thoughts. Emotions can be ornery. They often play us for the fool. When we are angry about being angry, we self-sabotage. We rage at our wrath until it overwhelms us. When we are afraid of being afraid, our resistance causes fear to bloat until it explodes. In both cases, what we resist not only persists, it multiplies with hurricane force. Something very different happens when we observe our feelings without judgment.

DISCOVER THE MIRACLE OF NEUTRAL OBSERVATION

When you observe the outbursts of a chronically angry co-worker with detachment instead of allowing the person to engage you in verbal combat, you feel pleased with yourself instead of emotionally distraught. Your self-esteem rises because you realize you didn't grab the individual's tempting bait. You didn't become defensive or combative. Over time, you develop compassion for this person who has limited skills for handling frustration. Because your behavior shifts their focus away from you, they may notice that their behavior is inappropriate. It is quite likely that there will be an opening in the future when you can deliver honest feedback with an open heart and it will be acccepted. In the meantime, the distraught person will no longer find you an attractive target.

You also receive excellent benefits when you witness your own negative feelings with detachment. Instead of wasting energy and time trying to manipulate your mood, *observe* your emotions. Remember that feelings form a constantly changing chain. One emotion is replaced by another, which is then superceded by the next.

Accept that you are part of the human race. Acknowledge your negative feelings without resisting them. Self-acceptance freezes resistance to change. When your mind chatters in an attempt to reinforce a familiar zone of fear, detach yourself. One very effective method is to remark, "The mind is sure busy right now!"

It is often said that fear is merely an acronym for *False Evidence Appearing Real*. Fear is propped up by fantasy, the illusion that it is possible to fail. It is really impossible to fail because every action you take will produce a result. Mistakes are magical tools for self-discovery and professional growth. To avoid genuine failure, we only have to stop labeling ourselves as inadequate when we don't achieve the result we want and then use a different approach. The next exercise will help you achieve a peaceful state instead of labeling negative feelings.

DISCOVER YOUR NEUTRAL OBSERVER

Use this exercise to calm your nervous system when you feel emotionally out of balance. It will help you observe, instead of judge, negative feelings.

Because the technique emphasizes the exhalation process, it cleanses physical toxins that exacerbate emotional tension.

You can use this tool at any time, even in a meeting, without calling attention to yourself. Of course, you can also do the exercise while sitting quietly with your eyes closed. The three simple steps usually only take a few minutes of your time.

1. Inhale for four seconds.
2. Exhale for eight seconds.
3. Repeat steps one and two until you feel calm.

CONCENTRATE ON RESPONSIBLE ACTIONS

You are always the commander of your actions, even when experiencing your emotions reminds you of riding a roller coaster.

You are not responsible for what you feel. You are, however, totally accountable for how you respond to your feelings.

Because managing your behavior creates healthy neural networks in your brain, you build self-esteem when you carefully choose your actions instead of unconsciously reacting to unpleasant situations. There is an additional wonderful side effect. Your responsible actions eventually alter how you feel about situations that previously frustrated you. Over time, unpleasant feelings fade more and more quickly.

ENJOY A BALANCE OF POSITIVE AND NEGATIVE FEELINGS

Instead of struggling to place a happy mask on your face when you are distraught, find value in the negative and focus on the positive. There will never be a shortage of negative events screaming for your attention at work. Positive emotions are often more subtle.

Since good feelings are associated with heightened creativity and awareness of new possibilities for solving problems, be aware of your positive and negative emotions. Notice when you spiral into negativity. As discussed previously, it is essential to honor (not indulge) negative emotions and to use them in constructive ways.

Your ultimate goal is to experience more joy at work. Psychologist Barbara Fredrickson's research indicates that a 2.9 or higher ratio of positivity to negativity is associated with flourishing in life instead of languishing.[2]   Notice and focus on what is working when you are on the job. When you nourish an attitude of gratitude, you foster more fun and eventually create a cycle of joy.

Experiencing more happiness at work will heighten your confidence and capabilities. Every time you choose contentment instead of chaos, life becomes less struggle. If you are like most of us, you will occasionally give away your power by forgetting that you have total control regarding how you react to situations. The solution is simple. Notice backsliding, without judging yourself harshly. You will eventually dismantle any remaining fragments of the socially-imposed toxic belief system that life is a struggle.

A gem cannot be polished
without friction.
Chinese proverb

CHAPTER 15

EMPOWER YOURSELF WITH ACTION

Only a hen lays down on the job and gets results.
Ancient barnyard proverb

SWIM TO YOUR SHIP

You will grow old and weary if you wait for an elegant cruise ship to float toward you, ask you to take command, and offer you 95 percent of the company's stock along with unlimited perks. Since you are the only person who can create your happiness, swim from the shore and claim your fair share of joy on the job.

When 360 employees of FCI Electronics of Pennsylvania learned their plant would close due to tough economic times, the workers took charge. They applied for a new company! The FCI employees promoted themselves on the Internet and in trade magazines as a made-to-order work force. They marketed their special attributes so they wouldn't have to separate from each other or leave the geographic area they loved. They advertised that they were offering hundreds of years of experience in specific technical skills and emphasized that most of the workers had never missed a day of work during the last eight years.

The FCI employees took action because they were committed to joy on the job. There were several reasons they succeeded.

✦ They were aware of their value.
✦ They searched for a solution that would benefit everyone concerned.
✦ They asked for what they needed.

Helen Houston also had an opportunity to feel hopeless and helpless but chose to move forward. Houston didn't receive the same signing bonus other employees received when they were transferred to a new corporate department. Instead of feeling like a victim or second-guessing the merits of her performance, she assumed she was entitled to the bonus and asked management when she should expect to receive it. Houston transformed a thorny situation into an opportunity. She presented a list of her accomplishments and clearly indicated how they contributed to customer loyalty and other aspects of the organization's bottom line. She also described the ways she had helped team members fulfill their responsibilities. The result? Houston not only received a retroactive bonus, she received a promotion.

When facing difficulties, employees who are happy focus on solutions. Those who are discontent usually feel hopeless or helpless. When you take action to resolve challenges, you feel you have some control over your circumstances. You validate yourself and build inner strength.

TO FAIL . . . OR NOT TO FAIL

> There was once a very cautious man.
> He never laughed or cried.
> He never cared, he never dared.
> He never dreamed or tried.
> And when one day he passed away.
> His insurance was denied.
> For since he never really lived,
> They claimed he never died.
>   Author Unknown

Failure is a secret ingredient

for happiness.

Most people shy away from risks because they fear they will make a mistake. They dread failure because they think it will rob them of confidence, but the opposite is true. Taking healthy risks builds self-esteem, even when you fail. On the other hand, when you don't leap out of your familiar zone, you reinforce a negative self-image and lower your confidence.

Joy on the job emerges when we purposely pursue activities in which we have never proven our ability to succeed and refuse to label ourselves as a failure if we don't immediately succeed.

When you were a small child learning to walk, you fell . . . over and over and over again. Even though you were often frustrated, you didn't worry about being a failure. You didn't feel worthless. Each new attempt to amble around was a hopeful, determined fresh start.

> When babies fall while learning to walk, they don't waste energy judging their performance as inadequate. They focus on what they want. They master many new skills quickly because they see, smell, hear, and taste the benefits of success.

Instead of feeling inadequate, babies concentrate on "I want to be held. I want to grab that cookie that will taste good. I want to see people smile at me and hear them laugh because I'm so cute. I smell something interesting in the next room, so I'm going there right now!"

> Usually, what we fear is pointing us to our next step in life. As Eleanor Roosevelt said, "You must do the thing you cannot."

WHAT HAVE YOU GOT TO GAIN?

1. Find a quiet place where you will not be disturbed for at least ten minutes. Sit quietly and breathe deeply.

2. Focus on a healthy risk you've wanted to take but haven't because you fear the possibility of failure. Note: Intelligent risks are not impulsive. Although the potential outcome is uncertain, you have previously considered the foreseeable consequences of your actions.

3. Close your eyes and imagine what life would be like if you did fail. Write a one-sentence description of how you would feel. If you were not successful, would you gain feedback that would allow you to improve your method or go another direction?

4. Complete the following sentence stem.

   "If I was not afraid I would fail,
   I would _____."

5. Close your eyes again. Imagine possible benefits of meeting your goal. Talk out loud, using

continued on the next page . .

rich multisensory language that describes what it would be like to achieve your desire. Speak in the present tense. Example: *I feel relieved because I am now comfortable sharing my opinions in a tactful way. I see a new sparkle in my eyes when I look in the mirror. I hear myself breathing deep, calm breaths. When I hold my favorite pen or smell freshly perked coffee, I remember how satisfying it feels to accomplish an objective. Each time I take a bite out of a delicious piece of food, I savor the sweet memory of the taste of success.* Pause a few moments to cherish the vivid images of achieving your goal.

6. Now imagine how it will feel if you do nothing. How will you feel if you just continue to experience what dissatisfies you?

7. Decide if you have more to gain by clinging to your familiar zone and not attempting to achieve your dreams or by taking a healthy risk.

> *If you don't risk anything,*
> *you risk even more.*
> Erica Jong

CHOOSE THE FOCUS THAT EMPOWERS YOU

Although the goal is to take action, happiness occurs as a by-product when you become absorbed in a challenge.

IDENTIFY YOUR PATTERN

During the next two weeks, observe your reactions to challenges. Once you acknowledge a problem, which of the following is your most common reaction?

DISEMPOWER YOURSELF

✦ Focus on the problem instead of concentrating on potential solutions

✦ Blame someone or a situation you don't like

✦ Feel hopeless

✦ Wait for the problem to be solved

EMPOWER YOURSELF

✦ Channel energy you might use to blame others in a positive way, such as attempting to identify a solution

✦ Consider potential ways to overcome difficulties or obstacles

✦ Take responsible action

✦ Evaluate the results of the strategy used

✦ Employ a new strategy if the first action fails

If you tend to focus on the dilemma instead of the solution, the next exercise will help you initiate a different pattern.

CHOOSE A FOCUS THAT EMPOWERS YOU

1. Remember the last time you solved a problem. The situation you are reviewing does not have to relate to a recent challenge at work.

   ✦ List the steps you took to resolve the challenge.
   ✦ Remember how you felt after solving the problem.
   ✦ **You have just proven that you are capable of resolving challenges.**

2. Complete the following sentence stems as you hold a current challenge in your mind. Write with your nondominant hand and keep your hand moving on the page. If no thoughts come into your mind, scribble until they do because this stimulates new feedback loops in your brain.

continued on the next page . . .

Keep writing until you receive insights regarding each question.

✦ I didn't think I could solve this problem because _____.

✦ If I could resolve this challenge, I would feel _____ about my-self.

✦ When this problem no longer exists, I will be _____.

3. With your nondominant hand, draw a symbol or cartoon character that represents an old identity that lives inside of you, such as *gotta be perfect, hopeless,* or *helpless.* Be absolutely truthful with yourself. All of us have old identities that don't serve us. Once we become aware of their existence, they begin to spontaneously change.

4. Complete the following sentence stems.

✦ When this old identity is no longer a part of my consciousness, I will be living in a way that is more aligned with my true capabilities. Then, I will feel _____.

✦ The following are some ways I can solve the current problem _____.

✦ The first step I will take to resolve this situation is to _____.

MAKE INDEPENDENT DECISIONS

Happy employees understand that making independent decisions fuels their job satisfaction. Today's workers are often confronted with overseers or electronic systems that stifle creativity and service. Satisfied employees triumph over such obstacles.

Every day, customer service personnel who are constrained by tracking systems that tally the time consumed by every call delight in discovering how they can treat customers with the respect they deserve. They go home at night proud they may have been the one person that day who remembered that the word *service* is part of their job. Physicians and therapists who have been told they can no longer independently treat their patients also feel good when they skirt the system. Their quest is to provide quality service, and they constantly invent ways to do so. The internal satisfaction they derive from their creativity lifts their spirit and elevates their self-esteem.

SPRING FORWARD

Leap and the net will appear.
Julia Cameron

Forego the social addiction to powerlessness. It is so much easier to feel that we are powerless to achieve our goals than to acknowledge the extent of our personal power and allow ourselves to have what we need to fulfill our true potential.

Although it is often important to seek advice or reach consensus, endlessly discussing problems drains creative juices and slows *go power.* Taking action invites additional ideas and resources to magically appear. Your forward motion may also inspire others to break out of the box and take action.

Use the following tips to ensure that you don't shortchange yourself or your abilities.

JUST SAY "NOW"

1. Write down your goal and take some action, no matter how small, toward achieving it. Support will emerge once you are firmly committed to forward movement. New resources will help you overcome any internal or external resistance to change.

2. Focus on the goal rather than worrying about how well you are doing. Performance analysis blocks progress by inviting your internal critic to babble. You may not always do a perfect job, but you can always do a good job.

3. Achieve one goal or sub-goal at a time. You will be proud of your achievements, and you won't beat yourself up for not having completed a long to-do list.

4. Center yourself and imagine yourself accomplishing your goals. Use multiple senses as you see, hear, and feel your success. Make your vision very specific and detailed because your brain is a pattern-recognition machine. When you combine imagination and emotion with clear and specific directions, your mind will precisely follow your orders. Imagination creates enthusiasm, which nourishes joy and success.

It is so rewarding to realize that you are in charge of your happiness and that you are the one person who can significantly improve your work life. Instead of waiting for your company to develop a more employee-friendly culture or languishing until your boss decides to please you, make choices today that structure your work life so it's more fun. Place yourself in *the zone* as often as possible and enter the state termed *flow* by Claremont Graduate University psychologist, Mihaly Csikszentmihalyi.[1] When you are experiencing flow, you are so absorbed in your job tasks and so fulfilled that you lose track of time. You forget to worry, and you often forget to eat or take breaks. Techniques for reaching flow are completely described in another chapter in this section of the book.

MARCH TO THE BEAT OF YOUR OWN DRUM
You have met many "sheeples." These individuals blindly follow the masses like a lamb, even when this requires them to march over the edge of a dangerous cliff and incur injury. Rather than trying to fit in, happy employees operate with a strong sense of personal integrity. Because their actions are aligned with their ethics and values, sleep comes easily at night, even when they are occasionally criticized by a crowd of conformists. Instead of taking unjust criticism personally, they engage in a conscious process of self-discovery. These self-reliant individuals are open to receive more information concerning how to live their soul's purpose at work, and they consistently receive priceless clues at just the right time. This primes them to listen to and follow the beat of their inner drum when no one else can hear or understand their personal melody. They take healthy risks and pursue their dreams.

CHOOSE TO CHOOSE
Give yourself the gift of conscious choices. Employees who make their own decisions—no matter how small their selection menu may be—feel a sense of control over their lives. They are three times more likely to feel satisfied than those who don't.[2]

CHOOSE CHOICE

✦ When you hear yourself complaining that you *have to* do something, remember that unless you have been sentenced to a prison cell, you aren't *forced* to do much of anything. Discover how different you feel when you use language that reflects a sense of autonomy. Your mind remembers everything you say, so feed it words that imply an internal locus of control.

✦ Listen to your inner dialogue. Notice the next time you think you *have to* do something. Then ask yourself, "How could this action provide value to me?" Consider your answer and then make a conscious choice whether or not to do the activity. This will clarify your options and priorities. Your mind will take note that you are *choosing* to act in a certain way.

✦ Special things happen when you recognize the positive effects of activities that you previously conducted begrudgingly or labeled unpleasant. Do you want to make it easier to work in a cramped cubicle with poor ventilation? Remind yourself of the happy expressions on your healthy kids' faces as they devour the nutritious food that your work allows you to provide them.

✦ Reinforce the fact that you always have choices by recalling the choices you made in the past that created your current scenario. What have you learned that will help you make even better choices in the future?

Recognizing the areas where you have autonomy—even the ability to make minor choices—will reinforce and energize you. You will begin to identify additional resources for improving your work environment.

SELECT A POSITIVE PARALLEL REALITY

You will not be happy when your current challenges disappear if you haven't developed the ability to be contented and peaceful in the midst of chaos, change, and problems. Since happiness at work is a choice, you can retrain your brain to move far beyond what social scientists such as Martin Seligman[3] call your genetic "setpoint" for happiness. The exercises throughout this book are specifically designed to assist you in doing so.

We are so much more capable than we have believed. We have perpetual power to select our thoughts with care. It is always our choice whether we respond to events in a mindful manner or react to situations in haste. This means we can be contented and peaceful no matter what is going on in our environment.

Scientists have proven that we live in a state of parallel realities.[4] We have the ability to select which environment we live in at any moment. Like Viktor Frankl, you can choose to experience peace and contentment no matter how dire your external circumstances. When you do, you will have far more energy and clarity to meet the challenges that life will inevitably present to you.

Consider setting the intention to enjoy your work, reframe negative thinking, and become more flexible. Be aware of problems but focus on desired outcomes. Make a commitment to swim to your ship. You are never limited to living out someone else's script.

The next exercise will help you achieve clarity so you can refine your focus.

READY FOR EVEN MORE JOY ON THE JOB?

1. Close your eyes and think of your definition of "happiness at work." Record your response.

2. What you didn't say is as important as what you said. Which of the following is closer to your first response?

   ✦ Well, happiness at work is sure not ____ _____.

   ✦ Workplace happiness is _____.

3. Just notice if you are more aware of what you don't want at work than of what you want. One of the greatest differences between happy and unhappy employees is that contented workers focus on what they want while dissatisfied workers focus on what they don't want. Your mind is so powerful that it consistently produces scenarios that you personally program with your focus.

4. Are your desires well-rounded? If your objectives are concerned only with aspects of work such as money and success, consider adding goals that will balance your approach. Include

continued on the next page . . .

objectives that will help you develop and maintain rewarding relationships so you can enjoy your success. Did you include goals of contributing to society or your local community? Are your business goals consistent with your physical fitness, personal development, and other spiritual goals? Look beyond material and career goals. Perceive the emotional payoff that achieving your goals will provide.

5. The first step toward finding true happiness is identifying your underlying needs. Review the results of the first exercise you completed in chapter one. When you clarify your unmet workplace needs, you take steps to fulfill them.

6. Evaluate the level of your passion to boost your workplace happiness. Use a scale from zero to ten. Zero represents the attitude, *"I'm not happy at work. Most people aren't. I doubt it's worth my time and energy to try to change things."* Ten, at the other end of the scale, reflects, *"I'll do whatever it takes to be happy at work."* There is no right or wrong answer. Just notice your current level of commitment to create more joy at work.

YOU HAVE THE POWER

Every one of us has the freedom to cling to negativity and to be unhappy 24/7 no matter what is going on in our world. That's personal power!

You also have the innate ability to do the following.

+ Be aware of problems but focus on what you want.
+ Notice and be grateful for what is working. This reinforcement will help you manifest much more of what you want with significantly fewer challenges.
+ Take one step after another toward a better future.

Because an unhappy state of mind is more stressful, it requires much more work to be unhappy and unfulfilled at work than to be happy and fulfilled! No matter which option you choose, the world is filled with unlimited possibilities that patiently await your discovery.

> *Build a little fence of trust*
> *Around today;*
> *Fill the space with loving work,*
> *And therein stay.*
> Mary Frances Butts

CHAPTER 16

BUST PROCRASTINATION

*It is not because things are difficult
that we do not dare;
it is because we do not dare
that they are difficult.*
Seneca

Willy: Aren't you tired of being stressed by over-
           due assignments? If you just do one thing
           at a time, you'll finish the project!

Nilly: I'm going to stop procrastinating . . . just as
           soon as I get around to it.

Procrastination is an opportunity thief. Each time we invite it into
our consciousness, it steals our time and confidence. We feel
self-doubt when we fret about what we dislike about a task instead of diving into the first step. When we ponder the pain of a
potential failure, our focus magnifies the possibility of incomp-
tency or defeat. We also cheat ourselves out of appreciating

the present moment because we reinforce the nagging feeling that we should be doing something else. Clearly, we feel more stressed when we put things off than when we take action. It is procrastination—not a task itself—that feeds fear and fatigue.

WHAT'S THE ROOT CAUSE?

1. The following are the most common causes of procrastination. Place a checkmark by the following reasons you sometimes put off activities that really need to be done. Be totally honest with yourself so you can gain the most value from this exercise.

   ___ Don't know how to accomplish a goal
   ___ Lack clear priorities
   ___ Not truly committed to a goal
   ___ Resources are overcommitted
   ___ Feel unsupported
   ___ Uncomfortable asking for help
   ___ Manage time poorly
   ___ Fear the unknown
   ___ Feel inadequate or unworthy
   ___ Fear being judged negatively if failure occurs
   ___ Addicted to the adrenaline rush associated with pressure to achieve at the last minute
   ___ Fear success. Note: This is really fear of change, so celebrate! It's time to shift your self-image from *unsuccessful* to *successful*.

continued on the next page . . .

> 2. Review the items you marked and keep them in mind as you read the rest of this chapter.

THE NEAR-LIFE CONUNDRUM

Near-death experiences produce profound changes. Most people who are given a second chance to live make a firm commitment to enjoy a life packed with pizzazz, meaning, and mirth. A near-life existence is quite different. Each mediocre day is a continuation of an empty yesterday. The following riddle illustrates the difference between the two.

Five fabulous, frustrated employees met one Tuesday after work to design a plan to create more joy on the job. After agreeing on the first step to take, they made a pact to meet again the next morning. At 7:45 a.m. on Wednesday, four members of the group decided to take the plunge into a new scenario before noon that day. How many of The Fabulous Five remained in their old reality at 1:00 p.m.?

Most people who answer this riddle guess either "one" or "none." They assume the hesitant worker either remained frozen in his current situation or felt pressured to follow the crowd. In truth, all five of the workers continued to endure their existing melodrama. All of them desired a more enjoyable future, but they acted like the group of world-class chefs who starved in spite of having a cookbook stuffed with splendid, fast, and easy recipes and a pantry loaded with mouth-watering ingredients. Not one of the cooks would take 10 minutes to prepare food!

Because The Fabulous Five didn't follow their decision with action, they continued to drool for a more fulfilling life.

We must use time as a tool, not as a couch.
John F. Kennedy

SAY GOODBYE TO
"SOME DAY I'LL . . ."

Sometimes we procrastinate because we want a guarantee of a positive outcome before we leap forward into our next phase of life.

1. Think of a task that you have been procrastinating on doing. Spend a minimum of five minutes writing your responses to each of the following questions. It is important to keep your pen or pencil moving on your paper, so write whatever comes into your mind. If you have no thoughts, just scribble until your thoughts become clear.

    ✦ I'm waiting until . . .

    ✦ I'll do it when . . .

2. Review your answers. How does *waiting* keep you from graduating yourself into more joy on the job?

3. What is the next step you will take so you will be more willing to live in the unknown with no need for assurance that your future will look a certain way?

Procrastination is the art of keeping up with yesterday. *Some day I'll . . .* and *I'm waiting until . . .* are usually followed by a regret-filled *If only I'd . . .*

Avoid the near-life syndrome practiced by The Fabulous Five. Make a decision and act! If you make a mistake, congratulate yourself for the courage to try. Then do something different. If you want to succeed, just pick yourself up more often than you fall down.

BECOME AN IMPERFECTIONIST

Perfectionism is the perfect partner for procrastination. When we assume our work must be perfect or not completed at all, we block creative problem-solving approaches from being perceived by a stressed brain. Then joy on the job seems impossible.

Thomas Edison, one of the most successful and prolific inventors of all time, recognized the perfection in being imperfect. Unlike perfectionists, who fear that the outcome of any task will make or break their career, Edison trusted that his hundreds of thousands of mistakes, one after another after another, would eventually lead to many wonderful products. Edison invented over 1,000 products that we still use precisely because this master inventor never expected to be perfect. He just became engrossed in doing every task and cherished the information he gained from each mistake.

A relaxed state of mind is associated with high levels of creativity and success. Because Edison worked in a calm state, he enjoyed his work on a consistent basis, not just on the rare days of a major success. If he had tormented himself by judging his failures or wasted energy and time trying to cover them up, he would have overlooked a multitude of ways to tweak his approaches a little bit here and there until the real solutions surfaced.

NOTICE THE DIFFERENCE

Think of an activity you feel comfortable doing when alone or with friends but uneasy doing in public. An example for many people is presenting an idea. They are at ease when describing the concept to a close friend but nervous when doing so as part of a public presentation. Is your performance better when you are uptight or when you are relaxed?

No matter how technical or demanding your occupation, your brain functions better when you are focused yet relaxed. Although it is true that brain surgeons, air traffic controllers, and Olympic figure skaters are effective because they function with precision, there is another essential ingredient in their recipe for success. They enjoy a relaxed alpha brain wave state. This is a condition in which the brain is alert and focused but it is also relaxed.

Why do champion athletes and world class musicians frequently enjoy flawless performances? It is because their skills and techniques bring them joy, not because they think perfection might make them happy.

Perfectionism produces

a painful paradox.

Perfectionism is based on a defense mechanism. The drive to achieve a perfect performance is fueled by a need to feel safe and secure. Since perfectionism feeds anxiety, the strategy backfires. The entire focus of perfectionism is fear-based: "I have to be perfect or something unpleasant will occur." Because our attention is riveted on what we don't want—the potentially unfavorable outcome—we lead ourselves straight into imperfection. We develop tunnel vision. We stifle our willingness to take healthy risks.

Perfectionism is based on a childhood script that reads: *If I'm perfect, I won't get into trouble.*

Since no one's perfect,

perfectionism becomes

glorified self-sabotage.

Striving to do our best is an excellent motive. It's also a hallmark that separates winners from whiners. Consistently expecting ourselves or others to be superhuman, however, is a superior setup for frustration and failure. Winners don't win because they struggle to be perfect. They excel because they understand that self-improvement is a never-ending journey. As Thomas Edison's story illustrates, high achievers who love their work devour the daily adventure of discovery. Instead of agonizing about a less than perfect performance, they consistently ask themselves: What can I learn from this? How can I grow as a result of this situation?

USE SELF-AWARENESS
TO OVERCOME PERFECTIONISM

1. Since perfectionism is usually clouded by unconscious motives, you can conquer it with self-awareness. Which, if any, of the following are results of nitpicking yourself and your performance?

    __ When I avoid going forward until I have a perfect product, I avoid taking healthy risks.
    __ Seeking a flawless performance provides the illusion of maintaining control over aspects of my job that I cannot change.
    __ I sometimes strive to be superior because I feel inadequate.
    __ Struggling to be superhuman provides an excuse to avoid intimacy with others.
    __ Striving for an impeccable record keeps me from acknowledging that I am lonely.
    __ Being a perfectionist reinforces feelings of unworthiness. Then I feel like a failure.
    __ The drive to be perfect has unhealthy effects on my body.
    __ Being a stickler produces difficulties in my relationships.
    __ Quibbling with all aspects of my work actually impairs the quality of my work instead of improving it.

2. Is there any real value in being a fussbudget?

What's the worst that can happen if you admit to yourself that we all make errors and that you will make more mistakes in the future? *People with a consistent error-free performance usually are doing tasks far below their level of capability.*

Unless you want to settle for boredom and mediocrity, embrace every mistake. Failures provide fabulous fodder for personal and professional growth

---

PRACTICE BEING PERFECTLY IMPERFECT

✦ Notice fear of failure or a tendency to base your self-esteem on your performance, but move forward with your work. Be aware of the areas in your body that tense up. Consciously relax them.

✦ Give yourself permission to be as imperfect as the rest of us. Each time you make a mistake, learn something valuable. Then redirect your efforts in a positive direction.

✦ Use your nondominant hand to throw a ball or write a letter. Notice that you don't expect a perfect performance when you engage in an activity for which you have no natural aptitude. Observe how easily you *can* excuse ordinary or poor accomplishment. This exercise can help you initiate a new neural network to squelch your tendency to judge your efforts harshly. Self-judgment leads to fatigue and failure. Laughing at silly ideas and ineffective approaches energizes you and spurs your creativity.

continued on the next page . . .

✦ Become another Thomas Edison. Recognize the perfection in imperfection. Perceive how flawlessly one error leads to another until an extraordinary solution evolves.

✦ Identify and honor your achievements instead of always downgrading your imperfections. Forget about what you might have accomplished if you had achieved an impeccable track record. When you live in the present, you discover the joy of the journey of your life.

✦ Because your new level of self-acceptance will be reflected back to you by others, notice that each time you drop a layer of perfectionism, those around you stop *appearing to* expect you to be perfect.

✦ Make a commitment to rediscover areas of your life that you've been ignoring because you've been trying so hard to succeed.

Learning to constantly quibble with so many aspects of your performance required a lot of focus and years of hard work before it became a habit. Don't mentally flog yourself for not letting go of perfectionism instantly!

Anything worth doing
is worth screwing up royally.
Marcia Menter

ENCOURAGE YOUR DONKEY

Farmer Dimwit and Farmer Enlightened lived on adjacent farms. Both raised corn and peas, and both used animals as part of their labor force. When Farmer Dimwit's donkey didn't want to work, he thrashed the poor beast and yanked its bridle while screaming violently, "You lazy, good-for-nothing animal! You *will* work or I'll never feed you again!" Farmer Dimwit's expertise was self-sabotage. His mistreated donkeys performed begrudgingly and their bodies wore out early, so the farmer's harvests were always mediocre.

When Farmer Enlightened's donkey balked at working, the kind farmer checked to make sure the animal wasn't injured or too fatigued to do good work. Once he made sure the donkey was okay, he petted it briefly and gently coaxed it forward with a treat until the animal became more willing to work. The farmer's children still remember their father's soft, loving tone of voice when he encouraged his animal workers, "Come on now, do just a little bit more for just a little while longer." Farmer Enlightened's cherished animals helped him achieve exceptional harvests, year after year.

Like Farmer Dimwit, when we chastise ourselves for procrastinating or lacking motivation to accomplish a task, we flog our own labor force. It is the same as judging a donkey as worthless and beating and screaming at it until we wear it out.

Self-judgment is self-inflicted poison. It is self-sabotage because we focus on what we don't want instead of concentrating on the results we want to achieve. Instead of judging yourself, just notice your resistance to move forward. Accept your human frailties. No one is motivated all of the time.

Encourage yourself forward. Instead of putting yourself down with, "You're so lazy" or "You're a loser," tell yourself in a gentle tone of voice, "I see what you're doing. Let's go just a little bit farther."

If you weren't raised with a great deal of patience, you probably aren't very patient with yourself. Notice the difference in results when you gently coax yourself forward instead of judging your behavior harshly.

ANOTHER VIEW OF PERFECTIONISM

Sylvia downgraded herself as she reformulated portions of a policies and procedures manual. The task was important to her, and she wanted to include all of the components that employee surveys said workers needed. In spite of interim feedback from proofreaders who rated the manuscript as excellent, Sylvia verbally beat herself up with expressions such as, "I'm so slow. Anyone else would have finished this project long ago. This perfectionism means I'm feeling incompetent."

A team member named Juan encouraged Sylvia to adopt a healthy new perspective. "You were selected for this job because very few people have the skill or can muster the commitment to write a comprehensive manual. Think about replacing your self-talk of 'I'm slow, so I must be feeling unworthy,' with 'I have unique skills and I have the passion to make this manual as useful as possible'."

Sylvia immediately comprehended the difference. Originally, she had felt like a failure. Now, she recognized her talents, passion, and dedication.

Juan continued, "Is it possible that what you fear isn't really failure? You may fear success because you will have to revise your self-image from *not good enough* to *good enough*. If you truly want to leave your old script behind, reframe how you describe yourself. Instead of saying, 'I'm too slow and this perfectionism must be because I feel inadequate,' you can choose, 'I passionately want this to be an excellent product that will truly be useful to employees'."

All of us have outdated self-perceptions that cause us to limit ourselves with negative self-talk. Even though everyone sometimes feel unsuccessful, it isn't true that we can't experience success and happiness. When we become conscious of negative self-images that don't serve us, they begin to change.

PROGRESS PAST PROCRASTINATION

The following suggestions are easy, proven remedies for procrastination and perfectionism.

❏ Make the Main Thing the Main Thing

If an activity needs to be done and it's your job to do it, commit to the goal. Reprioritize if you have overcommitted your resources.

Divide the task into small increments and concentrate on doing one subgoal at a time. Even though it can be beneficial to periodically reflect on how wonderful you will feel at the finish line, most successful racers focus on one marker at a time until they near the end of the race.

Assign yourself a certain time to do each task and follow through. Keep your schedule visible and stay on track. If you're digging for gold, don't decide to search for silver just before you reach the mother lode.

❏ Face Fears

Notice when you're looking busy but going nowhere like a dog that frantically chases its tail but stays in the same limited space. Forgive yourself and face any fears that are on the front burner.

YOU CAN DO

WHAT YOU'VE DONE BEFORE

If you are afraid you can't accomplish a task, think of an activity you once feared you couldn't learn or do but eventually did. Examples: Most people are apprehensive about learning a new skill or presenting a concept to others. You probably weren't confident you could land your first job.

Complete the following sentence stems.

✦ In the past, I didn't know I could _____
_____.

✦ Now I know I can _____.

✦ Since I've already proven I can learn and grow, I'll be able to _____.

When asked how they conquered their fear, heroes who step in the path of danger in order to save someone else almost always comment with surprise, "I was so busy, I didn't have time to be afraid."

> Action is one of the best
>
> antidotes to fear.

Most employees who face mass company layoffs spend their energy worrying about when their pink slip will arrive. Ivan Burnell took a different approach. He scoured the plant looking for work to keep him busy. The number of layoffs multiplied rapidly, but he concentrated on working. Because his focus was on working instead of being laid off, Burnell never got a pink slip. His boss noticed the nature of his focus and assigned other employees to him for supervision. Intelligent action conquered Burnell's fear and helped him build a better career. His advice to the rest of us? "When in doubt, do something!"[1]

❑ Place Analysis Paralysis on the Shelf

Stop waiting until every piece of your new plan is crystal clear or analysis will replace action. The best way to get started is to start. As long as you are sure you're on the right path, all you have to do is take one step forward at a time. Each step will produce feedback and offer opportunities to revise your path. Eventually, you will discover that you are too far along to turn back! Then the fun begins. You achieve one peak experience after another.

Start by doing what is necessary,
then do what is possible,
and suddenly you are doing the impossible.
St. Francis of Assisi

CREATE INSTANT SATISFACTION

No matter how tiny a step forward you take, moving toward a goal creates relief and gratification. Forward motion will also motivate you to continue traveling the path toward your desired endpoint. Even if you can only spend a few minutes on a task, begin it immediately.

Discover the benefits of this simple, powerful strategy right now by doing one small thing you've been putting off. Return a phone call or reorganize a small part of your desk so you feel like you have more energy and space to focus on what's important.

If you are anxious about a report you must write, instead of stewing about it, write five words. If you really feel stuck, write "By (your name)" and the date, and count them as words. Then write the name of the report. Notice that you feel better because you made an effort. Action changes behavior, so stay in motion by continuing to write.

When you overcome inertia, you invite life to leap forward to assist you. Build a new neural network—a brand new behavior pattern—by doing the same thing at home. Select a small task

continued on the next page . . .

you've been putting off and do it. It requires less energy to complete a minor task than to put it off. You also avoid the stress caused by the nagging voice in your mind.

Notice the difference in your overall stress level when you do this consistently. Life was never intended to be a constant struggle.

❏ Motivate Yourself With Benefits, Not Fear

Progressive physicians broke new ground when they discovered that patients with life-threatening conditions usually could not be motivated to change unhealthy behaviors if a doctor used fear tactics. When a patient had experienced a heart attack and was lonely and depressed, statements like, "You're going to have another heart attack and die if you don't stop smoking and lose weight" produced few, if any, positive behavioral changes. Telling unhappy individuals that they were going to become even more miserable was not a carrot on a stick.

An enlightened approach produced the opposite effect. Cutting-edge practitioners promised the same patients that they could feel good, be happier, and experience abundant energy. The rate of success was astonishing because the doctors connected patients with support groups, spent time educating them about healthy behaviors, and helped them prove the doctors' positive forecast to themselves.[2]

Even though fear is absolutely not an effective way to motivate people, most of us act more like Farmer Dimwit than Farmer Enlightened. The intelligent farmer coaxed his donkeys forward with support, kindness, and treats. The following exercise uses multisensory techniques that will help you develop enthusiasm about completing projects.

SENSE YOUR ACCOMPLISHMENTS

1. Close your eyes and breathe three deep, relaxing abdominal breaths.

2. Think of the last time you felt good about having successfully completed a project. Your example doesn't have to be related to work. The goal is to use all of your senses to create a memory you can recall on demand regarding how wonderful it feels to finish a task. Examples follow.

✦ *You hear yourself breathe a satisfying sigh of relief and you see a smile on a supervisor's face while you feel the texture of a report you hand him or her. You taste a delicious cup of coffee and smell its aroma while feeling pride about the quality of your work.*

✦ *You are pleased as you gaze at a beautiful lawn you just mowed. You smell the special scent of freshly trimmed grass. As you touch smooth, green blades of grass, you hear yourself say, "That was worth the effort!" Then you enjoy a refreshing drink of cool, clear water.*

continued on the next page . . .

3. Once you are in touch with the wonderful feeling of successfully finishing a previous task, shift your concentration to the benefits and feelings associated with effectively completing your current task. Feel how wonderful it will be to move beyond procrastination. Hold that focus with your eyes closed for at least 20 seconds before returning to work. Don't fret if your attention shifts to how difficult or distasteful the task may be. Just close your eyes until you regain the positive feelings associated with the benefits of completion. Over time, you will establish a new neural network. Then you'll be able to recreate this positive feeling instantly, with your eyes open.

Discover how you can benefit from providing yourself a carrot on a stick instead of the mental equivalent of a flogging whip. Instead of focusing on how uncomfortable you'll feel if you don't get a task done well or on misery you've associated with doing an undesirable task, concentrate on how great you'll feel when the job is completed. Good vibes will create an enjoyable reality because humans were designed to live more by their senses than their brains.

The next exercise provides additional techniques that will help you boost your progress when you lack clarity, energy, or motivation to complete a task.

IF YOU'RE REALLY STUCK . . .

➧ Substitute a More Unpleasant Task

If you really feel stuck, decide to do something less pleasant than your real task. It is amazing how motivated you can become if you alphabetize folders that need to be shredded or clean the toilet bowl!

➧ Engage in Stream of-Consciousness Thinking

Close your eyes and talk out loud, using rich multisensory language. An easy way to start the process is to say, "The way I finally did _____ was to _____." Conclude the exercise when you receive insights.

➧ Ask an Expert

Imagine that the answer to, "How would you accomplish this task?" is being answered by your favorite role model. Write his or her answers with your nondominant hand. Keep your hand moving on the page, even if no thoughts emerge. Keep writing until ideas concerning your next steps flow. Then, take action.

continued on the next page . . .

> ➠ Give Your Donkey a Break
>
> No matter how skilled you are at coaxing your donkey forward, it can only go so long without a refreshing break. When you take good care of yourself, your enthusiasm builds and your creativity soars.

❑ Cheerlead and Reward

Encourage yourself out loud. Tell yourself what you are going to do and acknowledge every step you do. Even if you are the only person who will deliver praise, gain some interim positive feedback.

Give yourself a small reward, even a mini-break such as a luxurious stretch at your desk, when you complete a significant component of a task you don't want to do. Take a bite of your favorite fruit or give your body the benefit of a short walk each time you complete a cold call. Promise yourself that you will call a friend or go outside as soon as you have completed your task. Write yourself a check or gift certificate to use for a fun night out.

Follow through with the rewards you pledge to provide. When we are honest with the little kids who live inside of us, the shrill voices that pierce inner peace with tantrums and screams of "No! I want to play, not work!" don't distract us when we really need to focus on adult stuff.

❑ Stimulate a Support System

Ask for help when you need it. If your pattern is to procrastinate on tasks you complete alone, involve others in the process. This doesn't mean they have to help you with the actual work. A mentor, coworker, or supervisor can offer advice. You can make a pact with a friend to call you and briefly check on your progress until you become so involved with your task that you can't put it down.

❏ Use the Power of Motion

Enrich your mind power and de-stress yourself when you take breaks by moving your body as if you are freestyle dancing. Consciously use this process to release tension and stimulate different areas of your brain to contribute ideas for your work. Make spontaneous chimpanzee noises as you move or wave your arms like a monkey. Communicate your true intentions to your brain by moving your arms in ways that symbolize engaging with the flow of life.

❏ Take a Stand in the Sand

Draw an imaginary line that represents the demarcation between *your intention to progress* and *your firm commitment to do so.* When you are 100 percent sure that you want to engage in your next step, stand up and walk past the line *with genuine enthusiasm.* This will unlock your passion and activate awareness of your inner resources.

Use a broad stride forward. Simultaneously complete the following two bodymind actions because they will direct your mind to assist you in moving forward.

✦ Say out loud with conviction, "Now, I'm committed!"

✦ Anchor your action by touching the tip of your thumb to the tips of your index and middle fingers. Repeat this neurological anchor later if your attention waivers from your goal. It reminds your brain that you have pledged to progress.

❏ Be Mindful

Become conscious of limiting self-perceptions. Resist the tendency to judge them, and they will spontaneously shift to a more positive self-image.

EXPECT GREAT THINGS FROM YOURSELF

Scientists have proven that we have virtually unlimited capabilities, so maintain a forward momentum once you are committed to action. Hold a vision of yourself as an "organizational athlete." Experienced marathon runners keep plodding along because they know they will receive the reward of a sudden burst of energy toward the end of their journey.

The turtle reached the ark
by taking action.
William Uhl

CHAPTER 17

CONFRONT CONTROL ISSUES

*Wisdom never kicks at the
iron walls it can't bring down.*
Olive Schreiner

Wayne: What's wrong with Moe? Ever since the company announced it's going to create a new evaluation system, he's become obsessed with installing anti-virus software.

Shayne: Isn't it smart to protect his computer data?

Wayne: He's gone way overboard. His files are protected as securely as the gold at Fort Knox, but he still spends his entire work day fretting about how to create data safety. He's so far behind on his real work that the entire department is suffering.

Shayne: Sounds like he's lost his focus because he feels out of control. He knows he can't influence the company's decisions regarding the way he'll be evaluated, so he's struggling to control what he can.

Wayne: Someone should tell the poor guy to concentrate on his real source of power. Even though he can't control the setup of the performance review process, he has total control over the quality of his own work. If he focused on that, it would be much easier to prove his value at appraisal time.

When life seems to be reeling out of our control, most of us want to call the shots in any way we can. We waste valuable time and energy worrying about things that aren't important so we won't worry about what does matter. The well-known *Serenity Prayer* stresses the importance of having the wisdom to know what you can and cannot control and letting go of circumstances that you cannot influence.

WHAT CAN YOU CONTROL?

In what areas of your work life do you feel the least control? Since most employees are concerned about interruptions that interfere with their ability to regulate their time and complete their work, this is a wonderful area to learn how you can own your power. The next exercise will help you identify how you can minimize and manage interruptions.

IDENTIFY WHAT YOU CAN CONTROL

1. Briefly describe a work situation that is bothering you. An example follows.

    I'm constantly interrupted, so I have a hard time getting my work done without staying late.

2. Draw a vertical line on a piece of paper. On the left side of the page, write the heading, "What I cannot control." On the right side of the page, write the heading, "What I can control."

What I Cannot Control	What I Can Control
✦ *Working in a cubicle*	✦ *How I respond to interruptions*
✦ *When people try to interrupt me*	✦ *The boundaries I set*
✦ *Who interrupts me*	✦ *The ways I interrupt my own work flow*

NEWSFLASH! YOU CAN
CONTROL INTERRUPTIONS!

continued on the next page . . .

✦ Respect your own time, and others will reflect your self-respect back to you.

✦ Treat others the way you want to be treated. Set appointments that are realistic. Be on time for meetings.

✦ Set the stage. Tell other parties in advance how long you are available for a conversation or meeting. When you don't have time to chat, ask the other person if you can talk later. Set up a definite appointment so you can temporarily let go of the interruption.

✦ When a customer or coworker rambles, ask, "What do you need?" or "How can I help you?" Keep discussions on point by tactfully using your body language. An erect posture, holding a pen in your hand poised to jot down a note, holding your briefcase in your lap, and standing up provide evidence that you have a serious agenda.

✦ Set and maintain personal boundaries instead of allowing others to control your time. If someone asks you to assist them but they really want you to do their work for them, say no *without guilt*. Don't reinforce dependency.

✦ When possible, stay in the driver's seat by planning your interruptions. Set aside definite times for telephone calls. Consider posting "open office hours" even if you are in a cubicle. Let people know the best times to disturb you.

✦ Use filters to avoid junk e-mail. Search the Internet as a reward after completing a task instead of succumbing to the temptation to search web sites before settling down.

YOU ALWAYS HAVE MORE CONTROL THAN YOU THINK

You may not be able to control the degree of autonomy you have at work, but you can always control the following.

✦ Your emotional state
✦ Acceptance of all emotions
✦ Your attitude
✦ How you respond to a situation

❑ Your Emotional State

Moe's frantic drive to control his life is not related to the challenges he is facing. His obsessive behavior is based on a misperception. He doesn't think he will be able to cope with every challenge life presents.

In truth, Moe has a fabulous inner guidance system. He is hardwired to spontaneously slap mosquitos·that buzz around his head. When he trusts himself, he uses the same innate ability to notice clues about his best next steps at work and to respond appropriately and with perfect timing. When he doubts himself or is uncomfortable confronting his fears, he misdirects his behavior. The result is self-sabotage.

Recognize your genuine
and spontaneous capacity
for responding to life
in a winning way.
Joseph Luciani

Moe thought he would lose control over his future when his company introduced a new evaluation system, and he was uncomfortable facing his fear of the unknown. To avoid feeling insecure, he concentrated his attention with laser-like focus on what he thought he could control. His strategy backfired. He wasted precious energy and he squandered a great deal of time. His attempt to resist feeling his fear—his desire to feel powerful—resulted in Moe feeling more powerless than ever.

CHOOSE WHICH WAY YOU RUN

Occasionally, all of us enact part of Moe's drama. We try to run our lives by running from them. Eventually, we discover that we are circling around and around a wheel of fear.

1. Think of an instance in which you want to control a situation that you cannot influence or control.

2. For a couple of weeks, observe any tendency to launch into compulsive thoughts or behaviors in an effort to divert your attention from uncomfortable feelings.

3. Become aware of your feelings. Notice related sensations in your body such as a queasy gut, clammy hands, tight jaw, or tense throat.

4. Without judging your behavior or your thoughts as bad, remind yourself that you can make a different choice.

5. Complete the following sentence stems.

   ✦ When I feel afraid of the unknown and I want to try to control the future, my first impulse is to _____.

continued on the next page . . .

✦ If I do this, _____ will happen.

✦ Therefore, I'm now choosing to _____ instead.

✦ I'm also going to reward myself for a different behavior by _____.

The desire to control our lives when we feel insecure is only a habit. Since any habit can be broken, you are the commander of your ship.

The above strategy will help you avoid the scenario of the wealthy venture capitalist who lamented on his death bed that he had experienced "a tidal wave of troubles" in his life. His loved ones were amazed that such a statement emerged from the lips of a man who had been surrounded by love, wealth, beauty, and excellent health until his last days. Puzzled, one of his sons finally countered the dying man's statement. "But, Dad, your life has been so carefree!

The embarrassed man hesitated before he finally answered, "I know. Almost every trauma I fretted about never happened. The more I tried to submerge my growing anxiety, the more it flourished."

A week later, the tycoon's shaken family was still impressed by the deceased man's stunning bedside statement. They enscribed his elaborate headstone with, "If he had known what he was so anxious about, he wouldn't have been anxious."

❑ Comfort with the Wide Array of Human Emotions

One of the most valuable approaches to life's uncertainties is to be at ease with the rich variety of human emotions. The key is to notice them rather than judge them. Neutral observation detaches us from the illusion that emotions can overpower us. In fact, feelings become profound tools when we learn how to purposely use them because humans create more by feeling than thought. Albert Einstein credited the discovery of the theory of relativity to his feelings. In fact, he said imagination is more powerful than thought. Our species was originally designed to live by our senses, not to be dominated by our neocortex.

As previously discussed, emotions exist in polarities. Examples are fear/self-confidence, anger/peace, and sadness/happiness. Because negative and positive emotions exist side by side in the brain, judging any emotion as bad stifles our ability to enjoy its opposite. When we resist feeling fear, we cheat ourselves out of an opportunity to become more confident.

The opposite effect occurs when we acknowledge negative feelings without trying to banish them. When we honor fear, sadness, and anger (recognizing them without indulging them) we allow the emergence of higher levels of their counterparts: confidence, peace, joy, and love. When we are not afraid to feel afraid while steering a ship headed into unknown territory, anxiety is soon overwhelmed by confidence.

Clearly, the objective isn't to banish or avoid negative feelings because they provide a doorway to more positive experiences. It is also important to notice the relationship between negative feelings and the focus of your thoughts. Use the following exercise when it is difficult for you to feel fear and move forward in your life at the same time.

ALLEVIATE ANXIETY WITH A NEW FOCUS

Next time the worrywart surfaces, pause and recall your previous thoughts. Were you focused on what you don't want or on what you want? If you were pondering a potentially unpleasant outcome, it is not surprising that you felt on edge. When you concentrate on favorable results, there is no room in your consciousness for fear and worry.

Each time you notice that you are concentrating on a possibility you dread, take a brief breather to acknowledge the negative feelings associated with your concern. Then gently shift your focus. Be aware that you have been unconsciously empowering a potentially undesirable outcome.

Imagination and emotions are two of the most powerful ways to create a given scenario, and you have been imagining how what you don't want would feel, look, sound, taste, and smell.

Detach the power of your senses from an outcome you don't want by enriching sensations associated with your preferred outcome. What would a desirable scenario look like? What sounds would you hear? What emotions would you feel? Imagine some of the textures, smells, and tastes that might be part of a positive picture.

continued on the next page . . .

The goal of the exercise isn't to program a specific way to achieve a result you desire. Neither is the objective to limit yourself to a certain outcome. That might play into a perceived need to control your life. You could inadvertently short-circuit magical processes that are working behind the scenes to produce consequences more favorable than your fondest dreams! The real objective of this exercise is to shift your thinking pattern and to alleviate anxiety until your experiences prove to you that you can always trust the process of your life.

With that in mind, consistently do the following.

✦ Notice when your unpleasant feelings are related to an unconscious focus on a potentially disagreeable outcome.
✦ Use multiple senses to shift your focus to a more desirable result.
✦ Notice how quickly your uncomfortable feelings diminish or disappear.
✦ Go on with your life and allow unseen internal and external forces to create a favorable outcome.

Constructive worries are based on realistic concerns. In this case, fear is just like a friend who alerts you to address an urgent issue. Useful worries lead to proactive problem-solving. *Obsessive, speculative worries* have the opposite effect. Repetitive thoughts such as, "I'll be devastated if this happens" or "How can I possibly cope if that happens?" sap the energy you need in order to meet genuine challenges. In addition, your mind is so powerful that your focus invites what you don't want to emerge in your life.

Your brain is hard-wired to ensure your survival in case you wander into the territory of a saber-toothed tiger. Even though this is impossible, it is a primal instinct. An untrained mind struggles to anticipate what dangers you might encounter next.

This becomes a biological loop it is best to avoid. The more often you think a specific negative thought, the more deeply it is etched into your brain. It becomes an automatic, learned neural pathway that you travel over and over. Unconscious, dysfunctional patterns of thinking and behaving emerge that inhibit your joy. A vicious cycle ensues because your biology, the soft wiring in your brain associated with the ingrained neural pathways, also influences your emotions. Like an ill-programmed robot, we can become unconsciously and automatically driven by ineffective thinking and action that continues to chissel a deeper encoding of a nasty, uncomfortable pattern.

Although this saga sounds hopeless, the opposite is true. Our brains are infinitely changeable. Many scientists call them "plastic." Awareness of our patterns combined with mindful behavior and a focus on what we want, instead of what we don't want, will spontaneously initiate a beautiful cycle of positive change.

The next exercise will be very beneficial if you, like so many of us, have an untrained brain. You will shift your mind's focus away from worrying as a default process and activate your brain's extraordinary capacity to create positive results.

DISCONNECT THE WORRYWART

1.   When an obsessive or speculative worry enters your mind, jot it down on an Official Worry List. Promise to give it your attention during "worry time," a prescheduled slot of time, such as from 7:30-7:45 that evening. Then immediately return your attention to a productive focus.

  If this is difficult, shift into an observer role. Each time the worry surfaces, notice it with detachment. Comment to yourself with a chuckle, "The mind is sure busy right now!" Using the phrase, *the mind* instead of *my mind* helps you disassociate from the worrywart.

  Without resisting any background mental chatter, focus your thoughts on what is important and productive. This will eventually defuse internal babble.

2.   Review your worry list during "worry time" and sort your concerns. Which worries are real? These fears will definitely materialize. Which worries are possible outcomes that may never happen? *These are products of your imagination. Studies have repeatedly concluded that well over 90 percent of what we worry about never actually occurs.*

continued on the next page . . .

3. If any of your worries are real—the situations you fear will definitely occur unless you act to circumvent them—take the following steps.

   ✦ Determine how to use fear to your advantage. What actions can you take to either prevent an undesirable outcome or prepare youself to cope with an obstacle? How can you build your competence and confidence? Can you learn a new skill or confront a challenge you have been avoiding?
   ✦ Remind yourself that you have handled difficult situations before. Recall a specific situation in the past that was frightening but helped you learn more about your inner strength. Reassure yourself that, based on your history, you know you will be okay no matter what emerges as a result of your current situation.

4. Distance yourself from imaginary worries. Observe them when they surface without identifying with them. One strategy is to notice the worry and comment, "Wow! That's interesting!" with a chuckle. Another is to embellish the worry until it is so outlandish that you roar with laughter.

continued on the next page . . .

The following is an example.

> If you are afraid your boss won't like a report you wrote, imagine yourself wearing tattered clothes and holding all of your worldly possessions in a battered box while you stand in a Great Depression-era unemployment line that stretches for blocks. Other unemployed people are trying to sell apples for five cents to those of you in the line. Sadly, none of you poor drooling, desperate people has a nickel—not a single nickel.

When you finish laughing, focus on your preferred outcome in a multisensory manner.

✦ Shrink your imaginary, life-threatening images to a tiny, blurry picture that you can barely perceive. Place them in an imaginary file cabinet under lock and key.

✦ Concentrate again on the scenario you want. Imagine how it looks, feels, sounds, smells, and tastes. Smile as you enlarge and embellish the picture of your preferred outcome.

Everyone sometimes feels insecure and afraid. The absence of fear isn't courage. It's evidence of brain damage! If you haven't undergone a lobotomy, learn to use fear as a tool. Then you will allow yourself to float peacefully and productively on the constantly changing river that is your life. Those who try to cling to the shore—their known reality—are dragged along by the inevitable, uncontrollable events of their lives. They miss amazing adventures because they fail to embrace the magic that can only unfold within the mystery of an unknown horizon.

> Recognize and use your innate abilities
>
> to respond to life in a winning way.

❑ Your Attitude

Two men look out through the same bars;
one sees the mud and one the stars.
Frederick Langbridge

Intelligent optimism is immensely helpful when we are confronted by situations we cannot alter. Anticipating the best when faced with such circumstances does not mean denying what exists. Intelligent optimists equally value negative and positive thoughts because they know the negative will help them stay grounded in reality. They acknowledge problems, but they don't allow themselves to be overwhelmed by factors they cannot influence. They make informed choices that contribute to inner peace. One of these is to adapt to situations they cannot control. At the same time, they hoist an antenna that will detect information about opportunities for creating a better future. This antenna is anchored with their attitudes and beliefs.

Intelligent optimists are convinced that a seed for the solution resides within the core of every challenge. Solving problems is exciting to them because they know the process will eventually produce personal and professional growth. Two actions help them hasten this outcome.

✦ Focus on how to be productive in the interim period
✦ Identify what can be enjoyed in the present moment

Familiar zones are dysfunctional comfort zones. They are actually *discomfort* zones, but we have convinced ourselves they are comfortable because most of us are creatures of habit and fear the unknown.

Have you ever avoided speaking up for yourself when you were treated unfairly because you didn't know how the other party would react? Do you know anyone with great potential who endures a dead-end job because they are anxious about entering unchartered territory? Unfortunately, most of us avoid change even when it is clearly to our advantage.

On the flip side, wasting energy being dissatisfied with what we can't change is also an example of a familiar zone that doesn't serve us. In this case, we are attached to our images of how life *should be*, so we moan about what exists. We fear the future, so we try to control what we cannot even influence. Because we don't trust the process of our lives, we place padlocks on the doors we must open if we are to enjoy the greatest adventures of our lives.

As the exercise below indicates, we can unlock these doors one at a time by savoring small successes and spontaneous sources of joy. We will be rewarded with a sweet series of unexpected positive changes.

FEED FLOWERS, NOT WEEDS

Most of us are masters at being dissatisfied with what exists. We are highly skilled in the arts of complaining and worrying. We have significant expertise in comparing ourselves to others in unfavorable ways.

The next step toward joy on the job is to accept ourselves, what we have, and what we do. Accepting what exists and what we cannot change paves the way for better circumstances. When we stop struggling and feeling victimized because life doesn't fit our pictures, we discover hidden gifts that we can only receive when we stop judging what exists. The focus that is required to appreciate each moment creates a neural network associated with intelligent optimism.

1. Identify what provides a sense of fulfillment or satisfaction at work. You can do this even if you dislike a task or don't enjoy the company of those with whom you work.

   ✦ Do you feel good about earning money to help those you love or to meet your own needs?

continued on the next page . . .

♦ Are you pleased when you do the best you can even if what you do isn't your dream job?

♦ Are you learning more about the world of business so you can make different choices in the future?

♦ Are you discovering more about your inner strengths?

♦ Which of your tasks are meaningful or enjoyable?

♦ What activities challenge you to reach your highest level of performance or learn new skills?

2. Review your list and decide how you can feed the factors that provide satisfaction and fulfillment.

3. Cultivate an attitude of gratitude. When you are grateful for what your conscious mind knows is working, you discover many things that have been working behind the scenes without your knowledge. What are you thankful for? What do you feel satisfied about? What do you enjoy doing? If answers to these questions don't come easily, think of something unpleasant that easily could have happened but didn't. Is that a reason to be thankful? Appreciating what exists is the first step to having what you want. People who live in harmony with their present circumstances attract a wealth of blessings.

No matter what you cannot control, you can always control your happiness because we choose 24/7 whether to accept what exists and go forward or whine and pine for the illusion of a perfect world that fits our limited, judgmental pictures of what *should* exist.

CONSIDER OPTIMISM

Optimism that is grounded in reality breeds happiness and success.

✦ Change is one of the most dependable components of life. Reflect on a list of situations in your life that you have judged as bad. Notice that, with time, the vast majority of them became something more enjoyable. When life at work seems difficult, can you enjoy a glass that is half full, instead of half empty, while you experience an imperfect world?

✦ Optimism is contagious. Hang out with optimistic thinkers who have proven their ability to ride the waves of challenge and change with enthusiasm. As if by magic, you will find yourself transforming while you enjoy their company.

Happiness is not something you will be awarded when your latest crisis ends. Nor will peace magically appear after you reform the circumstances or people that surround you.

Wherever you go,
there you are.
Jon Kabat-Zinn

If the grass seems greener on the other side of the hill, someone there is nurturing it better than you are tending your own area of concern. Joy on the job begins and ends with you.

Truly comprehending that you alone can transform your life provides an enormous sense of relief. Instead of feeling victimized, blaming others for your stress, or waiting for situations to change so you can have fun at work, you are 100 percent sure that you are in control of your happiness. Tweak your attitude when necessary so you can enjoy your innate power to enjoy your life at work.

❑ How You Respond to a Situation

The test of first rate intelligence is the ability to
hold two opposed ideas in mind at the same
time and still retain the ability to function.
One should, for example, be able to see
that things are hopeless and yet take steps
to make them better.
F. Scott Fitzgerald

How can we feel out of control and still take positive steps forward? We can let go of our expectations and demands concerning the outcome of a certain situation and allow, rather than trying to compel, an exquisite solution to emerge.

> Experiences don't
> cause disappointment.
> Expectations do.

Expectations are a breeding ground for disappointment. There is a parable about a man who was terrified when floodwaters gushed through his home. He crawled out of a second-story window, stood on the roof, and screamed, "Help me! Help me!"

Aid immediately arrived. A rescuer in a rowboat threw out a lifejacket and cheerfully called, "Climb aboard and I'll take you to safety." Instead of scrambling aboard, the stranded man refused assistance, but he kept shrieking hysterically, "Please help me!" After several more rescue attempts, the puzzled man in the rowboat paddled away to help others.

The rescuer was soon replaced by a helicopter crew that dangled a rope with secure foot and handholds at the precise level needed. A friendly and concerned rescue team urged the endangered man to climb to safety, but he waved the helicopter away just as he had dismissed the boater. Then the frantic man continued to bellow, "Help me! Save me!"

A large, bright red treehouse floated right by the forlorn man's roof. It was evident that a miracle was transpiring. The ladder, decking, and the house itself were in perfect condition. It would have been easy for the marooned man to step onto the ladder and ride comfortably to safety. The floodwaters continued to rise, but the desperate man ignored the magical offering. Instead, he perched on the roof of his rapidly disappearing home and wailed in a pitiful voice, "Help me! Please help me!"

Eventually, the man died and met his Maker in heaven. He bawled, "God, I was a good person. Why didn't you save me?" God patiently explained, "Your expectations got in the way. I sent you a rowboat, a helicopter, and finally a comfortable tree house with an exquisite deck. You were so attached to a certain answer that you missed the messages *and* the messenger."

We act in a similar way when we have rigid pictures of how life *should be*. Instead of exploring the unending mysteries and miracles of life with wonder and awe, we approach our challenges with the tunnel vision of a gopher. When what unfolds doesn't fit our preconceptions—which can only be based on our limited knowledge and experience—we feel devastated. We fear that our needs won't be met if we don't confine our journeys to a tiny, carefully folded map we've stashed in our hip pocket. It is the map of our known reality. Entire sections of this document are blank. Most of the markers that will signal us to cross from one path to the next won't emerge until the precise moment they are needed.

It is no wonder that our personal and professional growth screeches to a halt when we resist what exists. We stumble around in dark alleys instead of allowing every single situation we encounter to illuminate the path home. As you have proven to yourself when doing previous exercises in this book, with hindsight, it becomes clear that whatever happens is always perfectly in line with our present state of development. There is a master plan at work, 24/7, which we can enjoy without angst when we trust the process of our lives.

Letting go of expectations doesn't mean downgrading your dreams or adopting low standards. Nor does it mean slacking off. It means learning to trust that the same invisible forces that created you and led you to this moment are still working behind the scenes 24 hours a day, seven days a week to help you learn and grow. It means trusting that you were created with an abundance of amazing inner resources that you have barely begun to explore.

USE AWARENESS
TO DEVELOP
PEACE OF MIND

During the next few weeks, when you feel angry, frustrated, or want to blame someone for your discontent, ask yourself the following questions.

✦ Am I unhappy because I am assuming that what exists is not perfect in its own way? Is my discontent associated with lack of trust in the process of my life?

✦ Am I allowing myself to be frustrated by something I cannot control?

✦ What are the effects on my body, mind, and spirit of holding my sense of well-being hostage to this circumstance?

Be gentle with yourself. Don't judge yourself. Over time, you will become more conscious of the tendency to attempt to control what you cannot. You will spontaneously choose to remain peaceful when responding to situations out of your control. This will empower you to meet any challenge more easily.

> Suffering is caused by resistance to what exists. Uncontrollable aspects of our lives that we don't fret about usually change on their own. What we resist persists.

If you enjoy inflicting pain on yourself, resist a situation you cannot control. Judge it as bad, wicked, and awful. Struggle to change it to suit your fancy. Give away your personal power by allowing something outside of yourself (what exists) to be responsible for the degree to which you feel like a victim, want to blame others, and feel powerless. This is an exceptionally dependable recipe for long-term misery because you are focusing on what you don't want and can't control. You will feel unsuccessful and judge yourself harshly. Kicking at an iron wall is mentally, emotionally, and physically exhausting.

The alternative is to concentrate on what you can influence. Then you will feel hopeful and empowered. You will have the focus and energy you need to do your best work. You will still have preferences when you accept what exists, but discomfort will vanish and you will be more effective in initiating positive changes. Because you will be functioning at a more harmonious level, you will draw people and situations into your life that will help you create positive change. This is usually an effortless process because you allow, instead of try to force, change.

The next time you feel discomfort, notice that it is caused not by the event itself but by your judgment of what is occurring. Prove this by comparing the scenario to how you feel when you experience another situation that you don't judge harshly, even though the exact circumstances are not your preference.

Don't prolong your pain
by judging your resistance.
Flailing against resistance is futile.
Trust the process instead.
Blockages begin to change as soon
as we become aware of them.

A Tibetan monk was captured and tortured mercilessly by his guards. The tormented monk returned their rage with a cheerful expression. Puzzled and angry, the perpetrators relentlessly inflicted additional pain. Day after day, the monk maintained his sense of inner harmony and returned painful punches with a sweet smile. After months, the flabbergasted guards released the monk. As he departed, he smiled, bowed with respect, and wished his abusers well.

The overseer of the persecutors was furious and chastised the guards, "Why did you release your captive without breaking his spirit?" The confused captors could only mumble, "We were defeated. We were powerless to take his happiness away, so we finally had to let him go."

Of course, you won't be tested to this degree. However, it will be much easier for you to consistently own your inherent right to joy on the job by doing the following.

✦ Nurture your inner harmony.
✦ Accept responsibility for what you can control.
✦ Let go of what you cannot influence.

> Focus on your internal state of mind instead of on aspects of your work environment that you cannot control. When you don't allow external situations to affect you, it is impossible for anyone or any situation to harm you.

Just focus on living with integrity. You can always control how you respond to a situation. Approach challenges with the curiosity of a small child. When you dislike a task you are doing or think you were treated with disrespect, avoid the tendency to blame or judge. Instead, ask yourself one simple question, "I wonder what I can learn from this experience?" Negative feelings will vanish because you have opened the channel for joy on the job.

You gain power and freedom when you find meaning in everything that happens. If the significance of an event isn't readily apparent, trust that it will be. Ask for a sign and be open to receive it. Notice expectations that don't serve you. Make a decision to trust the process of your life.

> Your life will always be in harmony
>
> when you live in harmony with what exists.

REDUCE STRESS ABOUT THE UNCONTROLLABLE

We have tremendous personal power to reduce stress while we are exploring unknown pathways.

❏ Enrich Your Employment Options

Accelerating your ability to secure other employment causes other people to respond to you in a positive way. This indirectly provides more control over your work life.

Inventory your skills and marketability and develop new career goals. Stabilize your career ladder by engaging in educational activities that ensure you are trained and marketable. Work with a mentor. Build a solid support system by working with a mastermind group and networking with others who also value constructive feedback.

❏ Connect to Your Spirituality

You will be prone to worry and anxiety if your sense of well-being depends on what happens in the material world. Cultivate faith in the process of your life by exploring the meaning and opportunities for personal growth that reside within every challenge. We are here to make something out of our lives.

People who have a spiritual center are happier and less stressed. They also tend to be healthier, so they consistently perform better at work. Connect with your personal interpretation of a Higher Source and ask for guidance. Offer your concern to the Divine with a simple request, "Please show me the way to resolve this." Feel your Source taking the burden from you, and offer sincere appreciation that you will continue to receive guidance. Trust, and go on with your life.

Faith is to believe what you do not see.
The reward of faith is to see what you believe.
St. Augustine

❑ Pare Down Your Priority List

Learn to say no. Overloading leads to burnout. Gain a sense of control by doing one thing at a time in order of importance. Honor the commitments you make, and don't create unnecessary anxiety by promising more than you can commit.

❑ Exercise Your Way to Bliss

Exercise is often cited as the number one prescription for fighting stress and disease. Discover your preferred way to regularly take this easy-to-swallow pill that delivers magic benefits. Whether you choose walking, dance, weight lifting, or swimming, there is a perfect way for you to enjoy this reliable way to oxygenate your brain while flooding it with feel-good hormones. You might also reward yourself with magnificent connections with other people if you enroll in an exercise class.

❑ Practice a Blend of Deep Breathing and Focus

Studies have consistently endorsed yoga, tai chi, qi gong, and meditation as stress fighters. Each combines the benefits of deep belly breathing with focus. Taking deep breaths that fill every corner of your lungs before you slowly exhale balances your autonomic nervous system. Pause for a moment and prove to yourself how rejuvenating this can be.

The focus involved in yoga, tai chi, qi gong, and meditation distracts you from stressful situations, and you are much more capable of solving problems when you return to work. If you want to develop new friendships while relaxing, sign up for a class. Unlike some practices originating in Asia, Spring Forest Qi Gong is delightfully easy to learn.

❑ Put It in Perspective

Laugh at how seriously we treat even the smallest circumstances of our lives when we operate from our *discomfort zones*. When you lighten up, you are more optimistic, so you spontaneously attract people and circumstances that can make work seem effortless.

When you are frustrated about small uncontrollable aspects of life, ask yourself two questions.

1. Would I rather experience peace of mind or battle something I can't influence?
2. Will this situation really matter a year from now?

❑ Call in the Clowns

Happy children laugh hundreds of times a day until we teach them to be worker bees. Most human drones (adults like ourselves) manage a few smirks a day, but we have conditioned ourselves to bypass the deep gutteral laughs that heal stress and open our minds to dream up creative solutions to challenges.

It should make us smile that people who watched a funny video for 15 minutes felt twice as hopeful as those who viewed a neutral clip.[1] Sometimes the best strategy when you feel overwhelmed is to take a break with someone who makes you giggle, and the worst technique is to pound away at a problem. Laughter strengthens your immune system and increases your intellectual performance, so coping with challenges becomes much easier.

❑ Sing to Solutions

Most of us tense our shoulders or constrict our chest when we feel out of control. Both actions make it more difficult to breathe deeply. We begin to breathe short, shallow breaths when we need to be fully oxygenated to meet challenges. Singing can shift anxiety. It causes us to breathe more slowly and deeply. It relaxes our chest muscles. Singing can also rebalance our autonomic nervous system because it creates a positive balance between the oxygen we inhale and the carbon dioxide we exhale. Singing a song with upbeat lyrics can help you forget to worry. Since humor is one of the best ways to combat stress, sing an amusing song!

❑ Sooothe Yourself With Sweet Solitude

How will you hear the answers you so desperately seek when you are scurrying around in a noisy environment? Even short bursts of reflective time can replenish your energy and raise your confidence so you can achieve your long-term goals. Regularly enjoy the healing benefits of a quiet nature walk. Meditate, read inspirational literature, take a hot bath with lavender essential oil, or engage in other activities that keep your body healthy and feed your personal growth.

❑ Don't Cave in to Cravings

A yearning for high-fat, high-sugar foods when faced with challenges is based on an ancient need. Your body is requesting fuel for the battle with the saber-toothed tiger that became extinct long ago. Substitute easily digestible alternatives that accelerate your mindpower and help you solve problems. These include fruits, vegetables, and low-fat proteins.

Are you addicted to chocolate or another high-calorie, low-nutrient food as a wayward attempt to self-soothe? Bad habits beg to be broken.

Substitute healthy techniques that will truly prompt your body to produce positive, mood-influencing chemicals. The deep breathing exercises throughout this book take only a few minutes. They have no negative side effects such as the energy rush, energy crash syndrome associated with sugar and caffeine. Enjoy the feel-good release of serotonin and beta-endorphins you can trigger through laughter, deep breathing, luxurious stretches, aerobic exercise, and nature walks.

❑ Seek Help When You Need It

Avoid feeling isolated when you are stressed out. Ask for help when you feel overloaded. Those who assist you will smile as their self esteem rises.

Elevate your own self respect and your support system by working with a mastermind group or mentor.

Learn to recognize your personal stress triggers so you can take steps to prevent unnecessary wear and tear on your psyche. Seek professional assistance if you consistently experience difficulty sleeping, panic attacks, headaches, digestive difficulties, or aches and pains that are not associated with injury or diagnosed illness. If you don't feel deserving of the best that life has to offer, gain relief through professional counseling.

❑ Use Nature's Natural Release Valve

Tears are the natural cleansing system for your emotions. Tears release negative stress chemicals, including manganese and prolactin. Since weeping requires you to breathe deeply, tissue time is Nature's tonic for an imbalanced autonomic nervous system. Crying can also help you resolve challenges because it directs your focus away from stressors.

❑ Grow Blessings and Achievements

An observer always affects the outcome of an experiment. Even at the subatomic level, what you perceive and reinforce is what you get. Whether matter is a particle or a wave depends on the perspective of the observer. The object of your focus expands.

You are your personal experiment, so use your power to grow what you want. Begin by choosing your focus wisely because it will help you determine whether you live your fondest dreams or your worst fears. Even the smallest blessings and personal achievements will grow when you recognize and reinforce them. A focus on what you want gains results similar to using a tuning fork to prepare an out-of-tune piano for a recital. Explore how quickly gratitude can produce unexpected good fortune.

Use multisensory methods like those employed in the exercises in this book. When you catch yourself doing something right, a physical action such as patting yourself on the back and smiling while you look at yourself in the mirror can activate a neural network that stimulates feel-good endorphins.

❑ Practice Self-Care

Don't make unnecessary or big decisions when you are worried or stressed. Avoid stress by being aware that things that would ordinarily seem manageable usually seem difficult when your mood is foul. Give yourself healthy treats, such as frequent breaks, stretches, a massage, and connections with nature and friends. Engage in creative activities that bring you joy. Observe and manage your self-talk.

REV UP YOUR RESOURCES

✦ Which of the methods dissussed in the last few pages are you already using to reduce stress?

✦ How can you do more of what works?

✦ What new method will you explore this week?

> Control is a paradox. We have no control over anything except ourselves and the way we react to the events of our lives. This means we are in total control and can steer a steady ship.

PATIENCE PAYS

Intolerance creates irritability, but patience nurtures contentment and decreases stress. You can consciously cultivate patience as a source of job satisfaction.

In today's frenzied business climate, you may have forgotten that *you have an innate ability to be patient.* You may feel angry when a coworker is slow to answer your request for information but tolerant when equipment breakdowns occur. Perhaps you tend to be grouchy after three cups of coffee but are especially gracious and compassionate when someone truly needs your special work talents. Since you often lack control over aspects of your work life, the key to contentment is to discover the following.

✦ When are you *naturally* tolerant and easy-going?

✦ What fosters your innate patience?

✦ How can you stimulate your patience when you are challenged?

PROMOTE PATIENCE

❏ Step One. Recognize that you have a natural source of patience

Knowing that you have innate patience is the first step toward knowing how to stimulate it when a hurry-up world or other pressures challenge you. Take a few minutes to identify professional and personal situations in which you tend to be unhurried, compassionate, and understanding.

❏ Step Two. Identify factors that contribute to your patience

Determine your patience triggers. Use the following examples to jog your awareness.

✦ You develop compassion when you coach someone who has challenges similar to your own while learning a new skill.
✦ You know you are involved in the process of producing something valuable.
✦ Short-term results are recognized before completion of a final product.
✦ You have solved similar challenges in the past, so you feel confident you can do so again.
✦ You are fascinated by what makes a certain device work. Your curiosity entices you to

continued on the next page . . .

spend hours-on-end solving a mechanical problem.

✦ A creative action stirs something deep within your soul.

✦ You take pleasure in nurturing the personal or professional growth of others.

✦ You enjoy solving problems with like-minded people.

❏ Step Three. Pause and plan

Be proactive. Develop an action plan by thinking of how you can prompt a state of patience when you are challenged. Reflect on past situations that have stimulated your patience in the past. Use the following examples to help you do this.

✦ If curiosity feeds your tolerance, focus on what you can learn while solving a problem.

✦ If you are more broad-minded and accepting when you feel kinship with coworkers, ask open-ended questions designed to determine their perspectives.

✦ If you are more relaxed when you recall having resolved past difficulties, pause to reflect on pleasant feelings related to those situations.

✦ If you enjoy facilitating the professional growth of others, find ways to help other people thrive.

When a situation at work feels uncomfortable, our tendency is to want to leap in and force a solution to emerge. We are wiser when we cut a finger.

We have faith that, with proper care and a willingness to accept what exists, the damage will heal by degrees. We go on with our lives. Although we are conscious of the situation so that we don't exacerbate the problem, we don't obsess about the pain. As the healing process progresses, we don't slow down our rate of recovery by digging underneath a scab to make sure good things are happening.

Sometimes the fastest way to reach a goal is to travel the slowest route. Those who are the most contented at work have learned when to wait. They know impatience about what cannot be changed is a sure-fire recipe for unnecessary stress. They trust patience because it rewards them with the stamina they need in order to resolve difficult challenges. Patience provides the clarity required to recognize a true solution instead of grasping at a partial answer that will eventually magnify pain.

Answers emerge easily when we are focused *and* patient. When you are frustrated with what you cannot control, remember how patient you are while a wound is healing. Trust patience and time. They are two surprisingly powerful warriors for peace at work.

ACCEPTANCE + PATIENCE = POWER

Beware the fury of a patient man.
John Dryden

The power of patience and the wisdom of understanding what one can and cannot change have been grossly underrated. Resistance to what exists paves a perfect pathway to pain, but acceptance—acknowledging the realities of a given situation—allows new possibilities to emerge.

Beating on an iron wall will not magically transform it into an open doorway, so use a savvy strategy.

✦ Accept the realities of your situation.
✦ Decide what you can and cannot control.
✦ Take action to resolve problems that are within your control.
✦ Identify and employ your personal sources of patience.
✦ Discover the peace of mind that emerges as you bend with the uncontrollable whims of your work life. Maintain curiosity regarding what you can learn in the process. You will discover new possibilities hidden under the illusions of lack and limitation.

Embrace change.
We discover our true direction
within the winds of change.

CHAPTER 18

CASH IN
ON YOUR STRENGTHS

There is hardly anybody
good for everything,
and there is scarcely anybody
who is absolutely good for nothing.
Lord Chesterfield

Pat: I'm so excited about attending the design class! You're going, too, aren't you?

Nat: Nope. I don't have time. Why are you going? You're already good at design.

Pat: Because I want to get even better at what I do well. I know I have natural ability in design, and so do you. Don't you want to fully develop your talent?

Nat: I'm so busy trying to upgrade areas where I
          have weaknesses that I don't have time to build
          on my strengths.

Pat: I guess I think about things differently. I can
          spend my entire lifetime trying to be good at
          what I'm not, or I can manage my weaknesses
          while doing what brings me joy.

FOCUS ON YOUR STRENGTHS . . . OR ON YOUR WEAKNESSES?

Why is it often easier to identify our shortcomings than our strengths? It is not just because we have been taught to down-play our positive qualities and to praise those of others. Sometimes, we don't realize that our abilities are unique be-cause we have lived with them throughout our lifetime.

Once we acknowledge the significance of our special gifts, we feel compelled to fully develop them and to use them in ways that benefit others. As a byproduct, we become happier at work.

> *A funny thing happens when you*
> *connect with an aspect of yourself*
> *that has long been hidden or denied;*
> *it begs to be revealed, to be used.*
> Dottie Bruce Gandy

If your inner critic is trying to convince you that you might fail if you take the risk of exposing your talents to the world, remember that fear of failure is not the real issue. Most of us fear success far more than we fear failure because it is easier to play familiar roles, such as "I'm not good enough," than to acknowledge how special we are.

WHO'S THE FAIREST OF THEM ALL?

This exercise will initiate a process of breaking down social conditioning that may be standing between you and greater joy on the job.

1. Divide a piece of paper into two columns.
2. List your strengths on the left side of the page and your weaknesses on the right side.
3. Think of someone you admire. Repeat the process above, describing the other person's strengths and weaknesses.
4. Was it easier for you to identify the strengths of someone else than to identify your own assets?
5. Add to the list of your strengths by thinking outside of the box. Instead of only listing abilities that are also job responsibilities, such as marketing skills or computer proficiency, record additional talents. Examples follow.

   ✦ Compassion
   ✦ Can understand both sides of an argument
   ✦ High energy level
   ✦ Have a calming presence
   ✦ Concerned that customers receive value
   ✦ Good listener
   ✦ Patient
   ✦ Perceive hidden opportunities within adversities
   ✦ Curious about how things work
   ✦ Charismatic

continued on the next page . .

✦ Natural leader
✦ Consistently seek the truth
✦ Enjoy taking healthy risks
✦ Empathetic
✦ Sense of humor
✦ Good memory
✦ Passionate
✦ Can place names with faces
✦ Observant
✦ An attitude of gratitude
✦ Natural aptitude in _____.
✦ Feel compelled to make a difference when something occurs that is inappropriate

6. Review your list. Notice the difference in how you feel now and when you reviewed the list you made in step two above. Did you underestimate your strengths when you compiled the first list?

7. Continue to identify your assets during the next week. Also notice when you compliment others and when you belittle your own accomplishments. Observe patterns without judging or trying to change them. Trust that your awareness will create spontaneous change.

8. Make a commitment to do the following.

✦ Accurately identify your strengths.
✦ Play to your strengths while managing your weaknesses.

KNOW THY STRENGTHS

Never to be cast away
are the gifts of the gods,
which they give of their own will,
no man could have them for wanting them.
Homer

Although it is important to identify and strive to correct your weaknesses, it is even more important to identify and capitalize on your strengths. You can spend an entire lifetime focusing on ways to mend your weaknesses, but you will be much happier and more successful if you focus on the unique ways you can contribute to the world. Savvy organizations cross-train employees so they are prepared for emergencies, but they also recognize the wisdom of employees focusing on tasks that match their abilities.

Socrates said, "Know thyself" for a good reason. Feeling inadequate is stressful, but knowing you have unique gifts to contribute to the world of work provides immense satisfaction. The more you know about your strengths, the more you will be able to create a work life you enjoy. You will set yourself free to unleash the gifts your DNA has programmed you to deliver to a world that desperately needs your assistance. Identify your strengths so you can accomplish the following.

✦ Redesign your job so that it becomes more meaningful and fulfilling because it capitalizes on your strengths.
✦ Understand your life purpose. Then you will define yourself in terms of who you are rather than what you do.
✦ Allow knowledge of your life purpose to create a passionate work life that will feel more like play than work.

✦ Express your true self at work. This will escalate your self-esteem.

✦ Perceive additional work opportunities that reflect your heart's desire.

✦ Effortlessly promote yourself in ways that allow the new opportunities you desire to emerge.

The easiest way to achieve a balanced personal and professional life is to focus on your strengths. After Anita Willis and Rob Ryan identified their core talents, they convinced management to outsource, delegate, and eliminate other tasks from their workloads. How did two mid-level employees convince management to restructure their tasks so they could focus on what they did best while their coworkers wrestled with feeling overworked and overwhelmed?

Anita talked to her boss about how much more valuable she would be to the company if she focused 100 percent of her work time on activities in which she used her unique skills. She explained, "I find myself jumping up and down all day long to tinker with odds and ends. That breaks my focus, so the organization is paying me to take twice as long to accomplish the most important jobs I was hired to complete. I have a plan. I can train Laura and Mike to do the smaller tasks and they can establish a rotation system. You and I both know they are capable of doing this, and I can prove they have the time available. If either person is absent, I'll pitch in. And if my idea doesn't work, I'll go back to the old system without complaining."

Her boss had nothing to lose, and the organization had a good deal to gain. Anita won more freedom regarding her time and worked far less overtime. Laura and Mike also appreciated her efforts because she had created awareness that they were capable of higher-level tasks. Within four months, Anita proved to her boss that he was paying her less overtime and that she had eliminated unnecessary office tasks. Within seven months, she was given a raise.

Rob took a greater risk when outlining his plan to management. First, he outlined his concerns. Then he asked for assistance in restructuring his job "so I can be paid more to focus on what I do best." He proposed a timeframe in which he guaranteed his boss specific results. Rob's plan included outsourcing other tasks, and he concluded his proposal with, "I know we can save money when I use my time better. I'll prove that we will more than defray the cost of outsourcing. I'll also personally supervise it. If this plan doesn't work, I'll take a cut in pay after a six-month experiment. If it works, I'd like an increase in pay proportionate to the amount of increased revenue I can create with the new plan."

Rob's boss verified what research consistently indicates. Employees who do not comprehend their own value or stand up for themselves blend into the woodwork. Those who believe strongly in their abilities and take healthy risks are the most respected and supported by their bosses. Rob kept a careful accounting of the results of the new method, and he achieved his raise before the six-month trial ended.

Since our lives move toward the direction of our focus, you will receive the richest rewards when you support your strengths rather than warring against your weaknesses. When you concentrate on your most valuable talents and contributions, seen and unseen resources will help you accomplish your purpose.

HOW TO IDENTIFY YOUR STRENGTHS

Marcus Buckingham and Donald Clifton, coauthors of *Now, Discover Your Strengths*, differentiate talents from skills and knowledge. They define skills as steps of activities and knowledge as facts and lessons learned. Talents are special natural abilities and aptitudes that are innate. To identify them, observe yourself for consistent and spontaneous patterns of thought, feelings, and behavior that you can apply in a productive manner.[1]

The key to identifying your inherent strengths is to discover your authentic self. This requires stripping away layers of social programming, fear, and self-judgment that separate you from your True Self. The exercises on the following pages will help you do this.

❏ Find the Best in the Worst

Strengths are weaknesses.
Weaknesses are strengths.
We are all still polishing ourselves.
Jennifer Irene Moore

Only our belief systems and perceptions determine whether something is labeled good or bad. Our greatest strengths are usually also our most prominent weaknesses. This is balanced by the fact that our greatest deficiencies form a solid foundation for some of our most outstanding achievements.

The passionate person who is blessed with rapid, crystal clear visions of how to improve unpleasant situations is often cursed with intense impatience. He can't understand why coworkers don't flock around him to take advantage of his gift of prophecy. Why don't they line up to receive the benefits of his powerful, unique talent? His pushy posturing drives them away as if he were offering a bowl of delicious honey surrounded by a swarm of hungry bees. As soon as the soothsayer receives an "Aha!," he acts like a tethered, highstrung racehorse in agony. He gnashes his teeth because he has to wait until others finally comprehend his wisdom and slowly and carefully drag themselves onto the wagon he is chomping at the bit to tow forward at record speed.

Our most annoying characteristics are also often our greatest strengths. Every office needs *bull-headed* individuals who hold the focus until a difficult task is completed. *Lazy dreamers* can be invaluable in positions of creativity, research, and development. *Number crunchers* can keep a CEO and Board of Directors out of jail so the organization can thrive. *Nervous wrecks* can anticipate problems and design contingency plans while *clowns* ensure that the office is lively. Is it clear why labels should be reserved for jelly jars?

We are all brighter than we perceive ourselves to be, and our strengths and talents are often buried underneath what we judge to be inadequacies. Even high achievers are unaware of some of their greatest gifts. This was true for Win Wenger, author of *The Einstein Factor.* After decades of believing he was dull in math, he discovered his higher than normal mathematical abilities.[2] What do Walt Disney, Henry Ford, Alexander Graham Bell, Whoopi Goldberg, Albert Einstein, General George Patton, Nelson Rockefeller, Cher Bono, Hans Christian Andersen, and Leonardo da Vinci have in common? They discovered that dyslexia is much more of a gift than a disability.

Exercises scattered throughout this book will help you overcome premature and negative conclusions concerning your innate talents and abilities. Some of these were made by you and some by authority figures. You will also learn how to silence disparaging comments made by your inner critic. Its voice usually becomes louder when you are on the verge of discovering your inner genius.

SCAVENGER HUNT

1. Use the previous information to stimulate your thinking as you identify your strengths during the next few days. Reflect on the following.

   ✦ Characteristics of yourself that have been judged as negative
   ✦ Your past "worst experiences" at work
   ✦ Areas in which you or others have judged you to be incompetent

2. Identify hidden strengths and talents related to these experiences and traits.

3. Consider the possibility that your greatest "inadequacy" houses an undiscovered talent.

❑ Seek From a Different Source

The world is usually quick to educate us about our frailties and faults and often slow to help discover our virtues and untapped potential. Fortunately, how we feel about ourselves is much more important than how others feel about us.

Since your strengths can help you write your own ticket in the workplace, don't be a stranger to yourself. If you aren't clear about your strengths, the next exercise will help you step out of the box and access the information you need in a new way.

INTUIT IT

Sleep on It

Call for the assistance of your Oracle of the Night. Before going to sleep, ask yourself, "What are my unique gifts and talents?" or "How can I best use my special abilities at work?" Because your mind never sleeps, you will receive an answer upon awakening, so hold the intention to remember it. Have a pen and paper or a tape recorder handy so your sleepy state or a hurry-up response to your alarm will not keep you from gaining the answers that become available to you.

Write It Out

Use your nondominant hand to write answers to the following sentence stem. It may seem like nonsense, but the exercise will produce significant insights. Remember to keep your hand moving on the page even if no ideas surface in your mind. Continue to write your thoughts until you receive clarity.

✦ If I knew what my special gifts and talents are, I would know they are _____
_____.

❑ Witness Your Strengths

You can also discover your hidden talents by noticing your automatic reactions to stress. Since talents are innate and programmed into your DNA, use the exercise below to identify your strengths by observing your instinctive responses to challenges.

**SCOPE OUT
YOUR
SPONTANEITY**

Become a curious witness. Observe yourself for a couple of weeks and answer the following questions.

✦ What do you learn the most rapidly when you experience stress?
✦ What produces personal fulfillment when you feel pressured?
✦ What desires and responses differentiate you from others who experience similar challenges?

❑ Create a Commercial

Tutors often learn more than the students they teach because instructors must master material in order to be able to teach it. You will discover more about the significance and power of your strengths each time you place yourself in the position of selling them to another person.

SELL YOURSELF

Imagine you are producing a radio commercial to sell your talents.

Step One: Research the Product

Jot down answers to the following questions.

☆ What activities were fun and easy for you as a child?

☆ What were your most enjoyable challenges during your youth?

☆ How did you answer the question, "What do you want to be when you grow up?"

☆ What activities provide you with the greatest sense of accomplishment and joy at this time in your life?

☆ What tasks are easy for you but not for other people?

continued on the next page . .

☆ If you could be paid well to accomplish only three tasks each day at work, what would they be?

☆ What would coworkers and employers identify as your top three talents?

☆ What would you do if you had all of the time and money in the world?

☆ What needs can you meet by using your unique talents at work?

Step Two: Identify Strengths and Advantages of the Product

1. Design and produce the commercial by talking into a tape recorder.
2. Replay the tape after you have completed the commercial. Listen as if you are an objective person who has been observing your performance during the last year.
3. Continue to imagine yourself as an independent observer. Comment about the accuracy of the advertisement.
4. Write down strengths and talents you have identified through this process.
5. Decide which talents to focus on at work.

❑ Identify Your Talents By Observing Others

One of our greatest tools for self-discovery is observing how we mirror each other.[3] For example, if you admire and enjoy listening to great speakers, there is a good chance that you have a natural inclination to be a public speaker. Use the following exercise to take note when another person's talents evoke an emotional response within you.

DISCOVER YOUR STRENGTHS IN OTHERS

1.   Identify five individuals who are effective at work. Describe their strengths and talents.

2.   Review your list because each trait has a special meaning for you.

3.   Consider the possibility that you also possess these qualities. Then prove this to yourself. Carry your list around, and state the following when you observe the positive characteristics you have identified.

     I am willing to recognize in myself the positive traits I admire in others. These talents include _____.

continued on the next page . . .

If your inner critic makes a comment like, "Oh sure!," just notice its presence instead of trying to quell its voice. Over time, you will more quickly observe and appreciate your assets. When that occurs, other people will also notice your abilities more rapidly and more frequently.

4. The momentum behind what you reinforce expands, so take a few minutes each night to reflect on your day. Record the following.

☆ Your positive characteristics

☆ How you used them that day

☆ Evidence that you possess a favorable trait of which you were previously unaware

☆ When you think you have completed the exercise, ask yourself, "What else?" Then, record at least one additional strength or asset.

❏ Secure Feedback

If you have ever been told to be modest about your achievements, you may have overlooked how helpful it can be to gain external feedback. None of us perceives ourselves accurately. Take advantage of objective external feedback sources you can trust.

GAIN FROM GUIDANCE

1. If you are involved with a professional growth association, such as a mastermind group, ask members of the organization to describe your strengths. You can also ask friends, coworkers, and family members for their assessments. In addition, use the following sentence stem to appraise your progress.

    _____ *months ago, I didn't know I
    could* _____.
    Now I know I can _____.

    Note: Your answers don't have to be work related. For example, before 9/11, would you have thought you could cope in a workplace or world in which so many people feel unsure about the future?

2. If you have not discovered your unique talents and you do not yet know how you can enrich the world by using your special gifts, consult a career counselor. Ask the human resources department in your organization about tuition reimbursement programs, scholarships, or time off to attend local classes. A mentor may also be able to assist you in identifying your strengths.

REDESIGN YOUR WORK TO REFLECT YOUR STRENGTHS

To be what we are, and to become
what we are capable of becoming,
is the only end of life.
Baruch Spinoza

Now that you have identified your strengths, the next step is to believe in yourself so you will express your talents. This means taking action steps to build your livelihood around them. This process is much simpler than you may think, and it's never too late to begin. Grandma Moses began painting at age 75.

☆ Identify at least one talent or strength as a focus.

☆ Acknowledge your passion to excel in that area.

☆ Identify social or planetary needs related to your talents.

☆ Challenge yourself to continue developing your strengths.

☆ Learn from spending time with individuals who have similar talents.

☆ Take healthy risks so more of your true self can emerge.

Adam Sloan is a butcher whose skills and knowledge expand beyond the minimum requirements of his trade. Standing on a cold, hard floor all day long and receiving only occasional positive feedback from customers had drained his enthusiasm about his job. Adam determined that his core strengths included the following.

✦ Humor
✦ High energy level
✦ Concern that customers receive value

Developing a signature style transformed his job from an exhausting, routine occupation into personal fulfillment. He placed a basket, sign, cards, and pens above the meat counter encouraging customers to request customized packages of meat in advance. Each time he fulfilled a special order, he enjoyed getting to know the customer and telling jokes to lighten the person's day. Soon his mundane job became exciting. There was a steady supply of individuals to hear new comedy material he designed during his off time, and he used his high energy to tell his short humorous routines with a dramatic flair.

Adam developed a loyal following that was atypical in a fast-paced franchise grocery. His clients happily spread the word about him as they waited in checkout lines. Stressed-out shoppers were replaced by smiling, contented customers who circulated the news about the fun service they received. Adam had transformed a monotonous job into a meaningful career. Management received so much positive feedback from his efforts that Adam also received a raise and an expense-paid trip to present his ideas to other butchers at a national conference.

Darcy Bates provides another example. She is a very competent administrative professional who had grown quite weary of handling customer complaints. In addition to her knowledge and skills, Darcy identified core strengths that included the following.

✦ Curiosity
✦ An open mind
✦ Love challenges
✦ Enjoy taking healthy risks

Darcy's associates focused on outwitting a technology system that tracked their calls, but she threw caution to the wind so she could enjoy her job. She knew the complaints made by customers often glossed over the genuine reasons for their disgruntlement, so she devised a way to discover the real issues. She was confident that, once the root causes of problems were corrected, customers would have fewer grievances.

Darcy began by asking a series of questions designed to determine the underlying sources of problems. She kept track of customer responses and made recommendations regarding ways to prevent the same complaints from resurfacing over and over.

She followed up with recommendations to the research and development department. Instead of becoming discouraged when the department was too understaffed to follow through, Darcy developed a preliminary outline with suggestions for a prototype project. She also engaged in informal meetings with the personnel who would have to assume lead roles.

Her efforts were successful. She stimulated the interest of essential personnel and inspired new ways of developing and marketing products. In the process, Darcy developed new friends and gained respect for her unique talents. The new diversity in her work elevated the core strengths she had identified to even higher levels. Her self esteem and job satisfaction escalated.

In time, word traveled concerning her innovative style and she was offered a position at another organization. It was a tough decision for Darcy. Since she had redesigned her job into a challenging and fulfilling career, she chose to stay.

The exercise on the next page will help you change the way you approach work so that you can also do the following.

✦ Reinvent some of your work tasks so that the results you achieve reflect your core strengths.
✦ Develop a signature style that enables you to cash in on your strengths.

DEVELOP A
SIGNATURE STYLE

Your strengths are strong roots that will support your passion and your core activities as you reach to fulfill your dreams. This exercise will assist you in redesigning at least one aspect of your current job to capitalize on your strengths. Use the real-life examples of Adam Sloan and Darcy Bates to stimulate your thinking regarding how you can revise your own work situation.

☆ How can you use your core strengths to increase your joy on the job?

☆ Begin now by redesigning one small aspect of your existing job in a way that capitalizes on your strengths.

CAN'T EXPRESS YOUR TALENTS WHERE YOU WORK?

Consider a variety of strategies before concluding that your strengths are not a match for your organization. You may have to propose a new idea several times or to a number of different people. In the meantime, believe in your proposal, and regard each "no" as a stone you tread on the path toward "yes." Use the challenge as an excuse to learn new sales skills. Harlan Sanders heard hundreds of "no's" before anyone bought his idea to create Kentucky Fried Chicken.

Organizations are changing more rapidly than ever as they respond to global competition, so assume that possibilities are endless until proven otherwise. Before you jump ship, snoop around in house. Discover what your organization and clients really need. When you detect a product or service gap, imagine how your unique talents can plug the hole. Then design a simple but compelling proposal.

Instead of assuming that someone will invite you to submit a creative idea, tell management, team members, and other coworkers how your strengths and talents can benefit the organization. Notice and take advantage of informal grapevines.

If your talents are rare, such as those of many artists, approach special projects departments that need photography, layout, special effects lighting, electronics, recording, and other technical work that requires creative abilities and imagination. Large corporations often financially reward those who can entertain at special events for employees or clients. Although it may not become a full-time job, it can enliven your work and relationships to the degree that a routine job becomes exciting.

You may eventually conclude that you are a star and cannot contribute to an organization that only has square and round holes to fill. If that is true, decide to either express your gifts outside of work or design a plan to change employment. Muster your courage to travel a new path without a map . . . just for the joy of it!

ALLOW A BLOOM TO UNFOLD

Take action, whether you decide to use your special talents in your current position or elsewhere. Your special gifts are not accidental. They are essential ingredients for the joy that occurs when you meet your full potential. For every talent, there are related needs in the world, and you can help fill them. When you are doing a job where you use your strengths, you so enjoy what you're doing that you literally lose track of time. A state of bliss unfolds, and a wealth of unexpected resources and opportunities support your efforts.

> *You are a miracle. You have something to share that no one else has. To keep that hidden because of self-defeating ideas is to die less than you are.*
>
> *Don't let that happen. Your greatest responsibility is to become everything that you are, not only for your benefit, but for mine.*

Leo Buscaglia

CHAPTER 19

IT'S FLOW TIME!

Your work is to discover your work
and then with all your heart to give yourself to it.
Buddha

Theo: I stay on the lookout for UFOs when I'm on the job. Do you ever wish aliens would rescue you from work?

Leo: Nope! I'd send them away if they showed up. I crave parts of my job like a bear hungers for honey. In fact, I'd do some of my work even if I weren't paid to do it! When I'm totally wrapped up in a task, I'm in an altered state.

Theo: What's that like?

Leo: My focus is very intense, but I'm calm. I lose my sense of self because I become one with my work. I'm so mesmerized by what I'm doing that I don't notice what's going on around me. Hours go by like minutes. I forget to take breaks.

Theo: If you're not taking breaks, you must be exhausted at the end of the day.

Leo: Not at all! I'm ecstatic when I push myself to the limit. Achieving my peak performance produces an amazing high.

The heart of the business world beats joyfully when employees engage in work tasks that are meaningful and fulfilling. Happy team members merge into a group consciousness that buzzes with a creative flow of innovative ideas. Individual workers whose attention is riveted to a challenge lose track of time until they resolve a problem. They emerge from the experience with elevated self-esteem. For all of these employees, the importance of other aspects of their lives fade as they experience the joy of being completely absorbed in an activity.

They are participating in an optimal experience called *flow*, a state first identified by Mihaly Csikszentmihalyi, a psychology professor who was also an avid rock climber. Csikszentmihalyi was fascinated with the focus and elation he felt when he forced himself to excel by inching his way up a challenging rock face. After experiencing flow, he was baffled that the field of psychology was focused on human dysfunction instead of on joy and human potential.

Csikszentmihalyi knew humans pursue happiness more than any other goal. People strive to achieve wealth, influence, health, and beauty because they expect them to produce joy, but happiness is sought for its own sake.

> People will work very hard
> for the sheer joy of doing
> an activity they love.

Csikszentmihalyi's rock climbing was a perfect example of passion that fueled arduous labor. He spent decades investigating how people in all types of occupations experience flow.

His research explored the positive mental and emotional states that drive humans to perform at their peak capacity. When people are in flow, they are so involved in an activity that nothing else seems to matter. The experience itself is so rewarding that they will perform it whether they are paid or not, even at great cost or risk, for the sheer sake of doing it.

Csikszentmihalyi strapped pagers on thousands of individuals. When the pagers beeped randomly during the day, volunteers ceased their activities and completed a questionnaire measuring their mood and the level of involvement with what they were doing. After investigating more than 10,000 such snapshots of subjects' lives, Csikszentmihalyi was able to accurately describe the enjoyable state of mind in which people function at their optimum level.[1]

Flow experiences are demanding as well as rewarding. Subjects experience a heightened state of concentration and simultaneously increase their capabilities and confidence. People are the most creative, achieve at their highest productivity level, and learn the fastest when experiencing flow.

Csikszentmihalyi concluded that flow exists when one's body or mind is stretched to its limits in a voluntary effort to accomplish a task that is perceived as challenging or worthwhile. The task must be neither too easy nor too difficult. If it is too easy, the person becomes bored. If the task is too difficult, the individual becomes frustrated, which interferes with the ability to concentrate. A negative internal dialogue begins, and this can pave the way to defeat or self-sabotage.

Csikszentmihalyi's work has profound implications for our business and personal lives.

> We all *require* challenges. We *need* to be confronted with meaningful problems to solve and other tasks that are important to complete. We need jobs that stretch our limits in reasonable ways. If we are to enjoy our jobs and reach our highest levels of self-actualization, it is essential that we encounter activities that are difficult but doable. When we are in flow, we discover our true essence.

You have, no doubt, experienced the feeling of being in flow. Remember the last time you became so engrossed in an enjoyable or important activity that a set of unexpected, favorable events ensured successful completion. Perhaps you were passionate about solving a difficult problem. You knew the approach to take, but you personally lacked the financial or other resources to follow through. You discussed your idea with a friend who shared your enthusiasm but also lacked the funds or skills to carry out the project. Later, your friend casually mentioned your idea to other individuals who jumped at the opportunity to use their money, talents, or manpower to resolve the challenge.

You may have participated in a sailing, bicycling, or running event in which the odds were against your winning but you competed for the love of the game. During the last segment of the race when your excitement and an adrenaline rush surpassed your physical strength, you were assisted by currents of wind that literally pushed you forward while slowing the progress of others.

As the above examples indicate, when you are in flow, obstacles fall by the wayside and favorable circumstances propel you forward. The following factors contribute to your joy and total involvement in your project.

✦ You are accomplishing a task that is aligned with your interests and expands upon your current abilities. The activity is meaningful to you, and humans instinctively crave meaning in their lives. We are also hardwired to be attracted to activities that protect or enhance our species. Since a state of flow is meaningful and elevates our capabilities, we hunger for flow.

✦ You are authentic when in flow. You are passionate while fully using and developing your abilities.

✦ Although you are proud of your individual accomplishments, you feel connected to a force greater than yourself because significant, favorable coincidences occur. You feel supported by unseen forces that assist you in following your heart and achieving your goals.

✦ The altered state of consciousness you experience in a flow state causes your brain to release feel-good chemicals (beta-endorphins) into your central nervous system. Doubts and fears fall by the wayside.

> Flow produces positive cumulative effects. The more often you engage in flow, the less frustrated you become when confronted with new challenges.

One purpose of this book is to share how your work environment can support you so you can engage in meaningful tasks consistent with your abilities and interests.

DO-IT-YOURSELF FLOW

To experience flow, you must focus on satisfying goals that nurture your mind and spirit. Activities that produce flow vary from person to person. Some individuals thrive when they modify software, solve a mechanical problem, write a report, or train another employee. Others relish a good book or devour a chess game. Some people must be physically active. The next exercise will help you do the following.

✦ Discover how you currently reach a state of flow.
✦ Ensure that flow-producing activities are part of your life at work as well as your personal life.
✦ Communicate benefits of a flow state for the organization so your supervisor and team members fully support joy on the job.

FIND YOUR FLOW

This exercise can be done individually or with a team of people interested in self-discovery and maximizing job satisfaction. Insights are prolific when groups of individuals discuss their results.

1. For the next ten work days, record when you experience flow by using a chart like the one below. Set a device that will beep you once every 1 ½ or 2 hours. As soon as you hear the signal, stop and note the activity you are engaged in as well as your state of mind.

Date	Time Period	Activity	Level of Flow

Rate your level of flow as low, medium, or high. Determine your rating by considering your level of interest, absorption in the task, and enjoyment. Use a scale from one to ten, with one = low, five = medium, and ten = high.

continued on the next page . . .

2. Review your chart at the end of the ten-day period. Notice which activities produced the highest states of flow. Pay attention to surprises regarding your conclusions. Most people discover that at least some of the activities they dreaded the most actually produced flow because they were challenged and learned something new.

3. How can you ensure that your work schedule includes flow-producing activities?

4. Identify the ways your organization can benefit when you are involved in work activities that produce a state of flow.

5. What is your next step to communicate these potential benefits to your boss and team members?

6. How can you ensure that you also have flow-producing activities in your personal life?

One of the surprises in Csikszentmihalyi's research was that flow experiences and positive mood states were reported almost three times more frequently at work than during leisure activities. Employees felt happy, satisfied, creative, strong, active, motivated, and focused 54 percent of the time they were working. During leisure activities, however, they described themselves as experiencing negative states 82 percent of the time. They felt weak, dull, dissatisfied, and passive. *Even workers engaged in dull or routine tasks with little autonomy were more likely to report a state of flow than individuals engaged in leisure.*

Why? We love feeling useful, challenged, and skilled on the job. It is so important to reject the social conditioning that work is something you have to do or something you do for someone else's benefit. When you remember that work provides lifestyle choices and opportunities for personal growth, you realize you are getting paid to attend the School of Life.

SET THE STAGE WITH MANAGEMENT

If you need to sell the benefits of flow on the job to management, inform them that companies as diverse as Microsoft, Toyota, and Patagonia have recognized the economic advantages of workers experiencing flow.[2]

One of your goals is to become so involved in each work task that you forget about extraneous matters. The following steps will help you achieve this goal.

continued on the next page . . .

1. Assess your strengths and weaknesses so you can design a specific action plan.

2. Focus on a single activity that is doable but challenging. Select a task that matches your achievable skill and ability level. This task should provide feedback that will help you focus your attention in the most useful manner so you can self-correct as quickly as possible and improve your skills. This will build self-confidence and help you feel that you have a sense of control over your work. If you are climbing a steep mountain, each successful or unsuccessful foothold provides instant feedback. Although many work tasks, such as the spell check component of word processing, provide rapid feedback, others do not. Remedy this deficiency by setting up a system of regular feedback with management regarding your progress. This will ensure that the aspects of your workload that inhibit flow can be revised as rapidly as possible. The more timely feedback you receive, the better you will flow.

3. Make sure you, management, and team members agree on achievable goals that are to be accomplished one at a time. Flow and multi-tasking are usually incompatible. Make sure expectations for your performance are clear.

continued on the next page . . .

4. Ask for the additional support from manage-
    ment that you need, such as assistance min-
    imizing interruptions or lining up a mentor.

Have you been wondering how you can achieve flow when doing tasks you dislike? Most of the insights you need will be found below the level of your conscious awareness. Why weren't these pearls of wisdom available to you when you wailed, "This is the most boring task! Why can't my job be interesting?"

First of all, it is essential to focus on what we want instead of on what we don't want. Also, the conscious mind has limited abilities. It can only process five to nine bits of information at a time. The powers of the nonconscious mind are immense. This part of you can process millions of bits of data at a time![3]

Since inquiry can stimulate your innate genius potential, the key is to reframe your exasperation. Instead of asking a question that assumes the situation will never improve, substitute an empowering query designed to trigger your nonconscious mind to come to your rescue. You can ask, "How can I have fun doing this job?" with a genuinely curious mind. Since a playful approach will transform your state of mind, observe a delightful process unfold. Your nonconscious mind will unlock creative thinking that can inspire your next step toward joy on the job.

You will enrich your job significantly by transforming routine aspects of your work into an enjoyable flow state. The goal is to become completely absorbed by each activity so there are no unemployed brain cells that invite your inner critic to chatter about how bored or unhappy you are.

The next exercise offers you enjoyable multisensory ways to engage in flow on a daily basis.

EXPERIENCE FLOW EVERY DAY

The following additional tips will help you create the relaxed yet alert state that will increase flow and fulfillment.

❏ Engage in Alpha

When your brain is in the alpha state, it is naturally relaxed and calm, yet it is also alert and creative. Many studies have shown that this condition is the ideal mode for accomplishing most job tasks. It is certainly the ideal frame of mind for preventing job stress. The more you practice the simple exercise that follows, the more quickly you will reach an alpha state. As you continue to practice, you will notice that more and more of your waking time is spent in an alpha state.

1. Choose a location where you will not be disturbed. You may wish to listen to relaxing music while doing this exercise.
2. Settle into a comfortable position and close your eyes.
3. Take three deep breaths, inhaling and exhaling slowly.

continued on the next page . . .

4. Mentally count backward slowly from fifty to one while imagining that you are descending a staircase with fifty stairs.
5. Continue to breathe deeply when you reach the bottom stair. If your inner critic wants to voice an opinion, count from twenty to one until your mind is clear and you are peaceful.

❑ Look at the Bigger Picture

When you are in flow, the activity itself becomes the reward. Since flow is most often achieved when you know you are pursuing a goal that will serve society, identify the broader benefits of accomplishing each task. If social gains are not apparent, will part of your earnings support loved ones? Do you plan to donate a portion of your earnings to charity?

❑ Merge With Your Task

If progress seems slow, assume that your task has a consciousness. Ask the task what it wants and needs. Record the answers with your nondominant hand. Keep your hand moving on the page, even when no thoughts emerge. You will be surprised at the clarity you receive regarding how to most joyfully complete a task.

continued on the next page . . .

❏ Get in the Groove

A finger labyrinth can center your mind, calm anger and anxiety, stimulate creativity, and shift your perspective regarding a tough challenge or difficult emotion. It is a powerful tool because it meshes physical movement with a challenge to the left brain. Use your nondominant hand to "walk" through the labyrinth because you will stimulate different neural networks and provide easier access to your intuition. If you do not already have a finger labyrinth in your desk, pocket, or purse, you can find out how to buy or create one by searching *labyrinth* on the Internet.

❏ Orchestrate Your Mind

Certain types of music have been associated with heightened focus, concentration, and peak performance. Baroque, romantic, and classical music create the alpha and theta mood states in which Einstein spent most of his waking hours.[4] Companies such as Sound Health, The Relaxation Company, Inner Peace, New Earth, and Phillips, and composers such as Morry Zelcovitch offer outstanding collections of brain-entrainment music that induce these levels of consciousness. The strategy of using music to entrain your brain state is so successful that employees in many offices cooperatively select the recordings they play as background music.

continued on the next page . . .

You can also create a private brainwave symphony by using an iPod or a portable CD player and headphones.

❑ Follow Your Nose

Unique aromas produce distinct physiological effects and mood states. Essential oils and flower essences can dramatically affect your feelings because your olfactory sense is directly connected to the limbic area of your brain (the seat of your emotions). Employees frequently use essential oils to elevate concentration and arouse feelings such as peace and joy. Some Japanese companies diffuse lemon and peppermint essential oils to increase productivity. Sandalwood and nutmeg are used to dissipate employee stress. A blend of rosemary and lemon improves focus. Other oils, such as ylang ylang and bergamot, stimulate the production of the feel-good neurotransmitter serotonin. Lavender triggers alpha and theta brain waves. Chamomile, rose, and orange blossom are calming. Jasmine is said to imbue confidence in dealing with difficult problems, which can elevate your self-esteem.[4] Once you experience the benefits of aromatherapy, you will probably keep vials in your car and home as well as at work. When purchasing essential oils or flower essences, keep in mind that the quality of the product will determine its effectiveness.

GO WITH FLOW

Consistently reaching a state of flow will add an entirely new dimension to your work. Use the techniques described to make even the most routine aspects of your job more enjoyable and fulfilling. You will receive immense benefits, including elevated self-esteem, creativity, productivity, and of course—joy on the job!

There's no business like flow business.
Ann Marsh

PART THREE

MULTISENSORY, MIND-BODY TOOLS FOR A JOYFUL JOURNEY

CHAPTER 20

TOOLS FOR A
JOYFUL JOURNEY

If you have built castles in the air,
your work need not be lost;
that is where they should be.
Now put the foundations under them.
Henry David Thoreau

Because you are a unique and complex individual with mental, emotional, physical, and spiritual needs, this section provides you with tools that will facilitate a holistic approach for discovering happiness at work. Consistent with Thoreau's advice, you will be able to immediately use these proven techniques as a foundation to support your "castles in the air" by accomplishing the following.

❑ Avoid emotional roller coasters

❑ Substitute curiosity for:

✦ self-judgment
✦ expectations that are responsible for impatience or unnecessary frustration
✦ negative judgments regarding your experiences

❑ Access valuable intuitive hunches more quickly and easily

❑ Use whole-brain and whole-body techniques that link the rational and emotional areas of your brain

❑ More easily and creatively solve problems

❑ Trust the process of life

By the time you complete the exercises in these chapters, you will have access to a powerful internal support system. Your new resources will include the following.

❑ A curious witness
❑ An emotional anchor
❑ A powerful, positive resource state
❑ An intuitive edge
❑ Mind mapping

CHAPTER 21

MEET "C.W."

*"If only there were two of me," she thought,
"one who spoke and the other who listened,
one who lived and the other who watched,
how I would love myself! I'd envy no one."*
                                    Simone de Beauvoir

THE ADVANTAGES OF DETACHMENT

C.W. stands for the Curious Witness, one of the most effective and effortless techniques you will ever discover. By using your intentions, you can create C.W. as a personal assistant to help you approach challenges in fresh new ways. When you consistently use C.W., you avoid emotional roller coasters, self-judgments, and judgments of your experiences.

With C.W., you **observe** yourself having unpleasant feelings or experiences. You do not avoid or deny your emotions because what we resist persists. However, your emotions do not become a primary identity. Instead of becoming lost in anger, fear, or sadness associated with a difficult experience, you use C.W. to merely *acknowledge* your emotions. You experience them as sensations in your body. You still gain the benefits of emotions, including new insights. However, *you are very clear that you are not the anger, fear, or sadness. You just watch yourself experience the emotion.*

The process is similar to observing a stranger being injured. You have an emotional response, but you are one layer removed from the responses of those who are directly involved.

When you routinely observe yourself experiencing feelings in this way, you are actually more compassionate for yourself and others than when you ride the emotional roller coaster. Your perceptions are more accurate because you don't yearn for a certain outcome. More creative energy is available to you, so you act in a productive manner.

Because C.W. is a neutral, factual observer detached from emotional angst, negative feelings flow through very quickly. Since there is no resistance to counteract, you easily discover misperceptions about your circumstances and they gradually fade away. Inviting C.W. into your consciousness is like enjoying the company of a live-in umpire. You effortlessly avoid the temptation to judge your experiences as bad, unfortunate, or unnecessary.

This is similar to the choices you have when you approach a busy street corner in front of a tall building during 5:00 traffic. One option is to stand in the middle of the street, cursing the noise and congestion while shuddering with fear because you really could be hit by a car. Another option is to leave the street corner and take the elevator to the roof of the building. When you peer at the street corner from your new vantage point, you still witness traffic bottlenecks and hear angry horns. However, you realize they have absolutely nothing to do with you. From your new neutral position, you observe your environment much more accurately. You notice patterns in which traffic is sometimes stuck and sometimes clear, but you don't participate in the drama.

C.W. also helps calm the internal critic because you simply *observe* mental chatter. Instead of believing your critic's negative messages, thereby empowering its voice, the deeper, all-knowing part of you takes over. This part of you is totally detached from the critic. It calmly watches your "monkey mind" race around in circles until it wears itself out. Old perceptions of who you are (your ego-mind) dissolve, and your "bigger mind" (who you really are) downloads into your consciousness.

A wonderful and spontaneous transition occurs when C.W. consistently serves as your personal assistant. One day, you notice that you have substituted curiosity and the joy of learning for expectations that cause pain when they do not come to fruition. Eventually, you are hooked! You notice that you are having fun with two of the most exciting aspects of life—choice and challenge.

Because C.W. helps you experience life in the moment, you link with one of your best natural resources—your intuition. You steadily prove to yourself that you always have dependable inner guidance. Since happiness is a side effect of living fully in each moment and following your internal clues, you notice yourself smiling more often.

This one simple technique—developing and employing a personal witness—can help you let go of struggle or judgment and adopt bliss as a new familiar zone (a 24-hour a day lifestyle). Are you ready to begin?

CREATE YOUR CURIOUS WITNESS—

STAGE ONE

1. Discover the observer who already lives inside of you. Notice that you are analyzing the idea of a C.W. while you read this exercise. You have just proven that part of you is already playing the role of a neutral witness. This component of yourself is, and always has been, an aspect of your consciousness.

2. During the next two days, pay close attention to your neutral observer. Notice that your witness is ever-present and observes, instead of judges, what exists. Observe that your innate witness lacks concerns, problems, or worries.

MASTER YOUR CONSCIOUSNESS

Think of C.W. as a part of your consciousness that you can schedule to spontaneously appear:
+ when you want it to.
+ in the form you tell it to.
+ in a manner that will serve you—ways you are not yet aware of. Because C.W. is similar to a computer that can think, your instructions will result in benefits you haven't yet imagined.

You can become the programmer of the contents of your consciousness. Why would you want to do this? Mastering this aspect of yourself can ensure that you experience bliss on an ongoing basis.

In your present circumstances, you are involuntarily (unconsciously) responding to cues in your consciousness that have been programmed by the media and other aspects of society. The following are just two examples.

+ Subliminal messages in advertisements are designed to promote self-judgment so you will buy more products.
+ As a child, some adults taught you to pay more attention to errors in your performance than to what you did well.

Today, you can make different decisions—choices that will empower you. Rather than being *unaware* of the folders, file cabinets, and software in your consciousness, you can do the following.

+ Gain valuable self-awareness.
+ Clean your hard drive. How much of your old programming do you think is relevant today? When you become aware of erroneous software programs and misperceptions, you will be thrilled to delete them.
+ Take charge of your own life. That is the only way you will ever achieve happiness at work.

Instead of wondering why the messages of other people trigger unpleasant emotions or why you hunger for meaning and fulfillment at work, you can *purposely* create "automatic-pilot software." Because C.W. will increase your awareness, it will lighten your load in life.

You already have many subconscious programs that serve you. When you see a bottle of bleach that someone left on the kitchen counter next to a bottle of fruit juice, you know which bottle to drink from and which to avoid. Existing software tells you which substance will nourish and which will harm you. Now you can use C.W. to create a wider array of healthy mental and emotional programs that will serve you for years to come.

C.W. will be available to you every minute of every day. Based on your instructions, it will deliver whatever awareness or reminder you direct it to provide. It will always be under your control because you can retrain it at any time. If you want to equip yourself with this simple, powerful tool, set an intention that you want a C.W. to alert you regarding behaviors that do not serve you, including the following.

✦   Self-judgment
✦   Negative judgments about emotions, life, or
      other people
✦   Expectations or demands that life unfold in a
      certain way
✦   A perceived need to control or change what
      you cannot influence

You will still have preferences, and they may manifest more quickly when you observe life with curiosity instead of having an obsessive attachment to a certain outcome. We have more vitality when we are flexible. We are soft, supple, and spirited as babies. Most of us grow increasingly rigid until we become absolutely hard and stiff (a.k.a. dead).

There are many ways to establish your innate observer as a personal assistant. I simply had a talk with myself and set the intention to develop a C.W. Then, I programmed my observer to be humorous and emit a mental cue when I needed to become more aware of my ineffective behaviors. Now, when I perceive the phrase, "Caught ya!," I know C.W. is alerting me to notice my judgments, expectations, or attempts to control life. At that point, I chuckle and proceed in another direction.

CREATE YOUR CURIOUS WITNESS—

STAGE TWO

1. Determine your own objectives about developing a C.W. How do you want this part of your consciousness to help you? A couple of examples follow.

   ✦ Remind you each time you are confronted by challenges that your intention is to learn and grow from every event in your life
   ✦ Help you experience contentment on the job as often as possible.

2. Set clear intentions and then go about your day. Over time, you will observe that even when you are experiencing a negative emotion, *because you are detached from the unpleasant feeling and are not resisting it, you are simultaneously enveloped in a state of inner harmony.* The experience is similar to watching a movie. You have empathy for the characters who are struggling, but you do not fully engage with their emotional drama. During your own challenges, C.W. will remind you, "This is just another experience, so gain the wisdom that is available to you."

JENNA'S C.W.

All of us are stars and
deserve the right to twinkle.
Marilyn Monroe

Jenna was delighted to accept a supervisory position at a company that promised her autonomy, corporate support, and a hefty salary. By the time she arrived on the scene, the only thing that matched what she had been told during the interview was her salary level.

The sales goal for her department was ridiculous. It was four times the level of the actual achievement of her competitor, a national franchise. Written instructions from management stated that Jenna would have to gain chain-of-command approval for even routine actions that she and her sales force conducted. Although her department was distinctly different from other divisions in the store, she would have to follow standard corporate procedures that would inhibit sales. Even though the vast majority of Jenna's customers would be purchasing gifts, her employees were not allowed to stock gift-wrap paper and wrap packages because "every unit has to be consistent." The corporation's motto appeared to be, "one size fits all departments and customers."

Jenna was amazed and upset. She had resigned from another position and moved from out of state to accept the new job. For a couple of days she considered quitting. Instead, she completed the above exercises, *Create Your Curious Witness—Stages I and II.* Jenna employed C.W. as her personal assistant. She set the objective of learning and growing from her challenge so she could experience more joy at work.

Because C.W. promotes clear, rather than emotional, thinking, within a few days Jenna decided, "This is just another experience. It isn't what I think I want, but it may turn out to be that way. I'll take responsibility to make the changes I can and let go of what I can't control."

This shift in her perspective stimulated creative thinking. Soon, new techniques for resolving her dilemma became apparent. Jenna presented data to her boss concerning the unrealistic sales figures and countered other aspects of the situation that impeded the quality of service needed to create high sales. She began to notice areas of her job in which she had more leeway than she had originally thought. Regarding the remaining roadblocks to her effectiveness, she developed ways to openly but quietly beat the system. Today, thanks to C.W., Jenna is happily at work in the same position—with much greater support.

THE ROAD FROM FEAR OR ANGER TO EMPOWERMENT

When you get to the end of your rope,
tie a knot and hang on.
Franklin D. Roosevelt

C.W. is effective because it is similar to an internal piece of software. You personally program it as part of your consciousness, and it connects you with the most well-developed and aware parts of yourself. You begin to witness everything in your life accurately and without judgment. You notice your emotions but you do not engage in drama. Over time, you understand that fear and anger are usually related to misperceptions or the unwillingness to perceive and use our full capabilities (to own our personal power).

Our unconscious tendency is to cart memories of past experiences into the present without checking to see if the old programs and perceptions match our new circumstances. Since all of us are constantly changing, most of our automatic programs such as, "This was a problem last time, so I'm sure it will be so again" are invalid. Unfortunately, most of us continue to march forward like robots until a crisis—a wake-up call—triggers us to update our software.

For perspective, think of a situation in which two family members hold a grudge about something that happened twenty years earlier. Since the incident, both parties have gained two decades of new experiences and perspectives, but they operate as if time has stood still. They avoid each other and gossip to other family members in an effort to validate their perspectives and gain support. Because they are so attached to their old belief systems and a desire to save face, they are both cheating themselves out of getting to know a special person (each other). Neither wants to be the first to give in, so they both lose. It takes energy and focus to hold onto old issues. Both parties are unnecessarily stressing themselves out.

Jenna did not want to play that game. Her old program was "powerlessness." In past situations she felt incapable of addressing upper management. C.W. alerted her to notice what she was doing. Then she began to laugh because she realized she hadn't checked to make sure the new guidelines were truly inflexible. She paused to ponder. Perhaps her manager had been pressed for time and inserted boiler-plate text into Jenna's instructions. That turned out to be the case, and you already know the rest of the story.

Once Jenna's behavior changed (she sought assistance from management rather than merely feeling disempowered), her attitude about herself changed.

Technologies such as MRI scanning have proven that our brains are quite malleable. Experiences such as Jenna's change the neural associative pathways of our brains. C.W. helped Jenna cut a new groove in her consciousness, and this created permanent change in her behavior, attitudes, and self-esteem.

Like Jenna, you can direct your C.W. to warn you when you are attached to a familiar zone that is not serving you. Then you can consciously choose to experience more joy and less stress at work.

CURIOSITY LEADS TO JOY

Somewhere, something incredible
is waiting to be known.
Carl Sagan

Most people stop asking questions because they think they are supposed to know the answers. They miss many rich insights they would have gained by nurturing the peephole in the mind.

When everything else fails, curiosity can carry you forward. Jenna's true story is a perfect example of the hidden power of curiosity. What if she had not detached from her emotions and made a decision to learn from the experience? She probably would have walked away from what turned out to be a wonderful business opportunity.

The thirst for knowledge and new experiences is one of our most valuable tools for living in a state of joy and peace. It is also a significant source of creative solutions to challenges. Albert Einstein often denied that he was a genius. He said he was merely curious enough to sit with the problems he investigated longer than most people.

C.W. produces positive results by increasing your awareness of ineffective behaviors. A process of positive change is initiated the moment you perceive a pattern that is not serving you. All blind spots are corrected in this manner. *Once you have seen something, you can no longer not see it.*

Enjoy developing and programming your C.W. Since the Curious Witness identifies and corrects misperceptions, it can quickly increase wisdom and joy. The following exercise uses multiple senses to open your mind to new perceptions so you will be more aware of the insights provided by your C.W.

STRENGTHEN YOUR
PARTNERSHIP WITH C.W.

STAGE ONE

1. Breathe deeply for several minutes to calm and balance your autonomic nervous system.

2. Gaze at your surroundings.

3. Notice what visually appeals to you. A picture, plant, or pattern?   Identify vivid colors and interesting shapes. Observe pleasing lines, contours, and shadows.

4. Close your eyes and try to recall the scenario. Use all of your senses. Imagine the textures of the scene you were just reviewing. What did you smell and hear? What was the temperature in the room?   What images and colors were most vivid?

5. Open your eyes and compare the true image with what you remembered.

Notice how quickly you stregthened your perceptual abilities. You also enhanced multisensory memories. This will improve your ability to accurately interpret the world around you and tune into the wisdom of your C.W.

STRENGTHEN YOUR PARTNERSHIP WITH C.W.

STAGE TWO

Step One

Draw your perception of C.W. Is it a symbol, person, cartoon character, wizard, or pet? It is helpful to relate to C.W. in a multisensory manner rather than merely as an idea. One of my clients made his C.W. an icon on his computer screen. He programmed the graphic to move around as a subliminal message that reminded him of his intentions.

Step Two

Decide one task you want to assign to your C.W. Later, you can delegate as many tasks as you would like. For now, begin with one simple assignment so you can observe the process. Write down the following.

✦ The job you are assigning your C.W.

Example: I want C.W. to alert me if I try to control things about my work life that I can't even influence.

continued on the next page . . .

✦ What you expect to gain when C.W. completes the task.

>   *Example: I will be more content, less frustrated, and better use my time at work.*

Step Three

Engage in a mental conversation with your C.W. about its job assignment.

>   *Example: C.W., I want you to gently let me know each time I attempt to control things about my work life that I can't even influence. This will help me shift my focus into healthy efforts and better use my time. Then I will use my energy in ways that serve me instead of frustrating myself.*

Step Four

During the next few days, read what you have written each morning and night. Be mindful so that you will receive clues from

continued on the next page . . .

C.W., but go on with your life. Repeat the first exercise (*Strengthen Your Partnership With C.W.—Stage One)* each day to ensure that your multisensory perceptual channels are open.

Step Five

Review your assignment for C.W. on an ongoing basis and revise it at any time.

USE C.W. TO DEVELOP TRUST

*I think that we may safely trust
a good deal more than we do.*
Henry David Thoreau

Observing, instead of attempting to control, the journey of your life will help you develop significant trust in yourself as well as in the process of life. The following chart outlines the differences between employing C.W. and the popular concept called "create your own reality."

Employ C.W.

Strive to Create a Certain Reality

This approach is effortless and enjoyable. You become so curious about watching your "personal movie" instead of creating a mental movie that you enthusiastically watch each scene in your work life as it unfolds. You accept life on its own terms. This creates a profound sense of inner peace. You trust that your movie (your life) will continue to be interesting, so you have no desire or demand that it turn out a certain way. Since you have no attachment to a certain outcome, you witness your life in a calm, impartial manner. You avoid the emotional roller coaster.

Curiosity makes negative judgments disappear. This creates an open mind, so you easily meet challenges and recognize new opportunities.

Significant effort is required to control your life in ways that are consistent with predetermined outcomes. When you labor to create a certain type of reality, you must work. You must concentrate on holding a focus designed to achieve specific objectives.

This approach is usually based on stale thinking that can seriously limit your work experiences. You try to create an outcome you perceive to be ideal because you want to avoid an outcome you think would be unfavorable.

continued on the next page . . .

Employ C.W.

Strive to Create a Certain Reality

Possibilities are unlimited because working with C.W. is an open-minded exploration of the unknown.

Potential outcomes are limited to your known reality. You can only purposely create situations you can currently imagine, so you extrapolate aspects of the present into the future.

You are driven by curiosity and desire to learn and grow by stretching yourself in some new and unknown way. You trust the proess of your life.

The process is fear-based and linked to expectations. You feel disappointed if they do not come true. The process is based on fear that your life will not turn out the way you want it to unless you take steps to control events.

New discoveries and insights are frequent because of your open mind. When people begin to use C.W., they are often amazed at how inaccurately they have been perceiving reality. Once they expand their consciousness, they comprehend the infinite possibilities available to them. They are soon astounded to discover how many misperceptions have been programmed into their minds.

Rigid expectations prevent new insights. New discoveries are also inhibited by a preoccupation with assumptions, opinions, and preferences.

continued on the next page . . .

Employ C.W.	Strive to Create a Certain Reality
This approach makes it abundantly clear that wealth exists inside of you—in your mind, psyche, and consciousness.	This approach is often based on a desire to create prosperity. Unfortunately, rigid expectations often cause the participant to fail to perceive new, serendipitous opportunities to achieve abundance. Out of fear, the person is usually trying to avoid "lack of prosperity." When this is the case, the focus on "lack" creates the economic shortfall the person is trying to avoid.

A review of the chart above indicates the potential of C.W. for enhancing your contentment at work. When you cultivate your relationship with C.W. in the garden of your consciousness, you prove to yourself that your life is always on track. You trust the process of life so deeply that you develop profound peace of mind as you observe yourself meeting one challenge after another. Direct C.W. today to help you achieve the following.

✦ Nourish your curiosity so you can detect incorrect views of reality. We all have blind spots.
✦ Detach from fear or anger that no longer serve you.

USE C.W. TO CONNECT WITH YOUR HIGHEST ABILITIES

We know what we are,
but know not what we can be.
William Shakespeare

Carl Jung, founder of analytical psychology, argued that the most mature stage of adult development emerges when we lose our emotional attachment to misperceptions that we have considered to be reality.[1] In doing so, we detach from our fears, become an observer of our world, and elevate our level of consciousness.

You have now discovered some of the easiest and most powerful ways to achieve greater self-confidence and happiness at work.

✦ Notice that the observer within you is always paying attention to your surroundings.

✦ Connect with a deep sense of peace that is always present within you, even when your thoughts or emotions are in a state of turmoil.

✦ Permit C.W. to detach your attention from negative emotions and thoughts so that your life seems less intimidating and is easier to manage.

✦ Allow negative thoughts and moods to transmute more rapidly.

✦ Employ C.W. to assist you in achieving specific objectives.

Since the past is not the present and the future is unlimited, make a commitment today to consciously use C.W. to enhance your joy on the job.

CHAPTER 22

CREATE A POWERFUL, POSITIVE RESOURCE STATE

We all carry within us
supreme strength,
the fullness of wisdom,
and unquenchable joy.
They are never thwarted
and cannot be destroyed.
Haston Smith

Have you ever known exactly what you wanted to do but felt unsure of your ability to follow through? The following techniques will help you alleviate your anxiety when you stand your ground in a tough situation, propose a major change to coworkers, or ask management for assistance. The concepts are based on brilliant research conducted by Richard Bandler and John Grinder, who developed a process called *Neuro-Linguistic Programming* and Tom Kenyon, author of *Brain States.*[1]

The previous chapter described how to employ a Curious Witness to *prevent* anxiety by experiencing challenges without judging them. This chapter focuses on using two tools to relieve *existing* anxieties.

✦ An emotional anchor
✦ A positive resource state

These techniques will empower you because you will disassociate from unnecessary anxiety. Although it is possible to use the tools to create a desired scenario, you would not be continuing to read this book if you did not understand the following.

✦ You may not be able to instantly control your feelings, but you can always be responsible for your actions.

✦ The intensity of negative feelings changes when you accept them without resistance. They run their course and fade away.

✦ Managing your behavior can change how you feel about a situation. This can be as simple as transforming anxiety about writing a report by composing an outline and writing a few paragraphs.

There is far more to life than we currently perceive. You are on a quest to explore the breadth and depth of your life instead of limiting yourself. The following tools can help you.

✦ The emotional anchor and positive resource state will enhance your confidence by alleviating anxieties that are based on past experiences. (Most of us don't even remember these life-changing events!) Using these techniques will convince you that you are in charge of your life today.

✦ C.W. and your intuition are powerhouse techniques. They will help you develop healthy new perceptions.

An exciting new world packed with unexpected opportunities awaits your exploration.

ESTABLISH YOUR EMOTIONAL ANCHOR

Designate an emotional anchor you will be able to access when you are challenged. Anchors can involve any and all of your senses. They can be visual, physical, auditory, kinesthetic, gustatory, and/or olfactory.

If you will be speaking to your boss, you might keep an object with you that would be considered normal for you to hold, carry, or wear. Small objects such as a ring, pen, pencil, or notepad are ideal. Some people use their watchbands or a bracelet. Others simply touch their thumb to their index finger. Some people hold their palms together. Whatever you select, choose something you can consistently use without drawing attention to yourself.

You will eventually be able to create a positive resource state in virtually any situation. With practice, it can become an automatic response whether you are surrounded by unhappy coworkers and customers or racing to put out a fire. Until it becomes your default style, practice it in an undisturbed area while maintaining a quiet posture. You may want to enhance your learning environment with soothing music.

CREATE A
POSITIVE RESOURCE STATE

STAGE ONE

Please read all of the steps below before using the technique.

1. Sit in a comfortable position and breathe deeply. Close your eyes and visualize yourself in the area where you are likely to experience the challenge you have in mind. If you have no idea what the location of the event will look like, envision a neutral area such as a bare room.[2] Imagine that you are actually engaged in the activity. Notice tensions in your body, especially in the areas of your gut, heart, jaw, neck, forehead, and eyes. Notice your breathing. Is it shallow or deep?

2. Relax the tensions you have noticed. Do this by breathing slowly and deeply, with an even rhythm. At the same time, make a conscious choice to let go of the impressions and feelings you have associated with the work environment you have in mind.

3. Remember a time when you felt calm, self-confident, and relaxed. Perhaps you knew without

continued on the next page . . .

a doubt that you had produced excellent work. Maybe you were joyful because a loved one was happy. Perhaps you were lying on a warm beach, taking a hot bath, or receiving a back rub. Thoroughly enjoy the sensations of that feeling. If you are stressed and it is difficult to recall a real-life experience in which you felt calm and relaxed, engage your imagination. Your subconscious mind will follow your directions. It does not know the difference between actual events and fantasies, particularly when you are enthusiastic.

4. Disassociate from the memory of the above situation as you continue to feel relaxing feelings spreading throughout your entire body. Notice tension draining from your forehead, jaw, eyes, neck, chest, gut, legs, and feet. Imagine that your cells are expanding to release every bit of tension.

5. Keep breathing deeply, slowly, and rhythmically while you check in with yourself and continue to release tension. Imagine a warm glow shimmering around your entire body as if to protect you from any stress or anxiety.

continued on the next page . . .

6. Continue this process until you can re-create these feelings of relaxation with a simple inner command such as "calm now" or by using the anchor you previously established. Some people use both techniques. Others only touch their anchor. Decide on your command and recall your anchor.

7. Re-create the deep feelings of relaxation. When you are the most relaxed, *fire your anchor.* This means to hold your anchor in place, whether it is a gesture or object. Hold the position or article for five to ten seconds while you recall deep feelings of relaxation. Then release the anchor and bring yourself back to a neutral, non-directed feeling.

8. Practice re-creating relaxed feelings and then discharging the anchor for five to ten seconds when you feel the most relaxed. Do this several times. Research conducted by Tom Kenyon indicated that the key points are to: (a) hold the feeling of relaxation at its strongest level as you discharge the anchor and (b) hold your gesture or object in precisely the same way each time you repeat the exercise.[3] You are entraining your brain to build a new neural pathway that associates firing your anchor with feelings of relaxation, the opposite of anxiety.

continued on the next page . . .

9. Before you actually engage in the activity you have in mind, practice in non-threatening situations. This will ensure that your brain links your anchor with the feeling of relaxation. Discharge your anchor in front of a mirror or while talking to friends. If you feel more at ease after you ignite the anchor, the technique is working. Gradually elevate your perceived risks by practicing the activity you have in mind with a coworker. The more you use the technique, the more you will reinforce the association. Our brains eagerly carry out the tasks we give them. If you feel anxious as you continue to intensify your risk-taking, repeat the original practice steps.

10. Imagine yourself actually carrying out your planned activity. As you do so, fire and hold the anchor until you feel relaxed and you can instantly re-create feelings of tranquility.

In the exercise above, your positive resource state of relaxation is linked to your emotional anchor while you engage in an imaginary stressful situation. The next step will expand your new neural pathway and further enhance the power of your anchor.

CREATE A POSITIVE
RESOURCE STATE

STAGE TWO

1. Take a moment to stimulate your sensory channels. This will help you perceive situations more accurately and be aware of creative alternatives for meeting your goals. Gaze as far into the distance as you can see and then at the tip of your nose while breathing deeply. Then look at eight other distant points before looking back at the tip of your nose. Examples: upper right, upper center, upper left, left center, lower left, lower center, lower right, and right center. Make sure your posture is erect. Your head and neck should be balanced over your trunk, although your shoulders can be slightly dropped.

2. Envision yourself engaging in a challenge. This time, instead of actually firing your anchor, simply imagine doing so.

3. Notice your tension reducing as you feel more re-relaxed. It is neurologically impossible to simultaneously feel relaxed and anxious, and you have established a powerful positive resource state. Use it whenever you need to reduce or eliminate anxiety.

Now you can use the technique in Stage Three on the next page to further enhance your positive resource state.

CREATE A
POSITIVE RESOURCE STATE

STAGE THREE

Our brains respond beautifully to multiple sensations, so you can make this process even more powerful by remembering a time when you felt very confident. Holding an image in mind, remember the smells and temperature of the air, the clothes you were wearing, and the sounds and sights in that moment. Choose any time you felt confident. You don't have to select a workplace example. Your scenario could be as simple as a time when you knew an answer to a charades game pantomime before someone else uttered the correct answer.

Intensify the multisensory stimuli. Make the sights you see larger and the colors more vivid. Make the sounds louder and the smells more striking. Feel the textures of your clothes, the sensations on your skin, and any tastes on your tongue. Imagine seeing a movie screen in front of you. See yourself feeling self-confident while walking up to the screen and entering it. You are acting out a movie of yourself as a totally self-confident individual, and your brain will create new neural pathways that will serve you for years to come.

Richard Bandler and John Grinder developed a brief treatment for anxiety and phobias.[4] The brilliance of their method is its simplicity. Within just a few minutes time, the technique helped thousands of individuals disassociate from specific anxieties, and their symptoms did not recur. Bandler and Grinder believed that our fears hold us back when we have not allowed ourselves to dissociate from feelings of similar past experiences, whether we are conscious of the results of the experiences or not.

DISASSOCIATE AT THE MOVIE

Carol was too fearful to present her ideas to others in positions of authority. She avoided the risk of sharing her thoughts even though she knew her portion of the work process better than anyone else and her excellent ideas would have improved productivity. Everyone involved lost—Carol, her teammates, and the entire organization.

Since Carol kept her rich insights hidden in the recesses of her skull, she had no way of knowing if management would have accepted them. A vicious cycle began to whirl out of control. Carol's morale took a nosedive as she applied an inefficient work process one dreary day after another. Dismal days became bleak weeks. Months later, upper management was desperately searching for solutions, but Carol's fear was running the show. She had been labeled "not creative," "unmotivated," and "disinterested." Her gut churned each day with an unfulfilled desire to share her approaches with management. Instead, she despaired and complained to peers who were not in a position to improve her work flow. The situation was blocked, and so were Carol's opportunities for the positive recognition she needed.

Carol was the only person who could change her situation, but she had never learned how to dissociate from fear acquired during past experiences. Since she didn't know how to create new associations linked with pleasant memories, the negative pattern continued.

Carol didn't have to know exactly how her pattern of being afraid to talk to authority figures began. She only had to envision the feared activity of presenting an idea to others and reframe the incident with pleasant memories. This would create a disassociation from unpleasant memories.

Carol and I used a neurological process in which she repeated the exercise often enough and with enough focus that her brain molded a new *fearless* habit. As a result of establishing new neural pathways in her brain, her mind minimized and then forgot unpleasant memories. After that, only pleasant memories were triggered when she needed to present her ideas to authority figures.

Carol recognized that her anxiety about presenting her ideas was based on fear of rejection. I encouraged her to remember the earliest possible time in her life she had felt this fear. I reminded her that it didn't have to actually be the first time the anxiety occurred. We didn't need to psychoanalyze why she feared that she or her ideas would be rejected.

Next, I told Carol to follow the steps below.

✦ Imagine yourself sitting in the middle of a movie theatre. You are viewing a black-and-white photograph of yourself on the screen as you experience the situation you hold in your mind.

✦ Envision yourself moving from your seat to the projection booth of the theatre. From your new position, watch yourself continuing to sit in the middle of the theatre observing yourself in a still photograph on the screen.

✦ Imagine that the photograph on the screen transforms into a black-and-white movie. Watch the film from your seat in the middle of the theatre until the unpleasant experience ends.

✦ Stop the flow of the movie at its final frame.

✦ Imagine yourself leaping inside the picture and reversing the sequence of the movie as if you are pushing a rewind button. Notice that everyone and everything in the movie is walking and talking in reverse motion. Their voices sound bizarre. The entire backward flow of the movie only takes one or two seconds.

Carol quickly reported the same results other clients have communicated after using this technique. She laughed during the last step because situations that had previously resulted in fear appeared quite comical as they rolled across the movie screen in reverse. She felt a comfortable distance from past painful events because *she was merely watching herself observe herself in a black-and-white movie.* She also transformed fear into courage when she imagined herself jumping into the screen with an authoritative presence and rapidly running the picture backward.

After playing the scene as a comedy and moving so rapidly from "This is awful" to "This is great," her fears seemed absurd. The technique boosted Carol's confidence because she envisioned herself rapidly reliving a stressful event from the point of maximum discomfort backward to the point of no fear.

Carol felt detached from the past unpleasant experience. We played with the event a few more times until her brain substituted her new fearless pattern for her previous anxiety.

We added a few variations that are fun and easy to try. Your brain thinks in pictures rather than in words. Multisensory stimuli can help convince your brain that what you don't want is hard to envision and what you do want is easy and pleasurable to achieve.

In every instance in which Carol wanted to downplay the significance of painful events, she began to imagine that those scenes were dull and difficult to view. She made them black-and-white, fuzzy, blurry, and small. Every time she wanted to validate a scene, she introduced stunning colors and enticing scents. She also increased the volume and clarity of sounds. She added exquisite tastes, delightful temperatures, and textures she adored touching. Carol tricked her brain into being so attracted to the situations she preferred that the other scenes were difficult to focus on. They were boring, cloudy, and too tiny to attract her interest. You can imagine how unappealing it is to watch a difficult-to-view movie rolling backward.

Then Carol upped the ante. Each time she rolled the film backward, she made the screen smaller and smaller. Finally, it became too miniscule to see anymore. She also invented a variety of strange faces and odd voices for previously intimidating characters. Eventually, those actors faded away because our minds and memories don't know the difference between what is real and what is imagined.

After each new showing of the movie, Carol tuned into her feelings. She felt more confident after each screenplay. She also substituted new movies of herself for the old films. She recalled life situations in which she had felt very confident. She again used multiple senses—striking sights, appealing colors and sounds, alluring smells and tastes, and soothing textures. These sensations anchored a new feeling of high self-esteem as Carol established new neural pathways in her brain.

Most human behavior is designed to achieve pleasure or avoid pain. The techniques we used worked because Carol substituted pleasant memories for unpleasant ones. We easily and quickly created new associative pathways.

It has been several years now, and Carol reports that her past fears concerning presenting her ideas to others have not resurfaced. All evidence supports this because Carol is now considered an excellent public speaker.

TURN IT INTO HO-HUM AND FUZZY

The following exercise is included as a step-by-step summary of the process described above. Use the technique in the same way Carol did to gain freedom from past fears.

DISASSOCIATE

STAGE ONE

1. Think of a situation in which fear or anxiety caused you to avoid doing something that would be to your benefit.

2. Recall a time in your life, as early as you can easily remember, in which you felt fear or anxiety when undertaking a similar activity.

3. Imagine yourself sitting in the middle of a movie theatre. You are viewing a black-and-white photograph of yourself on the screen as you experience the situation you have in mind.

4. Envision yourself moving from your seat to the projection booth of the theatre. From your new position, observe yourself still sitting in the middle of the theatre as you watch yourself in a fixed photograph on the screen.

5. Imagine the photograph on the screen transforming into a black-and-white movie that you observe from your seat in the middle of the theatre until the unpleasant experience ends.

6. Stop the flow of the movie at its final frame.

continued on the next page . . .

7. Imagine leaping inside of the picture. Reverse the sequence of the movie as if you are pushing a rewind button. Notice that everyone and everything in the movie is walking and talking in reverse motion. Their voices sound bizarre. Allow only one or two seconds for the entire backward flow of the movie.

8. Describe your feelings regarding the activity. Did you find yourself laughing at the comical situation you produced instead of feeling afraid? Do you feel more detached from past anxiety? Do you feel empowered because you can literally freeze-frame, reverse, and otherwise change past events that used to feel unpleasant?

Repeat the above easy, short exercise until you have no more fear or anxiety concerning the challenging situation you have in mind. With each new practice session, add elements such as those described on the following two pages to your movie. The more you embellish your positive resource state with rich, detailed imagery and practice, the stronger will be your new supportive neural network. Eventually, you will have created a strong, automatic backup style based on positive associations and memories. You will face a variety of challenges much more easily, and your self esteem will reflect your positive resource state.

DISASSOCIATE

STAGE TWO

1. Paint funny faces on other characters or add bizarre voices until you have created a slapstick comedy.

2. Vary the speed of the acting and voices when you push the reverse-play button until the situation becomes more and more comical and you feel totally in control.

3. Add multiple sensations as Carol did until the scenes you don't wish to experience are black-and-white, fuzzy or blurry, and small. Make them smaller and more difficult to perceive during each iteration until the unpleasant scenes can no longer be perceived.

4. Then enrich the scenes you wish to experience. Saturate them with striking colors that lure you into the experience. Include clear, splendid sounds. Choose exotic or soothing textures. Each scene should contain yummy tastes, wonderful fragrances, and perfect temperatures.

continued on the next page . . .

5. Think about your current challenge again and repeat the process. Observe yourself in the middle of the movie theatre watching a black-and-white photograph of yourself on the screen before the challenge emerges. Imagine yourself in the projection booth. You are observing yourself watching yourself before you actually engage in the challenge. Now, turn your snapshot into a black-and-white movie. Watch the movie progress from the time you are feeling apprehensive until you complete the action. Freeze frame your movie and jump into the frozen scene. Reverse the movie at an extremely rapid rate. Continue until you feel detached from the original anxiety.

6. Your life is your personal movie, so continue playing with the scenes you create until they match your fondest dreams. Make pleasant experiences larger and much more colorful, alive, and captivating. This is your screenplay. Keep playing with it until you feel a warm glow inside.

7. When you feel complete with the experience, breathe deeply and enjoy the magnificent feelings that you, and you alone, have created. Associate your fond feelings with the emotional anchor you previously established. Inhale and mentally recall pleasant scents such as cinnamon, vanilla, or fresh pine needles. Your olfactory system will help anchor positive memories in your brain.

DISCOVER RICH INNER RESOURCES

You have now established new neural pathways of pleasant emotions. You will be able to recall them on command, so joy on the job can occur much more frequently.

In time, if you hear yourself say, "I can't" do something you want to do, you will immediately tell yourself, "Yes, I can do this!" Then you'll solidify your new point of view with multisensory techniques, including richly rewarding images associated with having achieved your goal. You'll treat your imagination to sumptious tastes that make your mouth water, textures that create a grin, emotions that curl your lips into a smile, exciting smells, and enticing auditory sensations. You'll be using *The Oomph Factor*—the power of focusing on what you want instead of on what you don't want.

If any self-doubt lingers, treat your mind and body as a resource instead of as a liability. Reopen your sensory channels as you did in step one of *Create a Positive Resource State, Stage Two.* Then ask your nonconscious mind to come to your aid by quizzing it with an empowering question. This is a question that assumes a solution is patiently waiting for your discovery. Begin with, "How can I more fully believe in my abilities?"

Combine your new skills for developing a positive resource state with the reframing techniques you practiced in chapter 13. Remind yourself that "bad things" can produce spectacular results. This is why Thomas Edison welcomed the thousands and thousands of failures that led to the development of his incredible inventions. Instead of labeling himself a loser, Edison invited his inner child to continue to dream and play.

Unlike Mr. Edison, most of us keep a tight reign on the playful, innovative child who lives inside of our controlled, culturally-cloned self. Not a good decision! When we are relaxed and playful, insights appear easily and spontaneously, and this elevates our self esteem. Invite the child who lives inside of you to come out and play. Discover how your kid's curiosity and awe can produce a "Eureka!" to resolve your most baffling dilemma.

Change your physical position frequently because this can also alter your view of yourself and your challenges. Thomas Edison worked from two desks simultaneously because he knew a physical shift can trigger a mental shift.

Edison also spent many hours that he could have used to criticize himself taking breaks. Time off triggered new intuitive hunches. Edison power napped. Both Edison and Einstein spent more time dozing than entertaining a negative self image. Both arose from catnaps with stunning new ideas to feed their playful antics—shenanigans from which we still derive benefit.

Creative approaches, such as reverse rolling a film of your personal drama, used in the previous exercises, stimulate our minds to let go of worn-out identities like "I'm not good enough." Innovative play generates more accurate ways of perceiving ourselves.

Invite your imagination to soar. Then watch problems become toys to play with as you explore an awesome array of potential solutions you can finally perceive. When you welcome your inner muse, what seemed impossible becomes possible. Dreams become bigger, bolder, and brighter. Eventually, they become reality.

DETERMINE THE COLOR OF YOUR EMOTIONS

The human spirit is stronger than
anything that can happen to it.
George C. Scott

You are now equipped with personal reminders and positive resource states, as well as easier ways to access your intuition and creativity. These powerful tools will help you stay enthusiastic, curious, and optimistic. This state of mind will definitely contribute to joy and peace of mind at work. In time, you will be able to spontaneously and automatically use each technique to dramatically improve your work life.

CHAPTER 23

MAP YOUR WAY
TO JOY ON THE JOB

A rock pile ceases to be a rock pile
the moment a single man contemplates it,
bearing within him the image of a Cathedral.
Antoine de Saint-Exupéry

Another outstanding tool for creating a more joyful worklife is a mind map. This powerful technique can break down barriers to creativity, learning, and memory.[1] You can use it to build new neural pathways and to help you make tough decisions. It is an enjoyable, free-flowing process that engages both your linear left brain, which thrives on thoughts and details, and your creative right brain, which easily recalls visual images. Creative ideas and solutions result when you develop new associations between your thoughts and the patterns, colors, and images of your mind map.

MIND MAP

STAGE ONE

1. Gather blank sheets of paper and a variety of colors of pens, pencils, or crayons.

2. Think of a challenge at work. Write a single major subject or focus question in the middle of a blank page. Usually, a question or sentence stem will stimulate your thinking more than a theme or single thought. You can also use a short phrase describing the subject.

    Examples:

    ✦ How can I discover more meaning in my work so I can experience more joy?

    ✦ Meaning = peace of mind

3. Draw a balloon around your question or sentence stem. This is your point of origin. It is a focal point for your brain and eyes. Here is an example.

    More meaning = greater fulfillment

4. Add a colorful picture or symbol to activate your right brain. Here's an example that reflects happiness at work.

Now that you have determined your focus, the process in stage two will liberate your thought process while activating new sources of creativity. This will retrain your mind. It will also help you silence your inner critic because this negative voice thrives on holding back, analyzing, and judging your actions. Mind mapping calls forth *The Doer*, the part of you that achieves remarkable results by taking healthy risks.

MIND MAP

STAGE TWO

You will now create a visual outline in which all of the ideas you generate will be directly or indirectly connected to your focal point.

Step One

- ✦ Write as short a description as possible of two or more main ideas.
- ✦ Surround the ideas with a balloon.
- ✦ Draw a line connecting each idea to your central theme.

Example:

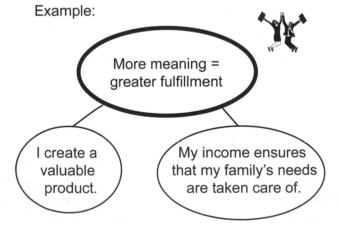

continued on the next page . .

Step Two

Engage in a free-association process. Write down or draw every idea that pops into your mind. Don't edit or evaluate your ideas and don't worry about spelling or grammar. Write as rapidly as possible without concern about the order of your thoughts.

Example:

✦ Make a difference
✦ Work on an interesting project
✦ Able to buy school clothes for the kids
✦ Work with people I enjoy
✦ Feel valued

Step Three

Connect each new idea to a previous idea or subject with a line, symbol, arrow, or dotted line. You are honoring every idea and thought fragment that pops into your mind without judging any of them as good or bad. Just write each new thought or answer somewhere on your page, draw a circle around it, and then draw a line connecting it to either your focal point or an idea that was generated afterward. Continue to build offshoots to main topics. Notice that the branches of your thoughts organize themselves as stems

continued on the next page . . .

and leaves as details flow freely from your consciousness and support your main thoughts.
Remember failure is impossible in this exercise.
You can delete anything you want to later. If you
fill up a page, just attach additional pages and
keep going.

continued on the next page . . .

Step Four

Continue to add details to your mind map. If your creativity wanes, ask yourself who, what, where, why, when, and how questions about what you have written.

You can usually stimulate new thoughts by drawing a new line from one of your previously recorded thoughts. The more questions you ask yourself, the more ideas you will stimulate.

If your thoughts stop when you are working on a side balloon, go back to your original focus thought or question and start again.

If your mind totally draws a blank, draw a related object upside down or put your pen or pencil in your nondominant hand and doodle on your page until new ideas or pictures emerge. Then connect them to a relevant idea somewhere else on the page.

Step Five

Add a rich array of vivid colors and additional symbols and pictures. Highlight some of your ideas with underlining, asterisks, or bold colorful letters. There is always room for new details.

You will feel a sense of completion when this stage of your map is finished.

Each new thought in the stage two exercise stimulated additional ideas. This is because mind mapping is based on research regarding how your brain actually works. It is a whole-brain approach that activates both hemispheres of your brain.

Your brain thinks in images and is fed by enthusiasm and imagination. It quickly links associations. The mental and visual pictures you create through rapid writing and drawing while mind mapping trigger positive memories. This stimulates your subconscious to focus on what you want instead of on what you don't want.

Our brains are hard-wired to link something new with an item that is already in our memory bank. The brain thrives by recalling information in the form of mental imagery—pictures, symbols, and shapes—as well as sounds and feelings.

The visual format you created in the stage two exercise helped you perceive the big picture as well as the detailed outline. Your brain established new neural pathways that reinforce your new perceptions.

Mind mapping is a wonderful process for purposely entraining your brain with new positive images and memories about a particular issue. Because your brain easily remembers symbols and pictures, new ideas and thoughts are linked in a nonlinear manner. You integrate logic with imagination, and this sparks extra brain power. Because of the branching process, your mind can more easily recall the specific details you outlined while it envisions the entire picture at a glance.

Mind mapping activates areas of your brain that you don't routinely turn on. Spontaneity heightens your creativity and stimulates your brain to build new associations. Your brain begins to think faster and faster as you freely associate words or phrases with what you've previously written. As discussed earlier, you also silence the inner critic. You can see why mind mapping is an excellent process for breaking old behavior and thought patterns.

MIND MAP

STAGE THREE

You will continue to retrain your mind in this exercise. Since you are the personal creator of your mind map, your imagination and enthusiasm will entrain your brain to do the following.

✦ Remember what you have created
✦ Quickly build new, empowering neural associations between your map and how it interprets future events

Step One

Color and pictures will stimulate your memory. Return to your mind map and enhance it with additional vivid images and colors.

Step Two

The mind map is also a technique that stimulates your intuition because it is *you talking to you*. You can prove this to yourself. Take a break and leave your mind map behind. Totally forget about it. Return to it the next day. You may be surprised at how much clarity you receive regarding the next steps you need to take at work.

continued on the next page . .

Step Three

It is just as important to *feel* the mind map as it is to intellectually be aware of its messages. Notice patterns and trends.

Step Four

Continue to stimulate your intuition. When you go to sleep, ask for additional information to come to you upon awakening the next morning. Have paper and a pen or a recording device by your bed so you can easily capture the wisdom you receive the next morning.

CHEAT SHEETS AND REMINDERS

Because mind maps use visual and sensory reminders in a pattern of connected ideas, you can use them like a road map. Many people use the technique to brainstorm an outline for a report or proposal. Mind maps make a fabulous cheat sheet when you are giving presentations. Taking notes during an important meeting becomes fun instead of a chore.

Since mind mapping is a whole brain approach that uses the natural language of your brain—symbols, pictures, and other images, you can deeply imprint associations in your brain's memory bank. Many excellent speakers who deliver lengthy presentations without notes sketch their main ideas, subpoints, stories, and other illustrations in a mind map before getting on the stage.

Consider using a mind map when you need to generate original ideas and organize them for easy recall. If you want to make sure certain questions are answered in a training or meeting you will be attending, draw a mind map of the points you want addressed.

The more colors and symbols you use to create visual images, the stronger your associations will be between disparate bits of information in your brain's memory web. In addition to strengthening your memory, striking imagery will help you perceive and make connections between ideas that seem unrelated at first.

Since the brain remembers vivid images, feelings, and symbols most easily, be creative and outrageous, as we were when creating a positive resource state in the previous chapter. Use lots of colors. Vary the size and boldness of words and images. Add symbols representing movement like a cartoonist does. The logo of employees jumping for joy illustrates another way to indicate movement when you only use a single image.

CONNECT THE DOTS

I have an existential map.
It has "you are here"
written all over it.
Steven Wright

As your new endeavors unfold, your intuition and your subconscious will recognize patterns of new incoming information and combine them with thoughts that are on the periphery of your consciousness. If you haven't previously used this process, you may be amazed at how quickly and precisely new perceptions and opportunities unfold. With that in mind, you will want to make mind maps often.

PART FOUR

JOIN THE MOST POSITIVE
AND POWERFUL REVOLUTION
ON PLANET EARTH

CHAPTER 24

YOU ARE THE MIRACLE YOU'VE BEEN SEEKING

Only fools and dead men don't change their minds.
Fools won't. Dead men can't.
John H. Patterson

JAW DROPPERS

In the past, we thought we had a genetic setpoint for happiness and an I.Q. that were set in stone. Now we know we are powerful alchemists. There is no limit to the degree we can increase our intelligence, and there is no cap on how much happiness we can experience.

Most of us are amazed to discover how much control we have over the level of joy we experience at work every day. Before doing the multisensory exercises, were you aware of your marvelous ability to send signals to your nervous system so you can be calm and contented even when surrounded by chaos or angry people? Before reading about Viktor Frankyl, would you have guessed that a concentration camp prisoner could maintain a peaceful state of mind? Was it a stretch to learn that Frankyl discovered profound meaning hidden within the grueling, revolting jobs he was forced to perform as a slave laborer?

Eye openers like these blast our illusions until we finally admit the truth and graduate ourselves from limited thinking. There is no ceiling regarding our ability to enjoy the work life we desire.

Whatever you are ready for is ready for you. New opportunities are already waiting for you. Make a commitment to notice and take advantage of them.

WAY TO GO!

You have contemplated and practiced almost 400 proven techniques that will help you claim your fair share of validation, fulfillment, and joy. Even if you haven't completed all of the exercises, you can trust the tools. They are still being used by employees in the 21 very diverse organizations. These individuals contributed their feedback so you can also enjoy more happiness at work.

Use the next exercise to validate your progress and set new goals.

Build a ladder to the stars
And climb on every rung.
Bob Dylan

WAY TO GO! . . . MORE TO GO!

You've practiced multisensory ways of doing the following. Which have you mastered? What are you still working on?

TOPIC	HAVE MASTERED	WORKING ON
Create meaning and fulfillment at work even when performing mundane or unpleasant tasks	_____	_____
Communicate my needs in ways that ensure I have the resources and support I need to do my best work	_____	_____
Create a flow state so my work is appropriately challenging and enjoyable and I develop new skills	_____	_____
Use the power of curiosity and neutral observation, including my Curious Witness, to reconnect with my innate source of inner peace	_____	_____
Take healthy risks	_____	_____

continued on the next page . . . . .

TOPIC	HAVE MASTERED	WORKING ON
Express my special talents in ways that ensure I am passionate about my work and well-compensated while I make a unique contribution to the world	_____	_____
Create a sense of autonomy even when I have no control over some aspects of my work	_____	_____
Gain new skills that facilitate fulfillment, productivity, and marketability	_____	_____
Enjoy rewarding professional relationships with coworkers, teammates, and supervisors	_____	_____
Receive support, coaching, and positive feedback, including during performance reviews	_____	_____
Creatively solve problems and resolve conflicts, including when I work with teams or "difficult people"	_____	_____

continued on the next page . . . . .

TOPIC	HAVE MASTERED	WORKING ON
Gain value from mastermind groups and mentors	_____	_____
Balance my personal and professional life	_____	_____
Prevent and reduce stress	_____	_____
Create emotional anchors and positive resource states that support me during challenges	_____	_____
Shield myself from workplace negativity	_____	_____
Reframe misperceptions and beliefs that cause joy blocks	_____	_____
Use multisensory approaches that develop new neural networks associated with peace and joy	_____	_____
Experience negative emotions in ways that benefit everyone concerned	_____	_____
Transform my inner critic into a virtual assistant	_____	_____

continued on the next page . . . .

TOPIC	HAVE MASTERED	WORKING ON
Accept my shadow side and unpleasant parts of life that I cannot change so they don't limit my happiness	_____	_____
Experience more compassion and patience. Judge myself and others less frequently	_____	_____
Decrease procrastination and perfectionism	_____	_____
Develop a signature style	_____	_____
Promote myself in ways that help me secure resources and advance my career	_____	_____
Capitalize on my strengths	_____	_____
Thrive during unexpected challenges and mandated changes	_____	_____
Live my personal mission (life purpose) and values while performing my job	_____	_____

continued on the next page . . . . .

TOPIC	HAVE MASTERED	WORKING ON
Identify hidden opportunities in adversities. Boost my resiliency	_____	_____
Control unnecessary interruptions. Set and maintain personal boundaries	_____	_____
Honor constructive worries and delete those that are unfounded	_____	_____
Easily and quickly create an alpha brain state so I can do my best work, fight fatigue, and elevate my confidence	_____	_____
Enjoy more laughter and humor at work	_____	_____

Other. List additional techniques you have learned or want to explore. Examples: situational optimism, inner genius, magical moments, strengths-based language, easy retrieval of nonconscious associations, focus management, the power of gratitude, downward comparisons, altruism, and selection of an alternate reality.

continued on the next page . . . . .

Use the Index and List of Exercises to find material related to the areas you are still mastering. If a specific strategy doesn't appeal to you, explore another method. All of us have unique learning and behavioral styles, and there are an infinite number of paths to joy on the job.

Enjoy continuing to develop your expertise related to the topics you identified in the previous exercise. Be as patient with yourself as you are when you explore a new hobby or help a child learn a new activity. Hardly anyone hits the bull's eye the first time, but the archer who trudges to target practice even when it's raining and cold eventually perfects the technique.

Work that begins as a struggle blossoms into a blissful state of flow. The archer merges with the tools of his trade, and he grins as arrows fly swifly to the center of his target. Spectators cheer wildly, but the archer hardly notices. He is attuned to a beautiful symphony that he alone can hear. It is the joyful beat of his heart singing the sweet melody of self-actualization.

You will also be richly rewarded when you passionately explore new goals with the intention of becoming your true self. A wealth of new resources and external support will spontaneously appear. As your confidence continues to soar, your response to new challenges will most often be an anticipatory smile representing a healthy, productive awe, "I wonder what I'll learn this time?"

Eventually, the intense fulfillment you gain from your work will have become so rewarding that you'll leap from bed before the alarm buzzes, excited about another work day. This is one of the most fantastic fortunes available on this planet. It's yours if you want it. Claim your prize with focused action.

YOU'VE ALREADY PROVEN YOU HAVE UNLIMITED ABILITIES

As you completed the exercises in the book, you validated the following.

+ You can be radiantly happy at work, whether you are in your dream career or working a temporary minimum wage job.
+ Your capabilities are unlimited. The fact that you can increase your intelligence exponentially with multisensory exercises can make "working smarter, not harder" a normal part of your life.
+ Even your personality is as flexible as that of a newborn baby. You can easily create new neural networks associated with joy and situational optimism.
+ You have an innate right to inner peace, and you have learned how to use conscious focus as one of your primary tools.
+ The world is a giant treasure chest twinkling with infinite possibilities patiently awaiting your discovery. Why settle for less than you want and deserve? You can be well-compensated for expressing your unique talents in ways that contribute to the lives of others.

You are the master weaver of your personal workplace tapestry. Become a passionate, attentive artist. Don't allow anyone else to dictate the details of your design.

DISCOVER A MAGICAL FORMULA

Personal responsibility will always be a key source of your joy, freedom, and power. You will receive amazing results when you do the following.

+ Question your perceptions and beliefs
+ Ask for what you need
+ Take action that will move you closer to your goals

Here's a great example. David Thomas of England was taunted as a child for being a "slow thinker." How did this individual with "limited abilities" become a World Memory Record holder and gain a Guinness World Record just eight months after buying a book to improve his memory? His original goal was to pass exams he had previously failed![1]

Thomas realized that most of our assumptions are inaccurate. He decided to graduate himself from "Yes, but . . . " to "What if . . . ?" thinking. He challenged beliefs such as, "There are reasons other people are more successful than I am. They must be able to do things I can't do." As the British say, Thomas decided to *give it a go.*

Thomas also questioned another assumption. Like most of us would do, he originally presumed that his competitor for the World Memory Record would never help a new adversary succeed. Why should a champ share his secrets? Thomas took a giant leap out of the tightly sealed thinking box most of us use for contemplation. He decided anything is possible and asked his rival for assistance. Thomas immediately received a free verbal download of the techniques the title holder had used to win the championship eight times in a row! Thomas beat his new friend in the next contest because he understood that reality rarely matches our perceptions.

Most of us restrict our happiness and our achievements because we believe life offers only a few meager options. We select what we think will be the best of several unfavorable alternatives without even asking "What if . . . ?". This is one of our most harmful self-deceptions. The true substance of our lives is bloated to the bursting point with infinite possibilities. We can always choose to experience a different potential, a new parallel reality.

Don't wait for everyone around you to become a psychic Mother Teresa of the Workplace. Instead of waiting for others to sense your needs and approach you about creating a more rewarding work life, notice and question "Yes, but . . . 's." Change them to "How can I . . . ?" As you discovered when doing the exercises in previous chapters, your mind will immediately act like a super sleuth. It will search for nonconscious associative links in your brain and promptly produce the answers you need.

Ask for help, using the win-win communication strategies we have discussed. This will help you continue to enrich your professional support system. You'll also be helping others because people feel validated when you allow them to assist you.

**BREAK FREE FROM
LIMITING PERCEPTIONS**

Practice the Magical Formula described above.

✦ Notice and challenge "Yes, but . . . " assumptions and beliefs.
✦ Identify the person you need to ask for assistance. When will you communicate with them in person or in writing?
✦ What step will you take this week that will move you closer to achieving your goal?

CHANGE YOURSELF . . . CHANGE THE WORLD

According to an ancient proverb, "When a bird flaps its wings in China, it is felt across the world." Like the fluttering bird, our energy—our actions, thoughts, and emotions—influence everyone with whom we come into contact.

There is no limit to the effects we create when passionate performance is backed by intentions born within a pure heart. Like the ripples created when a pebble is tossed into a pond, what we set into motion extends to an infinite number of people we will never meet. As scientific experiments have proven, everyone in the universe is connected as if we are one. In many ways, we are one.[2]

Each time we change ourselves in a positive way, we improve the world. Without saying a word to try to convert anyone else to our point of view or behavioral preference, our helpful example produces beneficial changes.

We may only perceive the favorable impact within a tiny inner circle of associates. However, as those individuals live their new truth, positive change travels. Eventually, it circles the world.

At birth, you were awarded very distinct, special aptitudes. This is your personal genius potential. The world desperately needs your assistance. Sharing your unique gifts will bring you joy at work whether you are a cheerful customer service worker who brightens the day of a very distraught individual or you invent a solution to a vexing global problem.

Each time you step up to the plate and aim to meet your full potential, an astonishing array of unexpected resources and opportunities will light your path home. Be mindful and you will continuously receive proof that unseen forces are continuously supporting your efforts to make this planet a better place to live.

YOU ARE THE MIRACLE

Use this exercise the next time you feel stressed out.

1. Sit or stand tall with your eyes closed. If you wear contact lens, you may need to remove them before doing the next step of this exercise.
2. Raise your eyes as if you are gazing through the top of your head at a spectacular sky studded by a sea of shimmering stars. Assume that every star is sparkling with you in mind. It is encouraging you to become all you can be because you have an important role to play while you are on Earth.
3. Keep your eyes closed and hold this posture until you feel a magnificent healing force surging through your entire body.

You have just induced an alpha brain state that connects you with your vast inner resources. Savor this splendid state of mind and perceive the truth about who you are, why you are on Earth, and why you hold the specific job you hold. You have unique talents to contribute to the world. You deserve, and have, the blessings and backing of the entire universe just so you can achieve your personal mission. Why? With every step you take to meet your destiny, you improve life for all of us.

In the previous exercise, in just a few moments, you replaced a negative state of mind with a resourceful state. Use this strategy regularly to help you reconnect with your true self and instantly melt stress. Notice after using the technique that it is almost impossible to feel anxious. (If any stress remains, repeat the technique.)

What lies behind us and what lies before us
are tiny matters compared to what lies within us.
Ralph Waldo Emerson

STAY IN TOUCH

The Joy on the Job Train only recently began to chug along, but it is already beginning to move at the speed of a jet plane. Jump aboard without hesitation. You will never regret accepting even more of the happiness the universe is eager to grant to you.

Stay in touch. Visit www.joyonthejob.info regularly because you are part of a great, growing community of people around the world who are absolutely certain that life will deliver as much joy as we can stand. We are on the cutting edge of the most positive revolution this planet has ever experienced. Share what's working for you and read newly posted articles and success stories written by others. Decide to untie the ribbons on the gifts that life brings to all of us each day.

REFERENCES AND RESEARCH NOTES

Chapter 1. Are You Happy at Work?

[1]   Gibran, Kahlil (1923). *The Prophet.* New York: Knopf.

[2]   Brodie, Richard (1993). *Getting Past OK.* Seattle, WA:Integral Press.

[3]   Even though the buying power of the average American has doubled since 1957, the percentage of people identifying themselves as happy has remained low. See Easterbrook, Gregg (2004). *The Progress Paradox.* New York: Random House. In most studies, employees rate the desire for higher pay behind their desires for respect, fair treatment, opportunities for advancement, and a friendly work environment.

Happiness at work has been associated with success, higher income, and greater productivity. See Koestner, E. L. & Ryan, R. M. (1999). "A meta-analytic review of experiments examining the effects of extrinsic rewards on intrinsic motivation." *Psychological Bulletin, 125,* 627-668.

A classic organizational psychology reference on this topic is Locke, E.A. (1976). "The nature and causes of job satisfaction" in M.D. Dunnette (Ed.), *The Handbook of Industrial and Organizational Psychology,* Chicago:Rand McNally. Since a state of flow and increased productivity can trigger happiness, savvy employers ensure that employees have the necessary resources to resolve job challenges. They remove obstacles to success and attempt to create job satisfaction.

Sirota Consulting tracked the stock prices of 28 companies that had monitored their employee morale during the past four years. Companies with high morale saw their stock prices increase more than five times (16 percent vs. 3 percent) that of the half-dozen companies with low morale. The stock performance of the high-morale companies also trumped the results of the industry average by a significant margin, 16 percent vs. 6 percent. High-morale companies provide fair treatment and promote a sense of achievement. Their employees have pride in their employer and compatible, productive relationships with fellow employees. Employees who work for companies where just one of these factors is missing are three times less enthusiastic than workers at companies where all elements are present. They are correspondingly less productive. For more information about the benefits of a satisfied work force, see Sirota, David, Mischkind, Louis, A. & Meltzer, Michael Irwin. (2005). *The Enthusiastic Employee: How Companies Profit by Giving Workers What They Want.* Wharton School Publishing: Upper Saddle River, New Jersey.

Also see "Happy workers pay off," *Spirituality and Health* Sept/Oct 2005 or David Batstone, http://www.rightrealty.com/wag.

Chapter 2. What's Different About This Book?

¹ While technological and other innovations and new management practices have escalated productivity, job satisfaction has plummeted.

In America, a 2003 study by The Conference Board determined the highest level of employee discontent since their first survey in 1995. Less than half of all workers who responded were satisfied at work. The decline was consistent among workers of all ages, across all income brackets, and across geographic regions. Special Consumer Report. Job Satisfaction. The Conference Board—September 2003. *Executive Action Report #68.* Also see the following websites: http://www.conference-board.org/utilites/pressDetail.cfm?press_ID=2227, www.careerbuilder.com, http://www.employerhealth.com, and www.watsonwyatt.com.

A study conducted by Integra, Inc., determined that one-fourth (23 percent) of American workers were chronically unhappy and stressed.

A study released July 2004 that was conducted by Robert Half Management Resources found that the top complaint of executives surveyed was hours worked. See http://www.roberthalfmr.com/Press Room?LOBName=MR&releaseid=1207 or call 1-888-400-7474.

A survey by Lee Hecht Harrison, a human resources consulting firm, surveyed 1,019 adults and reported that workers were exiting over unfair pay and too much work. See an article by Andrea Coombes of CBS Marketwatch, "In Surveys, Workers Cite Unfair Pay, Too Much Work." According to Coombes, "workers cited long hours and unfair pay as top complaints, and some were beginning to make the move to new positions, according to three new surveys." (This includes the studies by Lee Hecht Harrison, the AP survey conducted for the AP by Ipsos-Public Affairs, and the Robert Half Management Resources study.) Six percent of workers said they quit their job voluntarily for a new job in the second quarter, up from 5.3 percent in the first quarter of the current year and 3.8 percent the previous year, according to a survey of 1,019 adults conducted for the HR consulting firm, Lee Hecht Harrison. The survey conducted for Lee Hecht Harrison was done during July 7-11, 2004 by International Communications Research of Media, PA.

See www.LHH.com for more info. According to Coombes, "Those leaving their jobs might have been seeking an alternative to long workdays and unfair pay, top complaints cited by workers in two of the three surveys. Over half (58 percent) stated they would consider better job offers."

An August 16-18, 2004 Ipsos Poll on Worker Attitudes was conducted for the Associated Press (AP). Telephone interviews were conducted with 589 workers from all states except Alaska and Hawaii. Almost half (39 percent) of the respondents said their job was "something they did only to earn money" instead of "an important part of who they were as a person." Over one-third (34 percent) of workers were dissatisfied with the amount of job stress they faced. Other leading complaints included opportunities for advancement and issues concerning health and retirement benefits.

A study by Work & Family Connection during an economic downturn determined that 1/3 of employees surveyed were looking for a job and hoped to leave their current positions within six months. One-fourth of the respondents said they were "just putting in their time" and planned to continue to do so. "Companies were not getting their best effort—that discretionary effort that employees can choose to give or not; the effort every employer needs to compete in today's markets." See *Work & Family Connection News in Brief,* September 9, 2004. http://www.workfamily.com, page 1.

Also see an October 17, 2004 article by Teresa M. McAleavy in *The Record* of Bergen County, New Jersey, "Searching for happiness in your job." "About 30 percent of 1,600 workers surveyed by the CareerBuilder.com job-search site recently said they're unhappy with their career progress. Just under half of those in that group plan to leave their current jobs, and many expect to bail by the end of the year."

Dr. Howard Cutler, co-author of *The Art of Happiness at Work* with The Dalai Lama, (2003, New York: Riverhead) stated that western studies indicated that one-third of workers view their work as just a job, a paycheck. One-third view their job as a career and put emphasis on advancement and social status. The last third view their job as a calling and love to get up in the morning and go to work for the sake of the work itself. Assuming that these rough percentages are true, the fact that one-third of employees aren't fulfilled at work is high. Social costs occur because employees don't contribute in discretionary ways as much as they could. Thus, everyone suffers.

Thirty percent of German employees interviewed in one study "occasionally felt like strangling their bosses." Physical violence on the job caused thirty billion dollars of damages annually (two hundred billion dollars worldwide.) A study of angry office workers in a variety of industrialized countries discovered that workers spent up to 20 percent of their work time repairing malfunctioning computers or programs. In Norway, over 75 percent of engineering employees had recently endured harassment at work. Another study in America determined that 71 percent of employees interviewed had recently been accosted by hostile coworkers. See http://stats.bls.gov/. Also see Branham, Leigh. (2005). *The 7 Hidden Reasons Employees Leave*. New York: AMACOM.

[2]   Ibid.

Chapter 3. Avoid Delight-Deficiency Disorder

[1]   Sirota Consulting tracked the stock prices of 28 companies that had monitored their employee morale during the past four years. Companies with high morale saw their stock prices increase more than five times (16 percent vs. 3 percent) that of the half-dozen companies with low morale. The stock performance of the high-morale companies also trumped the results of the industry average by a significant margin, 16 percent vs. 6 percent. High-morale companies provide fair treatment and promote a sense of achievement. Their employees have pride in their employer and solid, productive relationships with fellow employees. Employees who work for companies where just one of these factors is missing are three times less enthusiastic than workers at companies where all elements are present. They are correspondingly

less productive. For more information about the benefits of a satisfied work force, see Sirota, David, Mischkind, Louis, A. & Meltzer, Michael Irwin. (2005). *The Enthusiastic Employee: How Companies Profit by Giving Workers What They Want.* Wharton School Publishing: Upper Saddle River, New Jersey.

Also see "Happy workers pay off," *Spirituality and Health* Sept/Oct 2005 or David Batstone, http://www.rightrealty.com/wag.

Also see Diener, Ed and Seligman, Martin, E.P. 2004. "Beyond Money," *Psychological Science in the Public Interest, 5*(1) p 1-31, American Psychological Society. Employee well-being has a significant positive influence on company profitability. Workers with well-being have better job performance and higher income and more often help other employees. They are also healthier, which cuts healthcare costs. Although well-being can cause higher income, higher earning does not cause happiness.

Also see "Why it's good to feel good," *Science & Spirit*, November/December 2004, pp. 58-60. Interview with Barbara Fredrickson by *Science & Spirit.*

Also see Howard, Julie, *The Idaho Statesman*, September 22, 2004, "Keeping Employees Happy." Interview with Yvette Ward, president of the Idaho Psychological Association (IPA) concerning IPA's meta analysis/data collected during sponsorship of the annual Healthy Workplace Awards.

Scientists have also found that happy workers are more successful because they tend to feel confident, optimistic, and energetic. Others find them likable and sociable, and the happy individuals benefit from these perceptions. Rather than success and accomplishments producing happiness, positive affect is one of several attributes that can lead to success-oriented behaviors, including high incomes, superior work performance, and promotions. See Lyubomirsky, Sonja. (2003). "The mechanisms of sustainable increases in happiness." Paper presented at the 3rd International Positive Psychology Summit. Findings were also published in the December 2005 *Psychological Bulletin* published by the American Psychological Association.

2   Ibid.

3   Bentall, Richard P. "A proposal to classify happiness as a psychiatric disorder." *Journal of Medical Ethics*, 1992; 18: 94-98.

4   Work in America: Report of a Special Task Force to the

Secretary of Health, Education, and Welfare. Cambridge: Mass: MIT Press, 1973. In 1997, Barbara Reinhold labeled the Monday morning worker death syndrome the "Black Monday Syndrome." See Reinhold, Barbara B. (1997). *Toxic Work*. New York: Plume, p. 3.

Also see http://www.mercola.com/2004/aug/21/health_happiness.htm, "Happiness helps the heart." Also in "Happy moments protect the heart," BBC News on April 19, 2005 reported from the April 19, 2005 *Proceedings of the National Academy of Sciences* (NAS). A team from University College of London and professor Peter Weissberg of the British Heart Foundation reported that happiness leads to lower levels of stress-inducing chemicals.

Also see Cortis, Bruno. (1995). *Heart and Soul*. New York: Pocketbooks.

Also see Steptoe, A., Wardle, J., & Marmot, M. (2005). "Positive affect and health-related neuroendocrine, cardiovascular, and inflammatory processes." *Proceedings of the National Academy of Sciences*, May 3, 2005, 102(18), 6508-6512.

[5]   Thousands of studies have concluded that primary sources of job satisfaction include interesting and challenging work, compatible relationships with coworkers, effective and encouraging supervisors and team members, supportive company policies, and opportunities for advancement. Regarding pay, findings have been that pay and other financial benefits must be "adequate." See Weiten, Wayne. (1998). *Psychology Themes & Variations*. Pacific Grove, CA:Brooks/ Cole Publishing Company, p. 707.

In chapter seven of Kohn, Alfie (1999) *Punished by Rewards.* New York: Houghton Mifflin, Kohn describes an excellent meta-analysis. In most research that relates salary to job satisfaction, employees rate the desire for higher pay behind desires for respect, fair treatment, opportunities for advancement, and a friendly work environment. A University of Warwick in England study indicated that rank and title tend to be more important than pay in determining how respected employees feel. According to an AOL Workforce Strategies poll regarding job satisfaction, both are dwarfed by the availability of a flexible schedule.

In spite of an abundance of studies indicating the opposite, as late as 2004, 90 percent of managers involved in a study of 19,000 departing and current employees *believed* employees left or stayed in their positions mostly for the money. That study was conducted by

Leigh Branham and reported in Branham's 2005 book, *The 7 Hidden Reasons Employees Leave* (New York: AMACOM). Branham's research indicated the real reasons employees were dissatisfied with their jobs related to the following. (1) Unmet expectations. Dissatisfied employees reported misrepresentations regarding job pay, hours, training, or promotions. (2) A mismatch between the employee and the job, which resulted in bored and/or stressed workers. (3) Inadequate feedback or coaching. (4) Inadequate growth or advancement opportunities. (5) Employees feeling devalued or unrecognized. (6) Stress from overwork and work-life imbalance. (7) Lack of trust in top leadership.

The buying power of the average United States citizen doubled since 1957, yet the investigations of Gregg Easterbrook, author of *The Progress Paradox* (2004, Random House), concluded that only one in three individuals could be described as "very happy." Researchers have repeatedly determined that people adapt to their circumstances, including their disposable income. After initial elation, lottery winners return to their normally happy or unhappy states. Once you earn a sufficient amount to afford the ordinary pleasures of the middle-class, more money usually does little to lift your spirit. For a point of reference, Abraham Maslow emphasized that, once a person's basic needs are met, they are more interested in self-actualization than income per se. Maslow, Abraham. (1998). *Toward a Psychology of Being. Third Ed.* New Jork:Wiley.

Middle-class employees tend to have more free time, exercise more, vacation more often, and belong to more social organizations than the average employee who holds a lower-class job. It is possible for leisure habits to make the middle class happier than those who worry about subsistence, but that is not necessarily true because happiness is a subjective term defined by each individual. See Flora, Carlin & Elins, Michael. (2005). "Happy hour." *Psychology Today 38*(1) p. 40-50, 95, 153. Also see Seligman, Martin E.P. (2002) *Authentic Happiness* (New York: Free Press).

For a review of other factors related to rising living standards correlated with a decrease in happiness (from 34 percent to 30 percent), see Koretz, Gene. "Does money buy happiness?" *Business Week*, October 16, 2000, which reports on a National Bureau of Economic Research study by David G. Blanchflower and Andrew J. Oswald in which they identified a cluster of social trends that overshadowed income gains.

Also see Jayson, Sharon. "Unhappiness has risen in the past decade." *USA Today*, January 9, 2006. The article reports on a National Opinion Research Center study (University of Chicago) that was part of the larger National Science Foundation-funded General Social Survey. According to the study's author, Tom Smith, and based on a 2004 study interviewing 1,340 people, unhappiness has risen in the past decade in spite of the author's anticipation that problems would have decreased since the good economic years of the 90s.

Some people who are dissatisfied at work blame their salary level, but many people who earn very little are quite content. In America at least, salary is definitely not an accurate indicator of how much joy we gain from our jobs. One survey of *Forbes's* 100 wealthiest Americans discovered they were only slightly happier than the average citizen. Most respondents believed that *money can increase or decrease happiness.* It is only one piece of the puzzle.

Regarding prestige, David Lykken, Ph.D., professor emeritus in psychology at the University of Minnesota, interviewed workers after they'd gotten a promotion they had desperately desired. Despite an initial boost in their joy, the moods of those interviewed generally returned to normal within a few months or a year. In a survey of 800 graduates of Hobart and William Smith Colleges in Geneva, New York, who ranged in age from their mid-20s to their mid-30s, alumni who ranked high income, job success, and prestige as their top priorities were twice as likely as other classmates to describe themselves as fairly or very *un*happy. For more information, see Lykken, David. (2000). *Happiness: The Nature and Nurture of Joy and Contentment.* New York:St. Martin's Press.

An Associated Press article, October 13, 2004, by Peter Svensson, "Economists say more money, more stuff won't make us happy" is relevant. Economists who analyzed surveys asking people how happy they were determined that money spent on tangible status symbols like larger homes and cars do not increase a society's happiness. Robert H. Frank, professor of economics at Cornell University wrote in an essay, "If we use an increase in our incomes simply to buy bigger houses and more expensive cars, we are not any happier than before."

Money can boost the reported life satisfaction of some individuals according to an Associated Press poll indicating that people who make more than $75,000 a year are far more likely than those who make $25,000 or less to say they are "very satisfied" with their lives—56 percent of the higher-income group compared with 24 percent of the lower-income group. However, in spite of the fact that average incomes have more than tripled in the last 50 years, average life satisfaction has held steady, according to the study which concluded that the U.S. economy has grown substantially, but happiness has not. (As reported earlier, other studies have identified an actual decline in life satisfaction and joy.) Robert H. Frank, professor of economics at Cornell University, concluded that if income affects happiness, it is relative, rather than absolute, income that matters. A related study was conducted by Princeton Survey Research Associates International for the Pew Research Center. A total of 3,014 people were polled from October 5 to November 6, 2006 concerning very wide income categories. Almost half (49 percent) of Americans with household incomes of $100,000 or more said they were "very happy" versus 38 percent earning $75,000 to $99,999, 33 percent earning $30,000 to $74,999 and 24 percent earning less than $30,000.

The thesis of Gregg Easterbrook (2004) *The Progress Paradox.* New York: Random House (even though the buying power of the average American has doubled since 1957, the percentage of people identifying themselves as happy has remained low) is compelling.

Most economists and social scientists agree that money can contribute to your happiness, but only on a short-lived basis and only as long as those around you don't also earn more than you do. In addition, because you get used to earning more money, after a while it doesn't cheer you up as much as it did at first. Humans adjust to their circumstances.

A recent survey of AOL subscribers asked how much more money they'd need to be free of worrying about money. Those with incomes over $100,000 thought they needed far more money than those with incomes under $40,000. The higher earners were five times more likely to say they needed at least another $90,000 annual income. When people adopt a more-with-more philosophy, they may never be satisfied with what they have.

Richard Koch, author of *The 80/20 Principle*, advocates focusing on "80/20 activities," activities of high value to others and one's self, simplifying lifestyle, and cutting out the trivial. His work promotes stepping off the treadmill, stopping comparisons to others, and enjoying challenges for personal growth instead of for adrenaline stress. One of his theses is that people who strive to help others are happier than those who strive to their stress point.

According to Ed Diener, professor of psychology at the University of Illinois, once basic needs like food, shelter, and health care are met, happiness related to an income increase rises very slowly. Richard Easterlin, professor of economics at the University of Southern California in Los Angeles, agrees. Easterlin believes money that isn't used well, for example, income spent on large homes and luxury goods, doesn't provide long-term happiness. However, other spheres of life, such as a reallocation of time in favor of family life and health, do contribute to our long-term happiness. See Diener, Ed and Seligman, Martin, E.P. 2004. "Beyond Money" *Psychological Science in the Public Interest,* 5(1) p 1-31, American Psychological Society.

Ed Diener and Martin Seligman investigated the relationship between well-being and money. They were also concerned that economic output has risen steeply for decades but life satisfaction has not. In fact, depression and distrust have increased (in ways not related to 9/11). They concluded that economic indicators were extremely important in the early stages of economic development, when the main issue was fulfilling basic needs. However, social relationships and happiness at work are more important in today's world.

Diener and Seligman concluded that employee well-being significantly influences corporate profitability. Workers with a sense of well-being have better job performance and higher income. They help other employees more frequently. These employees are also healthier. Well-being can cause higher earning, but higher earning does not cause happiness.

Other authors have investigated employee reports that shorter work hours and greater job flexibility are more important than salary. In an October 17, 2004 article, "Searching for happiness in your job," for *The Record* of Bergen County, New Jersey, Teresa M. McAleavy reported, "A separate survey found that in the past five years, 48 percent of workers took less money by shortening their work week so they could minimize their job-related stress and have more time with their families." The importance of having a flexible schedule, among the most important factors in job satisfaction according to a poll by AOL Workforce Strategies, was also reported in *Idaho Business I.Q.,* p 10, July/Aug 2004, "What workers like."

The previously described University of Warwick in England research study also concluded that rank and title are more important than rate of pay in determining how respected employees feel.

6   Sirgy, M. J., D. Cole, R. Kosenko, & H. L. Meadow. 1995. "A Life Satisfaction Measure." *Social Indicators Research* 34: 237.

See Peter Svensson, The Associated Press, October 13, 2004, "Economists say more money, more stuff won't make us happy." Economists who analyzed surveys asking people how happy they were determined that money spent on tangible status symbols like larger homes and cars do not increase a society's happiness. Robert H. Frank, professor of economics at Cornell University concluded that those who use an income increase simply to buy bigger houses and more expensive cars are not any happier than before.

According to Ed Diener, professor of psychology at the University of Illinois, once basic needs like food, shelter, and health care are met, happiness related to an income increase rises very slowly. Richard Easterlin, professor of economics at the University of Southern California in Los Angeles agrees. Easterlin believes money that isn't used well, for example what is spent on large homes and luxury goods, doesn't provide long-term happiness but other spheres of life, such as a reallocation of time in favor of family life and health, do contribute to long-term happiness. See Diener, Ed & Seligman, Martin, E.P. 2004. "Beyond Money" *Psychological Science in the Public Interest,* 5(1) p 1-31, American Psychological Society.

7   Niven, David, 2000. *The 100 Simple Secrets of Happy People.* New York: HarperCollins, p. 87.

8   The correlation between the work of Rupert Sheldrake and David Bohm and other physicists supporting this point of view was discussed throughout the *Brain/Mind Bulletin, Vol. IV,* 1979. (*Brain/ Mind Bulletin,* P. O. Box 42211, Los Angeles, CA 90042.)

9   Hawkins, David R. *Power vs. Force.* (2002). Carlsbad, California:Hay House.

Chapter 4. Delete Joy Blocks

1   Using your nondominant hand to conduct normal activities

requires you to engage the opposite side of your brain. The circuits, connections, and areas of your brain that are normally involved when you use your dominant hand are temporarily inactive. Their counterparts on the opposite side of the brain that are usually nonparticipative are unexpectedly required to direct your behaviors. Research has indicated that this creates a rapid and dramatic expansion of circuits in the parts of the cortex that control and process tactile information from your hand. Because you tend to think and perform in a more flexible manner, it also becomes easier to flow with the unpredictability of life. Katz, Lawrence & Rubin, Manning. (1999). *Keep Your Brain Alive*, New York:Workman, p. 44-45.

[2] Frankl, Viktor E. & Allport, Gordon W. (2000). *Man's Search for Meaning* (4th Ed.) New York:Beacon Press.

[3] The Monks of New Skete. (1999). *In the Spirit of Happiness*. New York:Little, Brown and Co., p. 313.

Chapter 6. Curiosity Creates Joy

[1] Fadiman, Clifton & Bernard, André (Eds). 2000. *Bartlett's Book of Anecdotes*, New York:Little Brown and Company, p. 180.

Chapter 7. Self-Awareness + Acceptance = Fulfillment

[1] Brown, J., & Dutton, K. (1995). "The thrill of victory, the complexity of defeat: self-esteem and people's emotional reaction to success and failure." *Journal of Personality and Social Psychology* *68*:712.

Chapter 8. Transform Blind Spots to Freedom

[1] When both eyes are open, you never notice that each eye can "see" what the other cannot. Of course, it is another misperception that we "see" with our eyes because it is the brain that receives input and creates sensory images.

[2] Bureau of Labor Statistics website. http://stats.bls.gov/ Reportedly, there will be labor shortages of up to 10 million workers by 2010. On January 15, 2006, *The Dallas Morning News* reported

that Lorrie Foster, research director for The Conference Board, stated in an interview, "Since 64 million baby boomers are poised to retire over the next decade, some labor analysts are predicting a shortage of as much as 10 million workers by the end of the decade." Also see "Number of jobs held, labor market activity, and earnings growth among younger baby boomers: results from more than two decades of a longitudinal survey summary." Report available at http://www.bls.gov/news.release/nlsoy.nr0.htm.

Chapter 9. Fulfill Yourself With Focus

1 　　　Wolfe, Fred Alan. (1989). *Taking the Quantum Leap*. New York: Harper & Row.
　　　Also see Tegmark, Max. "Parallel universes." *A Scientific American Special Report*. SCA 45026.

2 　　　Gladwell, Malcolm. (2005). *Blink:The Power of Thinking Without Thinking*. New York:Little, Brown and Company. Bargh's work about subjects being influenced to think they are old is discussed on pp. 55-57.

3 　　　Emoto, Masuru. (2005). *The True Power of Water*. Hillsboro, OR: Beyond Words Publishing, Inc. and (2004). *The Hidden Messages in Water*. Hillsboro, OR: Beyond Words Publishing, Inc.

4 　　　A 2005 Hewlett Packard study reported that employees lost 10 I.Q. points when multitasking (being interrupted by email bleeps). Also see Edelstein, Linda. (1999). *The Art of Midlife*. Bergin & Garvey.

5 　　　"What workers like" *Idaho Business IQ* July/August 2004, page 10.

6 　　　Barker S. & Raudenbush B., et al., "Improved performance on clerical tasks associated with administration of peppermint odor," *Perceptual Motor Skills*, (2003) Dec; *97*(3 Pt 1):1007-10.

Chapter 10. Own Your Power

1 　　　"Number of jobs held, labor market activity, and earnings growth among younger baby boomers: results from more than two decades of a longitudinal survey summary." Report available at http://www.bls.gov/news.release/nlsoy.nr0.htm.

Also see Pilzer, Paul Zane, *Unlimited Wealth*, (1991, New York:Crown). Economist Pilzer stated that employees will not only change jobs frequently, but half of the population will change careers every six years. Also see Wenger, Win and Poe, Richard. (1996). *The Einstein Factor.* Roseville, CA: Prima Press, p. 186 reporting a August 24, 1994 interview with Pilzer regarding this subject.

[2]   Bureau of Labor Statistics website. http://stats.bls.gov/
Reportedly, there will be labor shortages of up to 10 million workers by 2010. On January 15, 2006, *The Dallas Morning News* reported that Lorrie Foster, research director for The Conference Board, stated in an interview, "Since 64 million baby boomers are poised to retire over the next decade, some labor analysts are predicting a shortage of as much as 10 million workers by the end of the decade."

Chapter 12. Fully Embrace Life

[1]   Huxley, Aldous. (1942, 1998 reprint.). *Brave New World,* New York:Perennial.

[2]   Hendricks, Gay & Johncock, Philip. (2005). *The Book of Life.* Ojai, CA: The Transformational Book Circle.

Chapter 13. Reframe Versus React

[1]   Editor Henry Davidoff (1952). *The Pocket Book of Quotations,* report of an interview with James Russell Lowell by Julian Hawthorne. New York: New York Pocketbooks, Simon and Schuster.

[2]   Birkenbihl, Vera F. & Scheele, Paul R. (2001). *Memory Optimizer.* Minnetonka, MN: Learning Strategies Corporation.
Also see Schacter, Daniel. (1996). *Searching for Memory: The Brain, the Mind, and the Past,* New York: Basic Books.
Also see Nørretranders, Tor. (1998). *The User Illusion: Cutting Consciousness Down to Size.* New York:Penguin Putnam, Inc.
Note: The term "nonconscious mind" is used in this instance instead of "unconscious mind" for consistency with cognitive research (vis-á-vis psychological or psychoanalytical research).

[3]   Gelb, Michael J. (2002). *Discover Your Genius.* New York: HarperCollins.

Chapter 14. Use the Power of Negative Emotions

1   Pert, Candace (1997). *Molecules of Emotion.* New York: Scribner. Candace Pert discovered the brain's opiate receptors. In her book, *Molecules of Emotion,* she discusses her theory that neuropeptides and their receptors are the biochemicals of emotions. Dr. Pert claims that emotions are, in fact, one and the same as these neuropeptides that circulate around the body. Although her ideas were at first controversial, she is now considered one of the leading scientists in the world specializing in psychoneuroimmunology and the brain.

2   "Why it's good to feel good," *Science & Spirit*, November/December 2004, pp 58-60, interview with Barbara Fredrickson by *Science & Spirit.*

Chapter 15. Empower Yourself With Action

1   Csikszentmihalyi, Mihaly. (1991). *Flow. The Psychology of Optimal Experience.* New York:Harper Perennial.

2   Fisher, B. (1995). Successful aging, life satisfaction, and generativity in later life. *International Journal of Aging and Human Development 41*: 239.

3   Seligman, Martin E. (2002). *Authentic Happiness.* New York: Free Press.

4   Wolfe, Fred Alan. (1989). *Taking the Quantum Leap.* New York: Harper & Row.

Also see Tegmark, Max. "Parallel universes." *A Scientific American Special Report.* SCA 45026.

Chapter 16. Bust Procrastination

1   Burnell, Ivan April 7, 2004, "Are you afraid, worried, nervous, upset?" *International Personal Development News to Use! Yes Factor Monthly.* http://www.yesfactor.com/

2   Dossey, Larry. (1999). *Reinventing Medicine.* New York: HarperCollins.

Chapter 17. Confront Control Issues

1   Vilaythong, Alexander P., Arnau, Randolph C., Rosen, David H. & Mascaro, Nathan. (2003). "Humor and hope: can humor increase hope?" *Humor: International Journal of Humor Research 16:*1 (2003), pp. 79-89, 0933-1719/03/0016-0079.

Chapter 18. Cash in on Your Strengths

1   Buckingham, Marcus, and Clifton, Donald (2001*). Now, Discover Your Strengths.* New York: The Free Press.
2   Wenger, Win & Poe, Richard. (1996). *The Einstein Factor.* Roseville, CA: Prima Publishing.
3   Dobbs, David. "A revealing reflection." *Scientific American Mind* 17(2). April/May 2006, pp 22-27.

Chapter 19. Flow Time

1   Csikszentmihalyi , Mihaly (1991). *Flow. The Psychology of Optimal Experience.* New York:HarperPerennial.
2   Marsh, Ann, "The art of work." *Fast Company.* August 2005, pp. 77-79.
3   Note: The term "nonconscious mind" is used in this instance instead of "unconscious mind" for consistency with cognitive research (vis-á-vis psychological or psychoanalytical research).

Lewicki, P.; Hill, T.; and Czyzewaska, M. "Nonconscious Acquisition of Information." *American Psychologist*: American Psychological Association, Inc., 1992.

Also see Dixon, Norman F. *Preconscious Processing.* Chichester, NY: Wiley, 1981.

Also see Dixon, Norman F. *Subliminal Perception: The Nature of a Controversy.* London, NY: McGraw-Hill, 1971.

Also see DePorter, Bobbi. *Quantum Learning: Unleashing the Genius in You.* New York: Dell Publishing, 1992.

Also see Birkenbihl, Vera F. & Scheele, Paul R. (2001). *Memory Optimizer.* Minnetonka, MN: Learning Strategies Corporation.

Also see Schacter, Daniel. (1996). *Searching for Memory: The Brain, the Mind, and the Past*, New York: Basic Books.
Also see Nørretranders, Tor. (1998). *The User Illusion: Cutting Consciousness Down to Size*. New York:Penguin Putnam, Inc.

Chapter 21. "Meet C.W."

1   Jung, Carl F. (1933). *Modern Man in Search of a Soul*, Harvest Books, Dell, W.S. & Baynes, Cary F. eds., trans. New York: Harcourt, Brace.

Chapter 22. Create a Powerful, Positive Resource State

1   Bandler, Richard & Grinder, John. (1976*). The Structure of Magic, Parts I and II,* New York:Science & Behavior Books.
Also see Bandler, Richard & Grinder, John. (1979*). Frogs Into Princes*. Moab, Utah:Real People Press.
Since the original groundbreaking work of Bandler and Grinder, scores of scholarly research studies have validated and elaborated on their work. For an example, also see Kenyon, Tom. (1994*). Brain States*, Naples, Florida: United States Publishing, p. 168.
2   Kenyon, Tom (1994). *Brain States*. Naples, Florida: United States Publishing. p. 168.
3   Ibid.
4   Bandler, Richard & Grinder, John (1976*). The Structure of Magic, Parts I and II,* New York: Science & Behavior Book and Bandler, Richard & Grinder, John. (1979*). Frogs Into Princes*, Real People Press.

Chapter 23. Map Your Way to Joy on the Job

1   Mind maps were originally developed in the early 1970s by Tony Buzan, author of *Use Both Sides of Your Brain*. See Buzan, Tony. (1974). *Use Both Sides of Your Brain*. New York: Plume Books.

Chapter 24. You are the Miracle You've Been Seeking

[1] "Memorable lessons from a world-class mind," Issue #24 of the *Effort Free Newsletter and CD Series,* p.6, published by Life Tools, Sunrise House, Hulley Road, Macclesfield SK102LP, England. For more information, see David Thomas' book, *Essential Lifeskills: Improving Your Memory* (2003, DK Adult Press) or http://www.davidthomas.tv.

[2] Professor Brian Greene explained the scientific phenomenon of entanglement of photons that take off from the same location and cross the universe in different directions from each other in *The Fabric of the Cosmos* (2005, NY:Vintage Books). If something happens to one photon, the other is affected as if there is no time between the two. There is no speed of light to overcome because entangled particles, even though they are spatially separate, do not operate autonomously.

Dean Raiden, Ph.D., tested the relevance for human behavior in subsequent research. He discovered that all known forms of communication can be blocked and two individuals can still be entangled. When one party receives stimulus, similar brain activity is produced in the other individual even when subjects are in soundproof rooms in Faraday Cages that block cell phone and all other known frequencies of communication to the degree that vibrations created by a sledge-hammer in one room could not be picked up by seismic instruments in the other room.

In *Permanent Peace* (2002, Fairfield, Iowa: Institute of Science, Technology and Public Policy), Robert M. Oates described experiments conducted from 1988 to 1993 in which meditators reduced street crime by 23 percent in Washington, D.C. with focused thoughts, in spite of police doubts and a heat wave, which police said should have increased the crime rate. See "Effect of group practice of the transcendental meditation program on preventing violent crime in Washington, D.C.: Results of the National Demonstration Project, June-July, 1993) in *Social Indicators Research* 47:153-201, published in 1999 by Kluwer Academic Publishers.

INDEX

A

Absenteeism decreases when employees are contented, 48.

Acceptance *Also see: Embrace challenges.*

Act of accepting what can't be changed or influenced, 28-29, 32-36, 69, 73-78, 89, 93, 141-152, 154, 159, 170, 174, 177, 223-259, 305-323, 325.

Being accepted by others at work, 8. *Also see: Connections, Fear of rejection.*

Happiness is related to acceptance of what exists, 98-104. *Also see: Judgment, Resistance.*

Relationship of acceptance to positive change, 33, 35, 69, 73-78, 89.

Self-acceptance, 98-104. *Also see: Self-actualization, Self-judgment.*

Accountability, as related to job satisfaction, 136. *Also see: Act, Integrity, Self-responsibility.*

Act. Taking actions to improve one's circumstances, 33, 50, 126-134, 180-181, 183-199, 202, 214-215, 222, 257-258, 281-282, 358-370.

Addictions to unhappiness, 50-51, 78-79. *Also see: Unconscious addictions.*

Advancement. *See: Career Development, Professional advancement opportunities, Skill development, Training.*

Adversity. Turning setbacks into opportunities, developing resiliency, identifying hidden opportunities in disappointing circumstances, 92, 130, 141-168, 206, 237-242, 268, 307, 342. *Also see: Embrace challenges and life circumstances, Judgment, Resiliency, Resistance, Risk taking, Setbacks.*

Affirmations, limitations of positive affirmations, 173.

Allport, Gordon W., 383.

Alpha brain wave state. Benefits of being alert and relaxed regarding creativity, productivity, flow, focus, well-being, and success, 204-205, 283-298, 294-296, 298, 375-376, 381-382.

Altruism, as related to happiness, 51-52, 139, 368, 51-52, 381.

America On Line (AOL):

Survey regarding income and happiness, 380.

Workforce Strategies poll, 377, 381.

Analysis paralysis, 193, 214, 345.

Anchoring actions, thoughts, beliefs, and emotions. *See: Emotional anchor, Positive resource state.*

Andersen, Hans Christian, 268.

Anger, benefits of safely and constructively experienced anger; related techniques, 32, 169-182. *Also see: Emotions, Negative emotions, Negativity at work.*

Angry workers, 358, 375. *Also see: Hostility, Negative emotions, Negativity at work, Workplace violence.*

Anxiety, 324-342, 357-370. *Also see: Emotions, Fear, Negative emotions, Negativity at work.*
Appreciation:
  Being appreciated at work, 6, 10, 364, 367, 372-382. *Also see: Awards, Positive feedback, Praise, Promotion, Reinforcement, Rewards, Validation.*
  Benefits of a state of gratitude, 116, 119, 146, 149, 182, 238, 240, 249, 253. *Also see: Attitude, Choice, Gratitude.*
Arnau, Randolph C., 387.
Aromatherapy, as related to mood, stamina, productivity, and energy, 124, 252, 297, 384.
Assignments, 7, 61, 372-382. *Also see: Flow, Meaningful work, Priorities, Tasks, Workload.*
Associated Press polls and reports, 374, 379.
Assumptions, pitfalls related to assumptions. *See: Beliefs, Illusions, Misperceptions.*
Attachment, 78, *Also see: Desires, Expectations, Joyblocks, Roadblocks.*
Attitude:
  As related to happiness, control over one's life, and productivity, 25-35, 39-40, 119, 141-152, 227, 237-242, 296, 314-315, 324-342, 350, 357-370, 376. *Also see: Appreciation, Choice, Control, Gratitude.*
  Modify attitudes by altering behavior, 325.
Aurelius, Marcus, 112, 145.
Autonomic nervous system, how one can program their nervous system to relax and feel contented, 71, 180, 250-253, 287, 316, 357-358. *Also see: Emotional balance, Inner peace, Neural networks, Nervous system, Relaxation, Stress management.*
Autonomy:
  Job autonomy, 7, 12, 16, 25, 86-87, 183-199, 223-259, 291. *Also see: Control, Security.*
  New sources of autonomy, 26.
  The human desire for security clashes with the need for autonomy, independence, and personal growth, 31.
Awards, as related to happiness at work, 60, 66, 372-382. *Also see: Perks, Positive feedback, Promotions, Recognition, Reinforcement, Rewards, Status.*
Awareness as a key to spontaneous, positive change, 35, 41, 56, 74-78, 89, 94-97, 357-370. *Also see: Curious witness, Mindfulness, Neutral observation, Present Moment, Self-awareness.*
B
Balance. *See: Emotional balance, Inner peace, Work-life balance.*
Bandler, Richard, 324, 333, 388.
Bargh, John, 115.
Barker, S., 384.

Batstone, David, 373,376.
Behavior:
  Behavior is modified by assumptions, mental frameworks, perceptions, emotions, thoughts, and physiology, 153-168.
  Behavior modification alters emotions, 325.
  Behavior modification changes neural circuitry. *See: Neural circuitry, neural networks.*
  Behavior patterns. Techniques to shift dysfunctional patterns, 171, 189-192, 209, 215-216, 228-229, 233, 238-259, 309-310, 313, 315, 318, 326-342, 350. *Also see: Neural networks, Self-awareness.*
Beliefs:
  Affect thoughts and emotions, 157. *Also see: Beliefs that affect happiness.*
  Beliefs and interpretations as a cause of emotional pain (as opposed to circumstances or events), 154, 159.
  Beliefs that affect or limit happiness, 24-34, 88, 95, 103, 105-115, 127, 141-152, 182, 309-322, 357-370. *Also see: Illusions, Misperceptions, Priming experiments, Social programming.*
  Effects of unconscious beliefs on happiness and well-being, 105-111, 115, 153-168, 267. *Also see: Parallel realities, Priming experiments, Social programming.*
Bell, Alexander Graham, 268.
Benefits:
  Competitive benefits of happy workers to the organizations where they work (greater productivity and profits; discretionary efforts; better teamwork; more creativity; loyalty; assistance to others; fewer lawsuits; decreased absenteeism; lower healthcare, insurance, and disability costs; reduced turnover and tardiness, etc.), 47-48, 51-52, 291, 372-382. *Also see: Productivity.*
  Effects of employee benefits on job satisfaction, 377.
Bentall, Richard, 48, 376.
Bernard, André, 383.
Beta-endorphins. *See: Endorphins.*
Biology:
  Biology of beliefs, 153-168, 233.
  Biology affects emotions. *See: Biology of beliefs, Neural networks, Physiology affects emotions.*
Biological loop. *See: Biology of beliefs, Feedback, Neural networks.*
Birkenbihl, Vera F., 385, 387.
Black Monday Syndrome, 377.
Blake, William, 155.
Blame.
  Blame and victim game, 23-24, 28, 127, 148, 242, 245-246.
  Blame, as related to choice, 25, 119.

Blaming employees, organizational culture, or bosses for problems exacerbates them, creates blind spots, and prevents problem-solving, 22-24, 28, 39, 189. *Also see: Difficult people.*
Blame makes the one who blames feel powerless, 23, 39.
Blame, refusing to blame contributes to happiness, 25, 126, 189.
Blame. The relationship between blame and judgment, 29. *Also see: Judgment.*
Blanchflower, David G., 378.
Blind spot, 41, 105-111, 315, 322. *Also see: Illusions, Misperceptions, Myth, Perceptions, Social Conditioning, Social Programming, Truth.*
Bliss as a natural state, 56. *Also see: Emotional balance, Happiness, Inner peace.*
Bono, Cher, 268.
Body language, 226. *Also see: Body, mind, & spirit; Neurolinguistic programming; Physical movement; Posture.*
Body, mind, & spirit, 38, 86, 90,102, 114, 117-118, 149, 168, 207-208, 221, 226-228, 303-304, 327-328, 340-341. *Also see: Creativity, Exercise, Fun, Humor, Play, Massage therapy, Meditation, Mind power, Mood, Physical movement, Posture, Relaxation related to productivity, Resiliency, Singing, Stress management, Yoga.*
Bohm, David, 56, 382.
Boundaries. *See: Personal boundaries, Self-care, Work-life balance.*
Brain:
    A "pattern-recognition machine," 193.
    Associative links. *See: Nonconscious associations.*
    Benefits of relaxed yet alert alpha brain wave state re: productivity, creativity, well-being, focus, and success, 204-205.
    Entrainment, 196, 296-297, 329-331, 334-336, 340, 345, 350.
    Hardwired to link associations, 350. *Also see: Neural networks.*
    Hardwired to protect humans or improve the human species, 287.
    How it resolves conflicts between reality and misperceptions, 105-111. *Also see: Beliefs, Illusions. Social programming.*
    Link emotional and rational centers of the brain, 150, 304.
    Link left and right hemispheres via mind mapping, 343, 350, 352, 388.
    Link left and right hemispheres via nondominant hand writing, 296.
    Link left and right hemispheres via physical movement, 296.
    Malleability, 233, 314, 357-358, 365. *Also see: Neural networks.*
    Negative effects of brain's simplifying tendencies, 158.
    Processes information via mental imagery, enthusiasm, and imagination combined with sounds and feelings more than via words; humans create more by feelings than intellect, 335, 350, 352.
    Simplifies complexity to achieve efficiency, 158.
Branham, Leigh, 377-378.

Breathing as a stress management tool, 100-101, 124, 149-151, 180, 250-252, 327-328. *Also see: Autonomic nervous system, Emotional balance, Stress management.*
Brodie, Richard 4, 61, 372.
Brown, J., 383.
Buckingham, Marcus, 267, 387.
Buddha, The, 283.
Bullies at work, 15. *Also see: Harassment, Toxic employees, Toxic organizational culture.*
Burnell, Ivan, 214, 386.
Buscaglia, Leo, 282.
Butts, Mary Frances, 199.
Buzan, Tony, 388.
C
C.W. *See: Curious witness.*
Cameron, Julia, 192.
CareerBuilder.com, 374.
Career development, 9, 10, 12, 276, 372-382, 385. *Also see: Professional advancement opportunities, Skill development, Training.*
Career ladder, 9, 12, 126-134, 249, 372-382, 385. *Also see: Professional development opportunities, Skill development, Training.*
Carver, George Washington, 104.
Cathartic release of emotions, problems related to, 178. *See Emotions, Negative emotions.*
Challenge:
    Essential for personal fulfillment at work; strategies for embracing challenge, 85, 89-93, 238-259. *Also see: Change, Confidence, Flow, Fulfillment, Mandated change, Performance enhancement, Self-actualization, Self-responsibility.*
    How positive, appropriate challenges contribute to job satisfaction, 10, 53, 63, 64, 66, 73, 91-97, 141-156, 183-199, 283-298, 305-353, 364-370, 372, 377-378, 381, 383. *Also see: Flow.*
    Humans are hardwired to require challenge, 29, 30. *Also see: Change, Confidence is stifled by avoiding challenge, Mandated change.*
Change:
    Allowing vs. trying to force change, 34-36, 39, 97, 368.
    Benefits of, 91-92, 141-152. *Also see: Confidence, Creativity, Curiosity, Curious witness, Flow, Fulfillment, Judgment, Resilience, Resistance, Security, Self-actualization, Self-responsibility.*
    Changing jobs, 280-281. *Also see: Employee turnover, Resign.*
    Fear of change as it contributes to insecurity, 22, 53, 127-128, 201. *Also see: Fear of change, Insecurity, Security.*
    How positive changes occur, 36, 91-92, 97, 368. *Also see: Acceptance,*

Curious witness.
Mandated change, 30, 53, 86. *Also see: Challenge; Change, benefits of; Creativity; Curiosity; Curious witness; Flow; Resilience; Trust.*
Negative effects of trying to change someone else, 23, 36, 39.
Strategies for embracing change, 223-259. *Also see: Acceptance, Embracing challenges.*
The ability to change one's self creates external change, 68, 368.
The human brain craves challenge and change, 30, 91. *Also see: Challenge, Confidence is stifled by avoiding challenge, Flow, Mandated change, Resilience, Security, Self-actualization.*
Why it is virtually impossible to change other people, 23, 36, 39.
Chaos, 53. *See: Challenge, Change.*
Charisma, 133. *Also see: Personal power, Strengths.*
Chesterfield, Lord, 260.
Choice:
As related to control over one's life, 88, 119, 126-134. *Also see: Autonomy, Control, Interruptions, Personal organization, Personal power, Time management.*
Effects of choices on happiness, 88, 112-134, 141-168, 173-174, 183-199, 223-259, 309, 357-370. *Also see: Attitude, Autonomy, Control, Emotions, Interruptions, Personal organization, Personal power, Thoughts, Time management.*
When to avoid making decisions, 168. *Also see: Decision-making, Self-care.*
Civility, 255-259, 375. *Also see: Connections, Difficult people, Integrity, Patience.*
Clifton, Donald, 387.
Clutter, 125, 214. *Also see: Choice, Interruptions, Personal organization.*
Coaching, 9, 85, 256, 378. *Also see: Evaluation, Feedback, Mentor, Mastermind, Performance Review, Positive feedback, Professional support.*
Co-creation of circumstances, 147.
Coercion as related to job satisfaction, 57. *Also see: Myths, Power vs. force, Power over other people.*
Cohen, Alan, 139.
Cole, D., 382.
Colton, Charles Caleb, 83
Combinatory play, 165-167.
Comfort zone, 29, 95, 188, 238, 250. *Also see: Familiar zone.*
Commitment to positive change, 146, 198, 201, 209, 212, 221, 323, 358-370.
Communication.
Ability to communicate unmet needs to management or coworkers and to communicate negative emotions and opinions as well as benefits of

meeting employee needs, 8, 42, 136-140, 208, 288, 290, 366-367, 370.
Clarity, effectiveness and consistency of; communication styles, 13, 136-140.
Ways of communicating with one's self about circumstances and events influence quality of life, 153-168. *Also see: Internal critic, Internal dialogue, Self-talk.*
Problems related to gender or culture, 22.
Comparison:
How comparing one's self to others affects happiness at work, 55, 62, 65, 72, 74, 88, 100, 112, 238, 241, 380-381. *Also see: Possessions, Perks, Rank, Status, Title.*
Positive effects of downward vs. upward comparisons, 113-114.
Compassion, 51, 57, 66, 102, 113, 133, 160, 179, 256, 306.
Compensation re: happiness at work, 6, 54, 88, 143, 365, 372-382. *Also see: Income, Money, Pay, Salary.*
Competitive benefits of happy employees, 372-382. *Also see: Benefits of happiness at work.*
Competition, effects on job satisfaction, 59-60, 63-68, 113.
Concentration. *See: Focus.*
Confidence:
As related to job satisfaction; strategies for enhancing, 38, 66-67, 99, 110, 123, 132, 134, 144, 162, 173, 182, 185, 206, 210-213, 260-282, 285-298, 324-342, 377. *Also see: Body, mind, & spirit; Breathing; Creativity, Exercise; Fun; Humor; Massage therapy; Meditation; Mind power; Mood; Motion and physical movement re: stress reduction, mind power, & confidence; Physical movement; Play; Relaxation related to productivity; Resiliency; Self-actualization; Self-care; Self-improvement; Self-responsibility; Singing; Stress management; Yoga.*
Confidence is stifled by avoiding challenge and elevated by embracing change and challenge, 30, 90-93, 137, 139, 140, 230, 256-257. *Also see: Acceptance, Challenge, Change, Mandated change, Resistance.*
Conflict:
Between what employees want and need and management's perceptions of what workers want, including salary levels required for job satisfaction and employee retention, 372-382. *Also see: Employee-centered organizations, Employee morale, Fulfillment, Job satisfaction, Management styles, Motivation.*
Conflict resolution, 8, 375.
Connections:
With others; a natural and essential state of human beings, 56, 368-370.
Regarding productivity and happiness, 90, 123, 140, 149, 257, 250, 254, 277, 364, 367, 372-382. *Also see: Difficult people, Relationships.*

Conscious creating. Limitations of the traditional "create your own reality" approach, 119, 319-322, 325, 331.

Conscious mind, limitations of, 89, 100, 121, 195, 293, 325, 385.

Constructive worry. *See: Emotions, Thoughts, Worry.*

Contentment. *See: Emotional balance, Happiness, Inner peace.*

Contribute, making a positive contribution to society via one's work; relationship to job satisfaction, 6, 10, 21, 26, 66, 85, 88, 98-99, 102-104, 110-111, 135, 139, 140, 198, 256-257, 260-282, 291, 295, 365-370, 372-382. *Also see: Meaningful work, Strengths, Talents.*

Control:

As an illusion. Recognizing what one can and cannot control, 71, 74-78, 141-152, 207, 223-259, 310, 317-320, 341.

Control. Attempts to manipulate others as that relates to happiness at work, 57.

Control over one's work schedule, process, interruptions, tasks, etc., 7, 12, 26, 124-125, 86-87, 183-199, 223-259, 292-293, 372-382.

How one can program their nervous system to relax and feel contented, 71 ,180, 250-254, 357. *Also see: Autonomic nervous system, Emotional balance, Inner peace, Neural networks, Nervous system, Relaxation, Stress management.*

Interruptions can be controlled. *See: Interruptions.*

People can control their behavior but not their initial feelings, 178, 325.

People are in control of their thoughts, attitudes, choices, and happiness, 25, 72, 77, 126-134, 357-370.

Coombs, Andrea, 373-374.

Corporate benefits of happiness at work. *See: Benefits of happy workers to the organizations where they work, Competitive benefits of happy employees.*

Corporate culture, 6-17, 54, 89, 127-128, 372-382. *Also see: Employee well-being, Flexible schedule, Organizational culture, Organizational health, Organizational toxicity, Personal needs.*

Cortis, Bruno, 377.

Counseling, 253, 276. *Also see: Employee Assistance Program.*

Courage combats fear, 95, 237.

Create your own reality, limitations of the traditional approach; relationship of the approach to fear and insecurity, 119, 319-322, 325, 331.

Creativity:

Benefits of creativity as related to job satisfaction, 10, 40, 51, 91, 97, 123, 127, 142, 192, 254, 256, 281, 284-285, 291, 293-294, 296, 298, 304, 306, 313, 315. *Also see: Body, mind, & spirit; Curiosity; Fun; Humor; Physical movement; Play; Relaxation related to productivity; Humor; Resiliency; Singing; Stress management.*

Deterrents to creativity, 21, 204.
Happy employees are more creative, 48, 51.
Humans create more often by feelings, sensations, enthusiasm, and imagination than by intellect and thought, 102, 148, 218, 230, 352. *Also see: Brain, Emotions, Enthusiasm, Imagination, Multisensory.*
Relationship of creativity to positive emotions, 181, 342.
Strategies to enhance creativity, 51, 123, 165, 204,208, 343-353.
Critic, *See: Internal critic.*
Criticism by others, 6, 106, 194.
Csikszentmihalyi, Mihaly, 194, 284-286, 291, 386-387.
Cubicle, 195, 225-226. *Also see: Employee-friendly culture, Work environment.*
Cultivate a calm mind, 150-152.
Cultural creatives, 123.
Curiosity, relationship to happiness at work, 25, 61, 86-87, 91-97, 148, 177, 248, 256-257, 259, 293,304, 306-323, 341-342, 364.
Curious Witness, 80, 120, 141-152, 174-182, 230, 271, 304-323, 325. *Also see: Neutral observer.*
Customer satisfaction, 48, 52.
Customer service, 48, 192, 278-279, 368.
Cutler, Howard, 375.
Czyzewaska, M., 387.
D
de Beauvoir, Simone, 305.
de Vinci, Leonardo, 268.
Death statistics re: happiness at work, 51.
Decision-making:
  Related to job satisfaction, 12, 184-199, 202, 343. *Also see: Choices.*
  When to avoid, 168, 254. *Also see: Choices.*
Defense mechanisms, 40, 171,179, 206. *Also see: Difficult people, Emotions.*
Delaney, Sarah Louise, 80.
Delegate, 136.
Delight-deficiency disorder, 45, 47-68.
Denial, 171. *Also see: Defense mechanisms, Resistance.*
DePorter, Bobbi, 387.
Desires:
  As deterrents to happiness, 72, 74-78.
  Versus preferences, 74-78.
Detachment, 78, 169-182, 231, 234-235, 247, 305-323, 327-342. *Also see: Acceptance, Embrace challenges.*
Diener, Ed, 376, 381-382.
Diet as related to happiness at work, 149, 252.

Difficult people, 22, 39-40, 50, 53-54, 58, 86, 90, 179, 357-358. *Also see: Blame, Illusions, Mirror, Misperceptions.*
Disability claims. Employee happiness lowers claims, 48.
Disassociation from negative emotions, 324-342. *Also see: Curious witness, Detachment.*
Discomfort zone. *See: Familiar zone.*
Discretionary efforts contributed by contented employees, 48, 374-375.
Disney, Walt, 43, 268.
Dispositional optimism, 160.
Distortion, 57, 357-370. *Also see: Blind spot, Illusion, Misperception, Myth, Priming experiments.*
Diversity, 22, 39, 51. *Also see: Difficult people.*
Dixon, Norman, F., 387.
Dobbs, David, 387.
Dossey, Larry, 376.
Dostoyevsky, Fyodor, 140.
Downsize, downsizing, 53, 127-128, 130, 163, 214.
Dream job, 55-56, 111, 240, 340, 342.
Dryden, John, 258.
Duncan, Pat, 103.
Dutton, K., 383.
Dylan, Bob, 358.
E
Easterbrook, Gregg, 372, 378, 380.
Economic indicators re: job and life satisfaction, 372-382.
Easterlin, Richard, 381-382.
Economic state, 53, 58, 137. *Also see: Employee Marketability.*
Ecstasy, 127, 141, 284. *Also see: Happiness, Pleasure.*
Edelstein, Linda, 384.
Edison, Thomas Alva, 95, 204, 206, 209, 333, 341-342.
Einstein, Albert, 94, 165, 230, 268, 315, 342.
Elins, Michael, 378.
E-mail, junk, 226.
Embracing challenges and life circumstances and events as a key to happiness; negative experiences as gifts, 29, 60-65, 73-78, 80, 87-97, 112-113, 141-152, 159,169-182, 185, 193, 195, 204, 208, 223-259. *Also see: Acceptance, Adversity, Resiliency.*
Emergency mind-calming technique 77, 150-151.
Emerson, Ralph Waldo, 370.
Emotional:
Addictions, 56, 252.
Anchor, 42, 90, 221, 304, 324-342, 357-358. *Also see: Positive resource states.*

Balance, 56, 60-64, 67-68, 90, 97, 140, 141-152, 180-181, 227, 237-238, 248, 253, 285, 293-297, 306-342, 357-358.
Control, how one can program their nervous system to relax and feel contented, 71. *Also see: Autonomic nervous system, Inner peace, Neural networks, Nervous system, Qi gong, Relaxation, Stress management, Tai chi, Yoga.*
Emotional Intelligence, 90.
Emotional roller coasters, 96-97, 178, 304-323.
Emotional strength, 90, 93, 120, 357-358. *Also see: Emotional anchor, Emotional balance, Emotions as productive tools, Emotions—transforming negative into positive, Emotional control, Emotional intelligence, Positive resource state.*
Emotional triggers associated with past experiences, 168.
Emotional turmoil, causes of, 154, 168, 178.
Emotions:
Acceptance of negative emotions creates positive change. When negative emotions foster positive emotions, 120-121, 169-182, 230-233, 303-323. *Also see: Curious Witness.*
Actions are a choice, 169-182.
Effect of conflict between opposite emotions; effects of choice, 120.
Are modified by altering behavior, 325.
Are modified by altering thought, beliefs, and perceptions, 157, 172-174.
Are modified by physiology/biology, 233.
As one's primary identity, 306.
As physical sensations in the body, 175-176, 306.
As productive tools to create happiness when feelings are safely and constructively expressed, 8, 32, 90, 149, 169-182.
Effects on physical body and well-being, 117-118.
How resistance to what exists deters positive change, 169-182.
Humans create positive thoughts and emotions more often by feeling, sensations, imagination, and enthusiasm than by intellectual thought processes such as "positive thinking." Humans are hardwired to live by their sensations, 102, 148, 218, 230, 352. *Also see: Brain, Creativity, Enthusiasm, Imagination, Multisensory.*
Ideal ratio of positive to negative emotions, 178, 237-238.
Link emotional and rational brain, 90, 305-323. *Also see: Body, Mind, & Spirit; Whole-body.*
Modify perceptions and mental frames, 158-159.
Modify physiology, 157. *Also see: Biology of belief.*
Molecules of emotion. *See: Molecules of emotion.*
Negative and positive opposite states (polarities of emotion), 176. *Also see: Parallel realities, Polarities.*
Positive effects of appreciating all emotions, 141-152, 169-182.

Power of emotions, 108, 114-118, 169-182. *Also see: Enthusiasm, Imagination, Multisensory.*
Problems related to cathartic release of emotions, 178.
Transforming negative emotions into positive emotions, 29, 32, 90-93, 120-121, 141-152, 169-182, 303-342, 350. *Also see: Challenge, Change, Curiosity, Curious witness, Judgment, Mandated change, Negative emotions, Self-actualization, Self-responsibility.*
Emoto, Masuro, 115, 371.
Employee Assistance Program (EAP) services, 9. *Also see: Coaching, Employee-centered organizations, Employee-friendly culture, Feedback, Mastermind, Mentor, Positive feedback, Professional support.*
Employee benefits, effects on job satisfaction, 377.
Employee-centered organizations, 7, 9-16, 14, 48, 194, 372-377. *Also see: Corporate culture, Equal treatment of employees, Fair treatment of employees, Flexible schedule, Fulfillment, Job satisfaction, Management styles, Motivation, Organizational culture, Personal needs, Respect at work, Toxic organizations, Validation, Work environment, Work-life balance.*
Employee death ratio higher on Mondays, 377.
Employee decision-making as input to management, 12. *Also see: Autonomy, Management styles.*
Employee enthusiasm, 372-382. *Also see: Employee-centered organizations.*
Employee-friendly culture. *See: Employee-centered organizations.*
Employee marketability, 16, 126-134, 372-385.
Employee mobility. *See: Employee marketability.*
Employee morale, 16, 372-385. *Also see: Corporate culture, Employee-friendly culture, Employee well-being, Equal treatment of employees, Fair treatment of employees, Feedback, Flexible schedule, Management style, Motivation, Organizational culture, Personal needs, Respect at work, Toxic organizations, Validation, Work environment, Work-life balance.*
Employee motivation. *See: Motivation.*
Employee needs and preferences, 1, 5, 24, 39, 42, 135-140, 198, 372-382. *Also see: Conflict between what employees want and need and management's perceptions, Employee-centered organizations, Employee morale, Employee well-being, Flexible schedule, Fulfillment, Job satisfaction, Management styles, Motivation, Personal needs, Work-life balance.*
Employee recruitment and retention, 372-382. *Also see: Corporate culture, Employee-centered organizations, Employee turnover, Employee well-being, Equal treatment of employees, Fair treatment of employees, Family-friendly workplaces, Flexible schedule, Job satisfaction, Management styles, Organizational culture, Personal needs, Work environment.*
Employee shortages, 109.

Employee turnover:
   State of, 280-281, 372-382, 385. *Also see: Employee-centered
   organizations, Employee marketability, Employee mobility, Employee
   morale, Employee recruitment and retention, Employee well-being, Family-
   friendly workplaces, Job satisfaction, Management styles, Personal needs,
   Work environment.*
   Turnover decreases when employees are happy, 48.
   Why employees change jobs, 378-381.
Employee well-being:
   Relationship to higher performance, higher income, improved teamwork,
   and better health, 381-382.
   State of, 7, 9, 11-16, 362-385. *Also see: Corporate culture, Employee-
   friendly organizational culture, Employee morale, Equal treatment of
   employees, Ergonomics, Fair treatment of employees, Flexible schedule,
   Fulfillment, Job satisfaction, Motivation, Management styles,
   Organizational culture, Personal needs, Respect at work, Toxic
   organizations, Validation, Work environment, Work-life balance.*
Employment options. *See: Employee marketability.*
Empowering questions, 293, 341, 349.
Endorphins, 172, 252-253, 287.
Energetic versus fatigued, 168, 218, 220, 252, 258, 375. *Also see:
Breathing, Exercise, Oxygenate, Qi gong, Stress management, Tai Chi,
Yoga.*
Enthusiasm:
   As emotion and passion, 159.
   Positive potential and conscious use of enthusiasm, 108, 193, 221, 342,
   350-351. *Also see: Creativity, Emotions, Imagination, Mental imagery,
   Multisensory, Work environment.*
Environmental toxins, 15.
Epictetus, 141, 145-146.
Equal treatment of employees, 12-14, 16, 372-377. *Also see: Employee-
friendly culture, Employee well-being, Fair treatment of employees, Job
satisfaction, Management styles, Motivation, Professional support, Respect
at work, Validation, Work environment, Work-life balance.*
Ergonomics,15. *Also see: Employee-friendly culture, Employee well-being,
Physical environment, Work environment.*
Essential oils. *See: Aromatherapy.*
Ethics. *See: Integrity.*
Evaluation, 9, 67, 128-134,198, 209. *Also see: Criticism, Feedback,
Performance review, Positive feedback, Reinforcement.*
Excellence re: happiness at work, 57.
Executives often feel as vulnerable as employees, 24.
Exercise for stress reduction and as related to happiness, 10, 149, 221,

250, 378. *Also see: Body, mind, & spirit; Creativity; Exercise; Fun; Humor; Massage; Meditation; Mind power; Mood; Physical fitness; Physical movement; Play; Relaxation related to productivity; Resiliency; Singing; Stress management; Yoga.*
Expectations, problems caused by personal expectations, 73, 78, 80, 172, 202, 232, 238, 242-248, 304, 307, 310, 321-322, 380.
Experientially gifted, 146. *Also see: Embracing challenges.*
External sources of happiness at work, 52-67.
F
Fadiman, Clifton, 370.
Failure:
  Benefits of, 113, 143, 185, 208. *Also see: Mistakes.*
  Dodging mistakes leads to forfeiting joy on the job, 30, 179. *Also see: Mistakes.*
  Effects of expectations of failure, 103. *Also see: Mistakes.*
  Fear of failure, 147, 179, 201, 211, 348.
  Immunization against failure, 95.
Fair treatment of employees, 7, 9, 11-16, 372-382. *Also see: Corporate culture, Employee-friendly organizational culture, Employee morale, Equal treatment of employees, Evaluation, Feedback, Flexible schedule, Job satisfaction, Motivation, Management styles, Organizational culture, Performance review, Personal needs, Professional support, Respect at work, Toxic organizational culture, Validation, Work environment, Work-life balance.*
False self, 99-100, 191, 307. *Also see: Beliefs, Illusions, Misperceptions, Myths, Perceptions, Self esteem, Self-acceptance, Self-awareness, Self-image, Social conditioning, Social programming, True Self, Truth.*
Familiar zone, 27, 79, 95-97, 185, 188, 238, 307, 314. *Also see: Comfort zone.*
Family-friendly workplaces, 9, 11-12, 372-382. *Also see: Employee-centered organizations, Flexible schedule, Personal needs.*
Fatigue, 201, 218, 220.
Favoritism, 14. *Also see: Management styles, Toxic boss, Toxic organizational culture.*
FCI Electronics, 183-184.
Fear:
  As one's primary identity, 306.
  Beneficial effects of fear, 233-235.
  Coping strategies, 141-152, 169-199, 201, 212-214, 216, 228-229, 296.
  Effects of fear and methods of coping, 32, 116, 154, 169-182. *Also see: Addictions to unhappiness, Emotions, Priming experiments, Unconscious Addictions.*
  Fear of change, the unknown, or the future, 27, 50, 96, 173, 201-202, 211,

228, 238, 320-323.
Fear of failure, 173, 185-187, 201, 208, 348.
Fear of fear, 227, 230.
Fear of one's personal power, 27.
Fear of rejection, 32, 334.
Fear of success, 201, 211.
Relationship of courage to fear, 95.
Feedback:
    Constructive, 9, 16, 85, 91, 96, 130, 143, 214, 275-276, 292, 378. *Also see: Coaching, Employee morale, Evaluation; Feedback; Management styles, Motivation, Performance review; Positive feedback.*
    From employees to management, 12-14, 16.
Feedback loops in the brain, 70, 233. *Also see: Neural networks, Biology of belief.*
Financial benefits of happiness at work, 48-49, 51, 372-382. *Also see: Benefits of happy employees.*
Fisher, B., 386.
Fitzgerald, F. Scott, 242.
Flexibility, re: happiness, 133, 196.
Flexible work schedule, 9, 12, 54, 377, 381. *Also see: Corporate culture, Employee assistance program, Personal needs, Work-life balance, Work schedule.*
Flora, Carlin, 378.
Flow, reaching a state of flow at work, 63, 66, 91, 123, 133, 194, 283-298, 372-382, 387. *Also see: Challenge, Fulfillment, Performance Enhancement.*
Focus:
    Being focused yet relaxed as an avenue to fulfillment, flow, and productivity, 283-298, 369-370. *Also see: Alpha brain state.*
    Benefits of focusing on one's internal state of mind rather than on aspects of work one cannot control, 77, 258.
    Focus on what you want, not on what you don't want, 72, 74-78, 89, 92, 112-125, 136, 146-149, 184-186, 188-191, 196-197, 199, 206, 210, 218, 230, 236, 238-239, 246, 253, 293, 335, 350, 357-370.
    Having the ability to focus on one's work, 7, 87, 124, 204-205, 246, 283-298. *Also see: Alpha brain wave state, Flow.*
    The object gaining one's attention expands, 74-78, 116, 119-120, 149, 151-152, 172, 181, 189, 275, 322, 365.
    The value and power of focus at work, 32, 98, 112-125.
Force:
    Attempting to manipulate or control others, 57-58. *Also see: Power vs. Force.*
    Force creates counterforce, 23, 27, 36. *Also see: Power vs. Force.*
Ford, Henry, 120, 268.

Forgiveness re: happiness at work, 57.
Foster, Bill, 97.
Foster, Lorrie, 384-385.
Frank, Robert H., 379-380, 382.
Frankl, Viktor, 73, 96, 112, 134, 144, 196, 357-358, 383.
Franklin, Benjamin, 69.
Fredrickson, Barbara, 181-182, 376, 386.
Fulfillment:
  At work, 5, 17, 19, 42, 57, 135-136, 139-152, 357-370, 372-382. *Also see: Meaningful work.*
  As a tool for happiness, 24-43, 45, 54-55, 62-68, 74-78, 85-93, 98-104, 112-134, 143, 153-168, 183-199, 224-259, 271, 283-298, 309, 344, 346, 348, 372-382. *Also see: Life purpose, Meaningful work.*
Fun at work, 10, 42-43, 86-87, 91, 133, 182, 250-251. *Also see: Body, mind, & spirit; Creativity; Exercise; Humor; Laughter; Mind power; Mood; Physical movement; Play; Relaxation related to productivity; Resiliency; Singing; Stress management; Yoga.*
G
Gelb, Michael J., 372.
Gender conflicts, 22. *Also see: Conflict resolution.*
Generational conflict, 22. *Also see: Conflict resolution.*
Genetic setpoint for happiness, 55-56, 196, 357, 365, 368.
Ghandi, Mahatma, 27.
Gibran, Kahlil, 3, 359.
Gilman, Charlotte Perkins, 93.
Gladwell, Malcolm, 384.
Goals:
  Achieving performance goals set by management, 9, 85-86, 124, 137, 288.
  Goal setting by employee and achievement thereof, 20, 85-86, 126-131, 136, 143, 148, 186-188, 193, 197, 252, 257, 288, 291, 364-370.
  When goals limit achievement and happiness, 72.
Goldberg, Whoopi, 268.
Grandy, Dottie Bruce
Gratitude, beneficial effects of, 5, 55, 77, 116, 119, 146, 149, 182, 199, 215, 217-218, 238, 240, 249, 253. *Also see: Appreciation, Attitude, Choice, Contribute.*
Greene, Brian, 389.
Grinder, John, 324, 333, 388.
Guardian. *Also see: Critic, Inner critic.*
H
Habits. *See: Behavior patterns.*
HALT adage, 168.

Happiness. *Also see: Acceptance; Act; Appreciation; Body, Mind, & Spirit; Challenge; Change; Communication; Comparisons; Compassion; Connections; Contribute; Control; Curiosity; Curious witness; Ecstasy; Embrace challenge; Emotional strength; Employee well-being; Feedback; Flow; Focus; Fulfillment; Fun; Inner peace; Joy alarms; Joyblocks; Job satisfaction; Judgment; Laughter; Meaningful work; Needs; Neutral observation; Passion; Patience; Personal power; Play; Positive resource state; Reframing; Relationships; Resiliency; Self-acceptance; Self-actualization; Self-awareness; Self-care; Self-responsibility; Strengths, Stress management, Support system, Work-life balance, Uncertainty.*

As a choice, how choosing well-being fulfills and empowers, 25, 59, 72, 87, 126-127, 153-168, 169, 196, 241-242, 357-370. *Also see: Choice.*

As a side effect of meaning and challenge, 59, 87, 90, 188. *Also see: Challenge.*

As a state of mind and self-responsibility, 25, 68, 83, 183, 194, 357-370. *Also see: Inner peace, Self-responsibility.*

As related to management styles, 372-382. *Also see: Management styles, Professional support.*

As related to productivity and profit, 372.

As related to success, 372, 376.

Differences between happiness and pleasure, 49-50, 151-152, 378-379.

Internal and external sources of happiness, 47-68, 84-93, 126, 372-382.

Is defined and experienced in an individualistic manner, 71, 83, 378.

Long and short-term sources of happiness, 54-68, 83, 372-382.

Regarding living in the present and using one's intuition, 307. *Also see: Intuition, Present moment.*

Regarding relationships with coworkers, 54, 372-382. *Also see: Connections.*

Relationship between one's happiness and the actions of other people, 53-54. *Also see: Connections, Difficult people.*

Relationship to a state of flow, 372-382. *Also see: Flow.*

Relationship to organizational toxicity 53, 372-382. *Also see: Corporate culture, Organizational toxicity.*

Relationship of happiness to salary, title, rank, status, perks, possessions, meaningful work, purpose, flexible schedule, and aspects of corporate culture, 54, 372-382. *Also see: Corporate culture, Flexible schedule, Fulfillment, Meaningful work, Perks, Job satisfaction.*

Relationship to state of the job market or economy, 53, 372-382.

Roadblocks to happiness, 47-52, 69-80, 84-93, 357-370, 372-383. *Also see: Joy alarms, Joyblocks.*

Seeking happiness deters happiness, 71-72, 74-78.

The goal that is sought the most often and for its own sake, 284, 372-382.

What "creates" happiness changes over time, 83.

What does and does not create happiness, 47-68, 83-93, 126-127, 140, 152, 372-382.
Harassment at work, 15, 375. *Also see: Bullying, Management styles, Toxic organizational culture.*
Hawkins, David, 57, 382.
Healthy risks. *See: Risk-taking.*
Health, positive effects of job satisfaction, 91, 374, 377, 381. *Also see: Immune System, Illness.*
Health insurance costs decrease when employees are happy, 48.
Helplessness. *See: Learned helplessness.*
Hendricks, Gay, 385.
Hesse, Hermann, 153.
Hewlett Packard study, 384.
Hill, T., 387.
Hobart & William Smith Colleges study, 379.
Hoffman, Barbara, 152.
Holistic. *See: Body, mind, & spirit.*
Holmes, Oliver Wendell, Sr., 111.
Homer, 264.
Honesty. *See: Integrity.*
Hopeless. *See: Learned helplessness.*
Hostility at work, 375. *Also see: Anger, Harassment, Negativity at work, Toxic boss, Toxic employees, Toxic organizational culture, Violence at work.*
Howard, Julie, 376.
Humility as pride, 100.
Humor for stress reduction, well-being, and enhancement of productivity, 10, 42, 160, 208, 251, 387. *Also see: Body, mind, & spirit; Creativity; Fun; Laughter; Mind power; Mood; Play; Relaxation; Resiliency; Singing; Stress management.*
Huxley, Aldous, 143, 385.
Hydration related to well-being, clear thinking, and memory 149.
I
Identity, 164, 191, 201, 206-207, 209-212, 306-307,342. *Also see: Behavior patterns, Neural networks.*
Idaho Psychological Association, 376.
Illness. *Also see: Health.*
Illusions, 24-34, 41, 52, 57, 105-111, 139, 153-168, 179, 200, 207, 209, 211, 227, 237, 241, 267-268, 282, 357-370. *Also see: Blind spots, Misperceptions, Myths, Perceptions, Priming experiments, Security, Social conditioning, Social programming, Security, Truth.*
Image streaming. *See: Stream-of-consciousness thinking.*
Imagery. *See: Mental imagery.*

Imagination:
Effects of "reality" and well-being of using imagination with emotion and/or passion, 158, 159, 165, 193.
Value and purposeful use of, 86, 108, 116, 122, 230, 231, 234, 327-330, 335, 342, 350-351. *Also see: Creativity, Curiosity, Emotions, Enthusiasm, Mental imagery, Multisensory.*
Immune system, effects of happiness and job satisfaction, 91, 160, 251, 374, 377. *Also see: Health.*
Income as related to happiness at work, 4, 372-382. *Also see: Compensation, Money, Pay, Salary.*
Independence. *See: Autonomy.*
Industrial Revolution, 123.
Industry trends, 129-130.
Influence, personal, 132-134, 228, 246. *Also see: Charisma.*
Inner critic. *See: Internal critic.*
Inner dialogue. *See: Internal critic.*
Inner domain, 153-154.
Innate genius, 123, 244, 268, 293, 324, 341, 357-370, 385, 387.
Inner peace, 25, 59-61, 68, 73-80, 86-87, 89-90, 96-97, 99-103, 112-125, 141-152, 153-168, 230, 237-259, 294-298, 305-342, 344, 350, 357-370. *Also see: Emotional balance.*
Insecurity related to change, misperceptions, and happiness at work, 22, 109, 170, 173, 200-201, 204-210, 227-230, 237-238, 269,287, 324-342. *Also see: Blind spots, Change, Illusions, Misperceptions, Prejudice, Uncertainty.*
Integra, Inc. 360.
Integrity re: happiness at work, 57, 133, 170-171, 194, 248.
Intelligent optimism, 237-242. *Also see: Choice, Optimism.*
Intention, the power of, 56-57, 368-370.
Internal critic:
An internal negative voice, 33, 78-79, 86, 88-89, 100, 121, 170, 179, 195, 204-212, 216, 220, 234, 268, 275, 286, 293, 295, 307, 345, 350.
Befriending the internal critic and transforming it into a virtual assistant, 33. *Also see: Internal critic as an internal negative voice.*
Internal locus of control over one's life, 195. *Also see: Control, Personal power, Self-responsibility.*
Internal sources of job satisfaction or happiness at work, 52-67.
International Communications Research, 374.
Interruptions, experiencing and managing, 7, 15, 124-125, 293. *Also see: Choice, Management styles, Personal organization, Time management, Workplace environment.*
Intuition/inner guidance, 31, 60-61, 77, 90, 126, 130, 227, 270, 296, 304, 307, 325, 342, 352-353. *Also see: Inner genius, Nonconscious.*
Ipsos-Public Affairs research on worker attitudes, 361.

Isolation at work, 100, 103, 207, 252, 334. *Also see: Connections, Fear of rejection, Relationship.*
J
Jackson, Rick, 20.
Jayson, Sharon, 379.
Jewett, Sarah Orne, 104.
Job duties re: happiness, 58. *Also see: Assignments, Flow, Tasks.*
Job market or economy re: happiness at work, 53, 58.
Job satisfaction, 10, 21-22, 25, 27, 31, 34, 36-38, 54, 85-93, 103, 183-199, 283-298, 372-382. *Also see: Employee-centered organizations, Employee morale, Employee recruitment and retention, Employee turnover, Employee well-being, Flow, Fulfillment, Meaningful work.*
Job security, 127-134. *Also see Security.*
Job status or position re: happiness at work, 52, 58.
Job stress, 21, 372-382. *Also see: Stress triggers at work.*
Job title re: happiness, 54.
Johncock, Philip, 385.
Jong, Erica, 188.
Journal writing, 149.
Joy alarm, 48-49. *Also see: Joyblocks, Roadblocks to happiness.*
Joy quotient, 1-20.
Joyblocks, 49-50, 69-80, 127. *Also see: Joy alarms, Roadblocks to happiness.*
Judgment:
    As a self-created prison, a roadblock to happiness or problem-solving, 28, 69, 74-78, 91, 118, 141-152.
    Fear-based, 97.
    Negative effects of judging one's self, circumstances, other people, or emotions, 28-29, 32-36, 80, 88, 89-97, 103, 177, 195, 223-259, 304-325. *Also see: Acceptance, Judgment, Self-judgment.*
    Negative judgments by others. *See: Criticism by others.*
    The relationship between blame and judgment, 29.
Jung, Carl, 323, 388.
K
Kabat-Zinn, Jon, 242.
Katz, Lawrence, 383.
Keller, Helen
Kennedy, John F., 202.
Kenyon, Tom, 324, 329, 388.
Kiekegaard, Søren 68.
Kinesthetic modality, 326. *Also see: Neurolinguistic programming.*
Koestner, E.L., 372.
Koch, Richard, 380-381.

Kohn, Alfie, 377.
Koretz, Gene, 378.
Kosenko, R., 382.
Kudo folder
L
Labor shortages, 383-385.
Labyrinth as a tool, 296.
Lack, as a mental framework that blocks happiness, 74-78.
Langbridge, Frederick, 237.
Lantz, Walter and Grace, 144.
Laughter, 10, 86-87, 91, 208, 245, 250-252. *Also see: Creativity, Fun, Humor, Play, Stress management.*
Lawsuits decrease when employees are contented, 48.
Layoff. *See: Downsize.*
Leadership, 372-382. *Also see: Charisma, Management styles.*
Learned helplessness, 184, 185, 191-192, 246. *Also see: Beliefs, Behavior pattern, False self, Illusions.*
Lee Hecht Harrison, 373-374.
Leisure time as related to happiness, 12, 378. *Also see: Stress management, Vacation, Work-life balance.*
Leisure. When leisure is less enjoyable than work, 291.
Lerner, Alan Jay, 50.
Lewicki, P., 387.
Life purpose. Relationship between life purpose and job satisfaction, 31, 54, 88, 143, 194, 368-370. *Also see: Fulfillment, Meaningful work.*
Life satisfaction lags behind economic output and salary increases, 372-382.
Limiting beliefs; limited thinking. *See: Beliefs.*
List of exercises, xviii-xix.
Listening skills, 168.
Locke, E. A., 372.
Love regarding happiness at work, 57, 87, 230.
Lowell, James Russell, 155, 385.
Loyalty:
    Between employees and employers, 128, 131.
    Happy employees are more loyal to an organization or team, 48.
Luciani, Joseph, 227.
Lykken, David, 378.
Lyubormirsky, Sonja, 376.
M
Magical moments. Creating special moments as a tool for happiness, 26, 363.
Mandated change. *See: Change.*
Manage time. *See: Time management.*

Management:
Competency of, 14.
Styles and competency, 13-16, 21, 372-382. *Also see: Autonomy, Employee decision-making input to management, Employee morale, Employee recruitment and retention, Employee well-being, Equal treatment of employees, Fair treatment of employees, Feedback, Flexible schedule, Management competency, Motivation, Professional support.*
Mandated changes, 30, *Also see: Challenge, Change, Confidence is stifled by avoiding challenge.*
Marketability of one's skills, 53, 126-134. *Also see: Economic state.*
Marmot, M., 377.
Marsh, Ann, 298, 387.
Martin, E.P., 382.
Mascaro, Nathan, 387.
Maslow, Abraham, 378.
Massage therapy, 10, 254. *Also see: Body, mind, & spirit; Mood; Relaxation related to productivity; Resiliency; Stress management; Yoga.*
Mastermind group, 131, 249, 252, 276. *Also see: Mentor, Professional support, Training.*
May, Rollo, 127.
McAleavy, Teresa M., 374, 381.
Meadow, H.L., 382.
Meaning. Seeking meaning instead of happiness contributes to happiness, 25-26, 69, 73-78, 85.
Meaningful work:
As a motivational tool, 25.
As a tool for happiness, 5, 7, 10, 13, 19, 22, 25, 31, 42, 45, 50-51, 54-56, 61-68, 74-78, 85-104, 112, 126, 134-135, 139, 141-152, 248-249, 283-298, 309, 344, 346, 348, 372-382, 388. *Also see: Assignments, Contributions, Flow, Fulfillment, Life purpose, Meaning, Priorities, Signature style, Tasks.*
Meditation as a tool for happiness, 10, 100, 124, 149, 250, 252. *Also see: Body, mind, & spirit; Mind power; Mood; Relaxation related to productivity; Stress management; yoga.*
Meetings, required, 13. *Also see: Autonomic nervous system, Autonomy, Control.*
Meir, Golda, 169.
Meltzer, Michael, 373, 376.
Memory enhancement, 343, 350-353, 385, 387-388. *Also see: Inner genius, Mind power, Neural networks, Nonconscious.*
Mental abilities, 38. *Also see: Inner genius, Memory, Self-actualization.*
Mental chatter, 179, 195, 234, 293, 307. *Also see: Internal critic, Internal dialogue, Self-talk.*
Mental imagery, 100, 160, 165, 217-218, 231, 236, 350-353. *Also see:*

Emotional balance, Enthusiasm, Imagination, List of Exercises.
Mental frameworks as behavior modifiers, 159.
Mental structures and frameworks vs. facts as determinants of one's world view, 157-158.
Menter, Marcia, 209.
Mentor, mentoring, 131, 219, 221, 209, 241, 252, 257, 276, 293-297. *Also see: Mastermind group, Professional support, Training.*
Microsoft, 4, 61, 291.
Mill, John Stuart, 135.
Mind as inner sanctuary, 153-154, 159. *Also see: Inner peace.*
Mind is unable to differentiate between fact and fiction (imagination combined with emotion), 336, 338. *Also see: Brain, Mind power.*
Mind map, 304, 343-353, 388.
Mind power, 179, 195, 197, 252, 343-353. *Also see: Body, mind, & spirit; Creativity; Exercise; Humor; Massage; Meditation; Mood; Physical movement; Play; Qi gong; Relaxation related to productivity; Resiliency; Singing; Stress management; Tai chi; Yoga.*
Mind-body, 303-304. *Also see: Body, mind, & spirit.*
Mindfulness, 35, 80, 89, 94-97, 149, 173, 177, 196, 201, 209, 233, 307, 323. *Also see: Awareness, Present moment, Self-awareness.*
Mini-breaks, 220, 251, 254.
Mirror, others as a reflection of one's self, 37, 39, 53, 274.
Mischkind, Louis A., 373,376.
Misperceptions, 26-34, 40-41, 52 ,95, 99, 105-111, 153-168, 227, 237, 267-268, 306, 313, 315, 323, 325, 331, 342, 350, 377, 383-384. *Also see: Beliefs, Blind spots, False self, Illusion, Myths, Perception, Reframe, Self-image, Social conditioning, Social programming, Truth.*
Misperceptions, how the brain resolves conflicts between reality and misperceptions, 105-111. *Also see: Beliefs, Illusions. Social programming.*
Mistakes:
   Dodging mistakes and forfeiting joy on the job, 30. *Also see: Failure.*
   Relationship between mistakes and happiness, 100, 113, 143, 179, 185, 204, 208. *Also see: Failure.*
Mobility of employees, 126-134. *Also see: Employee marketability.*
Modality. *See: Neurolinguistic programming.*
Molecules of Emotion, 175, 177, 386.
Money, as related to happiness, 54, 58, 372-382. *Also see: Motivation, Rewards.*
Money and motivation at work, 54, 372-382. *Also see: Motivation, Rewards.*
Monroe, Marilyn, 312.
Montaigne, Michel Eyques de, 144.
Mood modifiers, 249-259, 293-297. *Also see: Anchoring actions; Body, mind, & spirit; Breathing; Creativity; Curiosity; Diet; Emotions; Exercise; Fun;*

Humor; Laughter; Massage therapy; Meditation; Mind power; Neurolinguistic programming; Physical movement; Play; Positive resource state; Posture; Relaxation; Resiliency; Singing; Stress management; Yoga.
Moore, Jennifer Irene, 267.
Morale. See: Employee morale.
Moses, Grandma, 125, 277.
Motivation:
    Effective motivational strategies, 13, 16, 25, 57, 210, 211-215, 218-220, 283-298, 372-382. *Also see: Compensation, Flexible schedule, Flow, Fulfillment, Meaningful work, Money, Motivate by . . . , Motivate with meaningful work, Perks, Rank, Relationships, Title.*
    Motivate by benefits and persuasion instead of control or fear, 14, 57, 216-218.
    Motivate with meaningful work, 25, 283-298.
    Related to employee rewards, 372.
Motion and physical movement re: stress reduction, mind power, & confidence, 38. *Also see: Body, mind, & spirit; Breathing; Exercise; Massage therapy; Physical movement; Singing; Stress management; Yoga.*
Multisensory approaches and abilities, 38, 100-102, 108, 148, 150, 158, 162, 186, 188, 193, 218, 231-232, 235-236, 253, 293-297, 301, 315-319, 326-341, 343-353, 365, 383. *Also see: Emotions, humans create more by feeling and sensations than thought and create positive changes more by pleasant feelings and sensations than by positive thoughts or words; List of exercises.*
Multitasking, effects of; why some organizations are reducing it, 123, 292, 384.
Music as it contributes to focus, concentration, creativity, relaxation, and peak performance, 296-297. *Also see: Brain entrainment, Singing.*
Myths, 24-34, 41, 57-58, 139. *Also see: Blind spots, Distortion, Illusions, Misperceptions, Perceptions, Social Conditioning, Social Programming, Truth.*
N
National Bureau of Economic Research study, 378-379.
National demonstration project on the effects of meditation, 389.
National Opinion Research Center study, 379.
Nature as a source of healing and happiness, 50, 252.
Needs:
    And preferences, 74-78, 139.
    Feeling comfortable meeting personal needs, 9. *Also see: Employee-centered organizations, Flexible schedule, Professional support.*
    Identify and meet personal needs, 85, 89, 139, 198, 367. *Also see: Employee-centered organizations, Flexible schedule, Needs—feeling comfortable meeting personal needs, Professional support, Unmet needs.*
    Needs versus desires, 4, 5, 72, 74-78, 139.

Negative emotions. *Also see Emotions.*
Ability to express negative emotions and opinions at work, 8.
Acceptance of negative emotions creates positive change and higher states of positive emotions, 169-182.
As part of the human experience, 170-171.
As related to social programming, 96. *Also see: Social conditioning, Social programming.*
Courage combats fear, 95.
Negativity at work as related to feeling others' emotions, 42, 175-176.
Problems caused by denial or suppression, 74.
Safe and constructive expression of negative feelings at work, 169-182
Transform negative emotions into positive emotions, 29, 100, 169-182, 305-342, 350.
Value of negative emotions, 169-172, 181, 230, 233, 237, 253.
Negative experiences as gifts, 29, 169-182. *See: Adversity, Embrace challenges, Setbacks.*
Negative thinking, value of, 170.
Negative thoughts, intentions, beliefs, judgments, and emotions re: happiness at work and personal power, 57, 112-125, 350. *Also see: Behavior patterns, Beliefs, Blind spots, Illusions, Internal critic, Judgment, Mind power, Misperceptions, Negative emotions, Perceptions, Reframe vs. react, Resiliency, Self-judgment, Self-talk.*
Negativity at work, 15, 42, 175-176. *Also see: Negative emotions, Toxic boss, Toxic corporate culture, Workplace negativity.*
Negativity, immunization against, 95.
Negotiating by saying no, 225-226, 249. *Also see: Personal boundaries, Self-care.*
Negotiations, 128, 136-140.
Nervous system, 38, 71, 180. *Also see: Alpha brain wave state, Autonomic nervous system, Emotional balance, Neural networks, Relaxation, Stress management.*
Networking, 129, 249. *Also see: Connections, Mentor, Mastermind.*
Neural networks, circuitry, and pathways:
   Related to happiness at work; associative links; modification of networks and links, 56, 70, 101, 107-108, 112, 150, 157, 165, 178, 181, 208, 215, 217-218, 221, 223, 239, 253, 296, 314, 329-331, 334, 336, 340-341, 343, 350-353, 365, 369-370, 382-383. *Also see: Autonomic nervous system, Breathing, List of Exercises, Stress management.*
   Effects on "reality," 153-168.
Neurolinguistic programming (NLP), 324-341.
Neurological anchor. *See: Emotional anchor, Positive resource state.*
Neuropeptides. *See: Health, Immune system, Molecules of emotion.*
Neutral observation as related to happiness and problem-solving, 118, 120-

121, 141-152, 169-182, 230-232, 271, 293, 305-323. *Also see: Curious Witness.*
Neutral witness. *See: Curious witness, Neutral observation.*
Nin, Anaïs, 105.
Niven, David, 382.
NLP. *See: Neurolinguistlic programming*
Nonconscious mind:
  Nonconscious associative links, 3, 164-165, 367, 385, 387.
  Nonconscious mind as more effective than the conscious mind, 293, 341. *Also see: Conscious mind, limitations of.*
Nondominant hand, value of using, 70.
Nonthreatening work environment, 10. *Also see: Corporate culture, Employee-centered organization, Employee morale, Equal treatment of employees, Fair treatment of employees, Job satisfaction, Management styles, Organizational culture, Organizational health, Work environment.*
Nørretranders, Tor, 385.
O
Oates, Robert M., 389.
O'Malley, Sandy, 168.
Obsessive, speculative worries, 233-234. *Also see: Emotions, Thoughts, Worry.*
Old identity. *See: Identity.*
Olfactory system, benefits and strategies of using direct links to one's emotions (limbic system), 108, 297, 340. *Also see: Mental imagery, Multisensory.*
Online courses, 131. *Also see: Career development, Professional development, Skill development, Training.*
Optimism, 54-55, 144, 168, 172, 237-241, 342, 365, 376. *Also see: Genetic setpoint, Intelligent optimism, Pessimism.*
Organizational athlete, 222.
Organizational culture, 6-17, 89, 127-128, 372-382. *Also see: Corporate culture, Employee morale, Employee recruitment and retention, Employee well-being, Flexible schedule, Organizational culture, Organizational health, Organizational toxicity, Professional support, Work environment.*
Organizational health, 6-17, 19, 53, 127-128, 372-382. *Also see: Corporate culture, Employee-centered organization, Employee morale, Employee recruitment and retention, Employee well-being, Equal treatment of employees, Ergonomics, Fair treatment of employees, Family-friendly organizations, Flexible schedule, Organizational culture, Organizational health, Organizational toxicity, Personal needs, Professional support, Work environment.*
Organizational toxicity, 6-17, 53, 127-128, 372-382. *Also see: Corporate culture, Employee morale, Employee recruitment and retention, Employee*

well-being, Negativity at work, Organizational culture, Organizational health, Toxic boss, Toxic employee.
Oswald, Andrew J., 378.
Oxygenation related to fitness and productivity, 250-251. *Also see: Exercise, Physical fitness, Stress management.*
Outsource, 136-137.
P
Parallel reality, 115, 141, 176, 195, 367-370. *See also: Beliefs, Illusions, Polarities, Priming experiments, Social programming.*
Passion, 32, 47-48, 54, 88, 93, 143, 198, 277, 287, 360, 364-370, 374-375. *Also see: Fulfillment, Meaningful work.*
Patagonia, 291
Patience, 40, 66, 120, 210-211, 255-259, 364.
Patterson, John H., 357.
Patton, General George, 268.
Pay. *See: Salary, Compensation.*
Peace. *See: Inner peace.*
Peak performance, 284-298. *Also see: Flow, Productivity.*
Pension fund, 131-132.
Perceptions:
    Effects of perceptions and misperceptions, 40-41, 153-168, 306-323, 325, 331, 350, 383, 387. *Also see: Blind spots, Illusion, Misperception, Myths, Reframe, Social conditioning, Social programming, Truth.*
    How perceptions affect "reality," 343, 366-367.
    How perceptions affect thoughts and emotions, 157.
    Perceptions directly related to one's beliefs, 155, 366-367.
Perfectionism, perfectionist, 35, 147, 191, 204-212.
Perfection of what exists. *See: Acceptance.*
Performance:
    Enhancement, 91, 123-124, 136, 185-199, 252, 384. *Also see: Flow, Professional support, Self-actualization.*
    Goals, 9, 292. *Also see: Goals, Productivity, Self-actualization.*
    Performance review, 6, 9, 42, 91, 128-134. *Also see: Evaluation, Feedback, Professional support.*
Perks, 54, 58. *Also see: Job status, Rank, Rewards, Status.*
Persistence, 95., 364-367. *Also see: Performance, Self-actualization, Self-responsibility, Willpower.*
Personal assistant (virtual assistant). *See: Curious witness, Virtual assistant.*
Personal boundaries, setting and maintaining, 11, 249, 225-226. *Also see: Negotiations, Self-care, Work-Life balance.*
Personal freedom. *See: Self-actualization.*
Personality, 42. *Also see: Identity, Neurolinguistic programming, Self esteem.*
Personal needs, ability to meet them, 1-20. *Also see: Employee Assistance*

Program, Flexible work schedule, Vacations, Work-life balance.
Personal organization, 125, 214. *Also see: Choice, Clutter, Interruptions, Time management.*
Personal power. *Also see: Autonomic nervous system, Charisma, Confidence, Control, Neural networks, Nervous system, Relaxation, Self-actualization, Self esteem, Stress management.*
  Ability to positively influence situations, 71, 223-259, 313, 357-370.
  As a tool for happiness, 25-29, 32, 42, 71, 87-88, 90-91, 93, 112-134, 148, 152, 355, 357-370.
  How one forfeits personal power, 70-71, 91, 182, 192, 246.
  Myths about, 26-27.
  Why people fear their personal power, 27, 127.
Pert, Candace, 175, 373.
Pessimism, 54-55, 160, 175. *Also see: Genetic setpoint, Intelligent optimism, Optimism.*
Phelps, Elizabeth Stuart, 81
Phobias, 324-342.
Physical environment that promotes well-being, 15. *Also see: Ergonomics, Work environment.*
Physical fitness related to happiness, 198, 250-254. *Also see: Body, mind, & spirit; Exercise; Physical movement; Oxygenation; Stress management.*
Physical movement and positioning related to job satisfaction or triggering a mental shift, 38, 221, 253, 296, 341, 353. *Also see: Body, mind, & spirit; Breathing; Exercise; Mind power; Mood; Motion and physical movement; Relaxation related to productivity; Singing; Stress management; Yoga.*
Physics, 114-115, 122, 253, 368, 389.
Physics, force creates counterforce, 23, 27.
Physiology:
  Affects emotions, 233. *Also see: Biology of belief; Body, mind, & spirit; Neural networks; Neurolinguistic programming; Physical movement.*
  Is affected by thoughts and emotions, 157. *Also see: Biology of beliefs; Body, mind & spirit; Neural networks; Neurolinguistic programming; Physical movement.*
Picasso, Pablo, 104.
Pilzer, Paul Zane, 385.
Play. Playful approaches to work, 10, 43, 47-48, 86-87, 91, 165, 168, 293, 341-342. *Also see: Creativity, Fun, Humor, Laughter, Stress management.*
Pleasure confused with happiness, 49-50, 61-63, 66-67, 151-152, 378.
Poage, William, 47.
Poe, Richard, 372, 374.
Polarities of life and emotions, 141, 176, 230, 242. *Also see: Parallel realities.*
Policies and procedures re: assisting employees to perform their jobs; fair

policies reflecting concern for employees, 9, 12, 19. *Also see: Employee-centered organization, Equal treatment of employees, Fair treatment of employees, Flexible schedule, Organizational culture, Organizational health.*
Position. *See: Perks, Job status.*
Positive affirmations, limitations of, 173.
Positive attitude, 38. *Also see: Emotions.*
Positive affect as it contributes to success-oriented behaviors, including high income, superior performance, and promotions, 376.
Positive emotions:
Alter mental frameworks, 158. *Also see: Choice, Self-responsibility.*
Beneficial effects of, 117-118. *Also see: Choice, Emotions.*
Positive feedback, 42, 58, 67, 372-382. *Also see: Feedback, Professional support, Reinforcement.*
Positive resource state, 42, 90, 217-218, 304, 324-342, 361, 369-370. *Also see: Anchoring actions, Neurological anchor.*
Positive thinking. *Also see: Dispositional optimism, Intelligent optimism, Situational optimism.*
Limitations of positive thinking, 160, 171-172.
Realistic positive thinking, 160.
Positive thoughts, beneficial effects of, 117-118, 125.
Possessions. The relationship between material possessions and happiness, 54-55, 372-382. *Also see: Perks, Rewards, Status.*
Posture, effects on mood and well-being, 114, 226, 331. *Also see: Biology of belief; Body, mind, & spirit; Neural networks; Neurolinguistic programming; Physiology affects emotions.*
Power:
Abuses of, 14. *Also see: Bullying, Difficult people, Equal treatment of employees, Fair treatment of employees, Harassment, Management styles, Toxic boss, Toxic employees, Toxic organizational culture, Victim mentality.*
Personal power, the ability to change one's self and to effect situations and other people. *See: Personal power.*
Power vs. force, 57. *Also see: Force re: attempting to manipulate or control others, Power, the myth . . .*
Powerful people, myths versus reality, 26-27.
The myth that the ability to manipulate or control others creates happiness, 23, 26-27, 39. *Also see: Personal power, Power vs. force.*
Powerlessness:
As an identity, 23, 27, 127, 227, 246, 314.
As a myth, 23, 26-27, 90.
Related to social programming, 192.
Why it does not create unhappiness at work, 26-27, 109. *Also see: Blind spots, Illusions, Social programming.*

Praise for one's work, 61, 66, 88, 372-382. *Also see: Awards, Feedback, Money, Pay, Positive feedback, Professional support, Raise, Recognition, Reinforcement, Salary.*
Prejudice, 109. *Also see: Beliefs, Blind spots, Difficult people, Illusions.*
Present moment (living in the present moment), 80, 89, 149, 173, 177, 201, 209, 238, 240, 307, 323. *Also see: Mindfulness.*
Presentations, enhancing preparation and delivery of, 138-139, 205, 213, 352-353.
Prestige, 55, 379. *Also see: Perks, Possessions, Rank, Status, Title.*
Primary modality. *See: Neurolinguistic programming.*
Priming experiments, 115, 371. *Also see: Beliefs, Illusions, Negative thoughts, Unconscious mind.*
Priorities, prioritizing, 13, 18-20, 201, 212, 215.
Problem-solving, relationship to positive emotions, 181.
Procrastination, 147, 187-188, 191-196, 200-222. *Also see: Action, Challenge, Choice, Insecurities, Prioritizing, Self-sabotage.*
Productive thinking vis-à-vis positive thinking, 172-173.
Productivity:
As related to happiness and financial benefits for both workers and organizations, 4, 48, 51, 133.
Enhancement of, 123, 149, 204-205, 297-298, 306, 352, 372-382. *Also see: Alpha brain wave state, Flow, Fulfillment, Goals, Meaningful work, Peak performance, Performance, Relaxation related to productivity.*
Professional advancement opportunities, 9, 10, 12, 85, 126-134, 276, 372-382. *Also see: Career development, Career ladder, Online courses, Skill development, Training.*
Professional support, 7-16, 19, 42, 85, 88, 90-91, 110, 130, 133, 135-140, 149, 168, 201, 249, 364-368, 372-382. *Also see: Connections, Employee Assistance program, Employee-centered workplace, Ergonomics, Family-friendly organization, Feedback, Flexible schedule, Management styles, Mastermind, Mentoring, Personal needs, Professional advancement opportunities, Relationship, Resources, Support system, Skill Development, Training, Validation, Work environment, Workload.*
Profits, 123. *Also see: Financial benefits of happy employees.*
Promoting one's self. *See: Self-promotion.*
Promotion re: happiness at work, 376, 378-379. *Also see: Positive feedback, Praise, Rewards.*
Promotion; receiving a promotion, 6, 55-56, 58, 61, 63, 66. *Also see: Awards, Raise, Rank, Recognition, Rewards, Status, Title.*
Psychoneuroimmunology, 386. *Also see: Health, Immune system, Molecules of emotion, Neural networks.*
Purpose. *See: Fulfillment, Life purpose, Meaningful work.*

Q
Qi gong, 124, 149, 250.
Quantum physics, 253, 368, 389. *Also see: Physics.*
Questions that empower; the importance of asking questions, 293, 315, 341, 349.
Quitting one's job. *See: Resign.*
R
Raiden, Dean, 389.
Raise (pay raise), 61, 66, 88, 137, 372. *Also see: Awards, Money, Pay, Perks, Positive feedback, Praise, Promotion, Recognition, Reinforcement, Rewards, Salary.*
Rank, 54, 372-382.
Realistic positive thinking; realistic optimism, 160, 172-173.
Raudenbush, B., 384.
Receive, willingness to receive (related to self-esteem), 149.
Recognition, level of recognition, 6, 55-56, 58, 61, 63, 66, 88, 372-382. *Also see: Awards, Job status, Promotion, Praise, Rank, Reinforcement, Rewards, Status, Title.*
Redesign or reinvent one's work, 277-280, 290.
Reframing:
    Dysfunctional beliefs, perceptions, and misperceptions, 26, 196, 211-212, 239-230, 295-296, 305-323, 350.
    Effects on "reality," 343.
    Versus reacting, 143, 153-168, 325, 334, 341.
Reinforcement, 58, 253, 372-382. *Also see: Perks, Positive feedback, Promotion, Status, Rank, Recognition, Reward one's self, Status.*
Reinhold, Barbara B., 377
Rejection, fear of, 32. *Also see: Connection, Fear of rejection, Isolation at work, Relationship.*
Relationship:
    With management, 8, 19, 127-128, 372-382. *Also see: Management styles, Professional support.*
    With one's self as the most dependable support system, 36-37, 88-93, 99-103. *Also see: Confidence, Personal power, Self-actualization, Self-care.*
    With one's self as a shield against workplace negativity, 36-37, 42, 103, 112-113. *Also see: Confidence, Personal power, Self-actualization, Self-care.*
    With coworkers, 8, 19, 51, 88, 139, 207, 372-382. Also *see: Connections, Feedback, Support.*
    Rewarding/positive relationships, 8, 88, 198, 372-382. *Also see: Connections, Feedback, Relationships with coworkers, Relationship with one's self, Support system.*
Relaxation related to productivity, focus, concentration, creativity, and

success; states of being relaxed yet alert, 10, 71, 204-205, 283-298, 327-331, 341. *Also see: Alpha brain wave state; Autonomic nervous system; Control, how one can program their nervous system to relax and feel contented; Exercise; Flow; Meditation; Neural networks; Nervous system; Peak performance; Play; Qi gong; Relaxation; Singing; Stress management; Tai chi; Yoga.*

Reorganization of a company or organization, 127-128, 130, 136.

Repetitive tasks, 66, 71, 359. *Also see: Assignments, Routine tasks, Tasks.*

Repplier, Agnes, 98.

Requesting assistance, 110, 135-140, 184, 201, 220, 252, 293. *Also see: Mentor, Mastermind, Professional support, Support system.*

Resign from a job, 280-281, 372-382, 385. *Also see: Employee recruitment and retention, Employee turnover.*

Resiliency, 30, 51, 53, 71, 143, 153-168. *Also see: Autonomic nervous system; Body, mind, & spirit; Breathing; Confidence; Control; Creativity; Exercise; Fun; Humor; Massage; Meditation; Mood; Mind power; Neural networks; Nervous system; Physical movement; Play; Qi gong; Relaxation; Self-actualization, Self-improvement, Setback, Shadow side; Singing; Stress management; Tai chi; Yoga.*

Resistance to change or life experiences, resistance inhibits positive change, 23, 34, 36, 69, 74-78, 89, 97 120, 154, 170-171, 177-179, 210, 244-247, 258, 306, 311, 325. *Also see: Acceptance, Change, Judgment.*

Resource states, positive emotional states. *See: Positive resource state.*

Resources, adequacy of, 7. *Also see: Management styles, Professional support.*

Respect, receiving respect at work, 6, 8, 12-16, 54, 140, 147, 372, 377-382.

Restructuring:

An organization, 21. *Also see: Downsize.*

A job. *See: Flow, Redesign or reinvent one's job.*

Retirement, 384. *Also see: Employee turnover, Employee recruitment and retention, Resign.*

Retirement benefits that pertain to job satisfaction, 374.

Rewards:

Effects on employee motivation, 372-382. *Also see: Awards, Motivation, Perks, Positive feedback, Praise, Promotion, Recognition, Reinforcement.*

Feeling deserving of receiving rewards. *See: Insecurities, Self-doubt, Self-judgment, Self-sabotage.*

Rewarding one's self, 220, 229, 250, 253, 283-298. *Also see: Self-care.*

Risk taking, taking healthy risks instead of limiting one's self by clinging to the illusion of safety and security, 31, 119, 186-188, 194, 200, 206-207, 209, 277, 330, 337, 345. *Also see: Challenge, Insecurity, Security.*

Roadblocks to happiness, 47-52, 103.

Robert Half Management Resources, 373-374.

Rockefeller, Nelson, 268.
Roosevelt, Eleanor, 186.
Roosevelt, Franklin D., 313.
Routine tasks; transforming routine tasks into a state of flow, 66, 278-280, 293-297. *Also see: Assignments, Repetitive tasks, Tasks.*
Rosen, David H., 387.
Rubin, Manning, 383.
Ryan, R.M., 372.
S
Safety, 31, 147, 206. *Also see: Beliefs, Change, Employee-centered workplace, Illusions, Insecurity, Security, Uncertainty.*
Sagan, Carl, 315.
Saint-Exupéry, Antoine de, 343.
Salary:
   As related to happiness at work, 54, 58, 372-382. *Also see: Compensation, Income, Money, and Pay.*
   Relationship between employee well-being and salary, 381.
Sanders, Harlan, 281.
Schacter, Daniel, 385, 388.
Schedule—work schedule, 7, 9. *Also see: Fair treatment of employees, Flexible schedule, Workload.*
Scheele, Paul, 385, 387.
Schreiner, Olive, 223.
Scott, George C., 342.
Secrecy leading to distrust, 16. *Also see: Management styles, Toxic organizational culture.*
Security:
   As a side effect of healthy risk taking, curiosity, change, challenge, and uncertainty, 30, 91-92. *Also see: Challenge, Challenge, Risk taking, Uncertainty.*
   As an illusion and a trap, 29-31, 77, 119, 206. *Also see: Beliefs, Illusions, Insecurity, Job security, Social programming, Uncertainty.*
   Needs for autonomy, independence, and personal freedom clash with the need for security, 31, 119, 135, 206.
   Peace of mind, self-responsibility, meaning, and fulfillment provide security, 29-31, 127-134. *Also see: Emotions, Fulfillment, Inner peace, Meaningful work, Self-responsibility.*
   The wisdom of insecurity, 91-92, 119. *Also see: Beliefs, Confidence, Illusions, Mandated change, Uncertainty.*
Seeker's syndrome, 69, 71-73.
Self esteem, 64, 66-67, 144-152, 179, 181, 185, 208, 252, 260-282, 284, 314, 324-342. *Also see: Confidence, Self-actualization, Self-responsibility.*
Self-acceptance, 98-104, 152, 171-172, 179, 204, 206, 208-210, 237-238.

Also see: Acceptance, Self-actualization.

Self-actualization, 24-43, 38, 53, 66-67, 91-93, 95-96, 98-111, 137, 144, 171-172, 183-199, 206, 210-212, 237, 260-282, 312, 323-342, 357-370, 378. *Also see: Body, mind, & spirit; Breathing; Challenge; Change; Confidence; Creativity; Exercise; Flow; Fun; Humor; Mandated change; Meditation; Mind power; Mood; Physical movement; Play; Relaxation; Resiliency; Security; Self-awareness; Self-improvement; Self-responsibility; Skill development, Stress management; Yoga.*

Self-awareness:
  As a key to happiness at work, 66-67, 112-125, 144, 209-210, 222, 227, 233.
  As a key to spontaneous change, 35, 191, 223-259. *Also see: Awareness, Mindfulness.*
  As it contributes to positive change, 35, 98-104, 305-323. *Also see: Awareness, Inner peace, Mindfulness.*

Self-care, 11, 91, 136, 168, 210, 225-226, 249-254. *Also see: Confidence, Personal boundaries, Self-actualization, Self-responsibility, Work-life balance.*

Self-doubt. *See: Insecurities.*

Self-expression, 14, 47. *Also see: Confidence, Emotions, Feedback.*

Self-image, 96, 98-103. *Also see: False self, Illusions, Misperceptions, Social programming, Self-actualization, True self.*

Self-improvement, 33, 38, 66-67, 98. *Also see: Act; Body, mind, & spirit; Career development; Confidence; Creativity; Exercise; Flow; Fun; Humor; Meditation; Mind power; Mood; Physical movement; Play; Professional development opportunities; Relaxation; Resiliency; Self-actualization; Singing; Skill development; Stress management; Yoga.*

Self-judgment, 28, 29, 32, 95-97, 99-100, 171, 179, 185-186, 201, 204, 208, 210-212, 222, 245, 304, 305, 309-310, 345. *Also see: Acceptance, Insecurity, Judgment.*

Self-judgment, immunization against, 95. *Also see: Acceptance, Self-respect.*

Self promotion, 66-67, 110, 133, 139, 280-281.

Self-respect as a dependable support system, 37. *Also see: Personal power, Relationship with one's self, Self-actualization.*

Self-responsibility, freedom associated with, 25-26, 53, 90, 126-140, 171, 178, 180, 183, 305-323, 357-370. *Also see: Accountability, Self-actualization.*

Self-sabotage, 79, 147, 152, 159, 206-207, 210, 227, 286.

Self-talk, 153-168,195, 203-204 206, 208-213, 217-218, 220-222, 254, 286, 293, 313-314, 341, 351. *Also see: Internal critic, Internal dialogue.*

Selfish software, 51-52. Also see: Altruism.

Seligman, Martin, 196, 378, 381-382, 386.

Seneca, 200.

Sensitivity, feeling others' emotions, 175-176.
Sensory channels, use of multiple senses to foster well-being. *See: Autonomic nervous system, Emotional balance, Multisensory, Neural networks.*
Serotonin, 252, 297. *Also see: Emotional balance, Autonomic nervous system, Neural networks.*
Serve, being of service at work. *See: Contribute, Strengths, Talents.*
Setbacks, turning setbacks into opportunities, 51, 130, 141-152, 153-168, 206, 238-259, 307, 342. *Also see: Adversity, Resilience.*
Setpoint for happiness. *See: Genetic setpoint.*
Shadow side. Strategies for honoring and working with unfavorable human characteristics as tools for personal growth and resiliency, 30, 36-37, 171-172, 179. *Also see: Resistance, Resiliency, Self-acceptance.*
Shakespeare, William, 323.
Shame, 32. *Also see: Emotions.*
Sheerin, John B., 62.
Sheldrake, Rupert, 56, 382.
Signature style, 26, 66, 278-280.
Simplifying lifestyle, effects on happiness, 372-382.
Singing for stress reduction, 10, 251. *Also see: Body, mind, & spirit; Creativity, Flow; Fun; Humor; Mind power; Mood; Physical movement; Play; Qi gong; Relaxation; Resiliency; Stress management; Tai chi; Yoga.*
Sirgy, M.J., 382.
Sirota Consulting, 372, 374-375.
Sirota, David, 373, 376.
Situational optimism, 160, 365.
Skill development opportunities, 9, 10, 12, 16, 85, 128-131, 249, 276. *Also see: Career development, Career ladder, Employee-centered workplace, Employee recruitment and retention, Professional advancement opportunities, Self-responsibility, Strengths, Training.*
Sleep quality re: well-being, 11, 149, 253. *Also see: Stress management, Work-life balance.*
Smith, Haston, 324
Smith, Tom, 379.
Social conditioning, 41, 50-52, 79, 90, 96, 116, 291. *Also see: Blind spots, Illusion, Misperceptions, Myth, Social Programming, Truth.*
Social costs of unhappy employees, 375.
Social programming that encourages unhappiness or fear, 26, 96, 109, 116, 192, 309, 314. *Also see: Beliefs, Illusions, Myths, Priming experiments, Social conditioning.*
Social class issues regarding life satisfaction and income, 378.
Social trends. Negative social trends have outweighed economic advances, 378-379, 382.

Socrates, 264.
Solitude related to well-being, 252.
Sources of happiness at work—internal and external; short and long term, 54-68.
Spinoza, Baruch, 277.
Spirituality at work, 54, 98, 135, 194, 198, 249, 287, 368-370. *Also see: Acceptance; Accountability; Act; Alpha brain wave state; Anchoring actions; Appreciation; Attitude; Autonomic nervous system; Autonomy; Beliefs; Behavior patterns; Body, mind, & spirit; Breathing; Career development; Change; Challenge; Choice; Compassion; Connections; Contributions; Control; Creativity; Curiosity; Curious witness; Detachment; Embrace challenges; Emotions; Exercise; Flow; Fulfillment; Fun; Goals; Gratitude; Happiness; Humor; Inner genius; Inner peace; Integrity; Intelligent optimism; Intuition; Laughter; Life purpose; Magic moments; Mind power; Mindfulness; Mood; Music; Nature; Negotiation; Neural networks; Neutral observation; Passion; Patience; Persistence; Personal boundaries; Physical fitness; Physical movement; Play; Positive resource state; Positive thinking; Present moment; Reframing; Relationship; Relaxation; Requesting assistance; Resiliency; Risk taking; Self-acceptance; Self-actualization; Self-awareness; Self-care; Self-respect; Self-responsibility; Skill development; Solitude; Strengths; Situational optimism; Support system; Talents; Thoughts; Trust; Values, Willpower; Win-win solutions; Work-life balance.*
St. Augustine, 126, 249.
St. Francis of Assisi, 214.
State of the job market or economy re: happiness at work, 53-54.
Status (social status) as related to happiness, 52, 54, 58, 362, 366-369. *Also see: Position, Perks, Possessions, Rank.*
Stone, W. Clement, 153-154.
Storytelling as a tool to reframe mental frames, 158. *Also see: Image streaming, Imagination, Mental imagery, Perceptions, Reframing, Stream-of-consciousness thinking.*
Stream-of-consciousness thinking, 219. *Also see: Imagination, Mental imagery, Image streaming.*
Strengths:
  Having one's unique strengths appreciated at work, 6. *Also see: Contributions, Talents, Validation.*
  Identifying one's strengths so one can capitalize on them, 37, 132.
  Using personal strengths as a tool for happiness, 6, 88, 93, 98, 110, 113, 132, 135, 136, 143, 162, 173, 240, 342. *Also see: Contributions, Self-actualization, Validation.*
Steptoe, A., 364.
Stress:
  Management of, 10, 12, 38, 51-52, 86, 89, 91,101, 123, 150, 151, 160,

201, 204, 221-222, 215-216, 225-226, 247, 249-259, 271, 294-298, 314-315, 323-342, 368-370, 382. *Also see: Acceptance; Act; Alpha brain wave state; Anchoring actions; Appreciation; Autonomic nervous system; Autonomy; Body, mind, & spirit; Breathing; Change; Challenge; Choice; Compassion; Connections; Contributions; Control; Creativity, Curious witness; Curiosity; Detachment; Embrace challenge; Emotions; Exercise; Flow; Fulfillment; Fun; Goals; Gratitude; Happiness; Humor; Immune system; Inner genius; Inner peace; Integrity; Intelligent optimism; Intuition; Laughter; Life purpose; Magic moments; Massage; Meditation; Mind power; Mindfulness; Mood; Music; Nature; Negotiation; Nervous system; Neural networks, Neutral observation; Passion; Patience; Persistence; Personal boundaries; Physical fitness; Physical movement; Play; Positive resource state; Positive thinking; Present moment; Professional support; Qi gong; Reframing; Relationship; Relaxation; Requesting assistance; Resiliency; Risk taking; Self-acceptance; Self-actualization; Self-awareness; Self-care; Self-respect; Self-responsibility; Singing; Situational optimism; Skill development; Solitude; Strengths; Stretching; Support system; Tai chi; Talents; Thoughts; Trust; Values, Willpower; Win-win solutions; Work-life balance; Yoga.*
Stress related to technology, 21, 22, 123, 362.
Stress triggers at work, 21, 253, 372-382. *Also see: Job stress.*
Stretching as related to stress reduction, 252-254. *Also see: Body, mind, & spirit; Exercise; Physical fitness; Physical movement; Oxygenate; Stress management; Tai chi; Yoga.*
Strindberg, August, 113.
Struggle; self-imposed struggle, 34, 74-78, 182. *Also see Acceptance, Embrace challenge.*
Subconscious mind, power and effects of, 74-75 115-116, 121-122, 328, 350, 353. *Also see: Unconscious mind.*
Success:
As a result of living with integrity, 104. *Also see: Integrity, Values.*
As related to focus and happiness at work, 4, 120, 125, 146, 185-186, 193, 201, 204, 206, 209, 212, 372, 376.
Support system, 42, 85, 88, 90-91, 110, 130, 133, 135-140, 149, 168, 216, 220-221, 249, 252, 364-368. *Also see: Connections, Feedback, Management styles, Mentor, Mastermind, Professional advancement opportunities, Professional support, Relationships, Skill Development, Training.*
Svensson, Peter, 379, 382.
T
Tai chi, 124, 149, 250.
Talents, personal talents re: creating happiness, 21, 26, 42, 88, 135, 240, 365, 368-370. *Also see: Contributions, Strengths.*

Tardiness decreases when employees are happy, 48.
Tasks, meaningful and aligned with employee interests, abilities, and achievable skill level, 7, 22, 287-293, 295. *Also see: Assignments, Flow, Meaningful work, Priorities, Workload, Work Schedule.*
Task-specific job contracts vs. long-term contracts, 128.
Teamwork:
  Positive teamwork affects job satisfaction, 377.
  Strategies for enhancing teamwork; communication with team members, 13, 139, 288, 290, 292, 333.
  Teamwork improves when employees are happy, 13, 48, 51-52, 382.
Tech stress (stress related to technology), 21, 22, 123, 375. *Also see: Stress management.*
Technical skills, 38. *Also see: Skill development.*
Tegmark, Max, 384, 386.
The Conference Board, 373, 384-385.
The Dalai Lama, 375.
The 80/20 Principle, 380-381.
The Monks of New Skete, 73, 383.
Thomas, David, 366, 389.
Theta brain wave state, 296, 298.
Thoreau, Henry David, 303, 319.
Thoughts:
  How choice relates to control over one's life, 119, 196. *Also see: Attitude, Choice, Mind power, Positive thinking, Situational optimism.*
  How thoughts affect physiology, emotions, and "reality," 112-125, 153-168.
  Mastery of thoughts; choices that lead to happiness, 25, 120.
  Thought prayers, 146,159.
Time management, 7, 86, 124, 200-202, 225-226, 258. *Also see: Choice, Interruptions, Personal organization.*
Toxic work situations:
  Boss, 6-16, 21-22. *Also see: Blame, Bullying, Difficult people, Harassment, Management styles, Mirror, Negativity at work, Organizational culture, Personal power, Work environment.*
  Employees, 6-16, 22. *Also see: Blame, Bullying, Connections, Difficult people, Harassment, Mirror, Negativity at work, Organizational culture, Personal power, Relationship.*
  Organizational culture, 6-16, 21-22, 58, 73. *Also see: Blame, Bullying, Difficult people, Harassment, Negativity at work, Organizational culture.*
  Work environment, 6-16, 22, 73. *Also see: Blame, Bullying, Difficult people, Harassment, Negativity at work, Organizational culture.*
Toyota, 291.
Training. *See: Career development, Career ladder, Professional advancement opportunities, Skill development opportunities, Strengths.*

Tranquility. *See: Emotional Balance, Inner Peace.*
True Self, 99-102, 191, 277, 307, 342, 364, 370. *Also see: Beliefs,
False self, Illusions, Misperceptions, Self esteem, Self-acceptance, Self-
awareness, Self-image, Social conditioning, Social programming, Truth.*
Trust:
  Of coworkers, 8.
  Of management and the organization, 9, 13-14, 16,19, 378.
  Of self, 319-322.
  Of life, 35, 53, 56, 74-78, 87, 89-91, 119, 141-152, 172, 174, 199, 232,
  238, 244-249, 304, 319-322.
Truth, 41, 153-168. *Also see: Beliefs, Blind spots False self, Illusions,
Misperceptions, Myths, Perceptions, Self-image, True self.*
Turkel, Studs, 49.
Turner, Steven, 171.
Turnover. *See: Employee turnover.*
Twain, Mark, 54.
U
U.S. Bureau of Labor Statistics, 82, 109, 132, 383-385.
Uhl, Bill, 222.
Uncertainty, 127-128. *Also see: Change, Insecurity, Security.*
Unconscious mind. *Also see: Addictions to unhappiness, Behavior patterns,
Beliefs, Illusions, Mind power, Misperceptions, Myths, Perceptions, Social
conditioning, Social programming, Subconscious mind, Thoughts, Truth.*
  Unconscious addictions and motivations; unconscious choices to be
  unhappy, 50-51, 79, 201, 207, 212, 252, 231-233.
  Unconscious beliefs, assumptions, behaviors, and thoughts that affect
  happiness, 105-111, 148, 155, 165, 252, 231-233, 313, 333, 357-370.
  Unconscious mind, power and effects of, 74-75, 115-116, 121-122, 385,
  387-388.
Unfair work practices or policies, including pay inequities, 372-382. *Also see:
Policies.*
Unhappiness at work, prevalency of, 21-22, 372-382.
University of Warwick study, 382.
Unmet employee needs related to workplace happiness and to negative
behaviors, 1-20, 24, 39, 42, 135-140, 198, 372-382. *Also see: Bullying,
Conflict between what employees want and need and management's
perceptions, Employee-centered organizations, Employee morale, Employee
recruitment and retention, Employee turnover, Employee well-being, Equal
treatment of employees, Fair treatment of employees, Family-friendly
workplaces, Flexible schedules, Fulfillment, Harassment, Job satisfaction,
Management styles, Motivation, Work-life balance, Work schedule.*
V
Vacations, 12, 378. *Also see: Leisure, Stress management, Work-life*

balance.
Validation:
At work, 6, 8, 12, 19, 42, 45, 53, 126-134, 378.
Internal sources of, 65-67, 127-133.
Value of:
Healthy risks. *See: Healthy risks.*
Value of negative emotions. *See: Emotions, Negative emotions.*
Value, being valued at work. *See: Awards, Praise, Promotion, Recognition, Reinforcement, Rewards, Validation.*
Values, living one's values at work as a key to happiness, 68, 85, 88, 103-104, 126, 194, 380. *Also see: Integrity, Self-responsibility.*
Victim mentality, 28, 126, 146, 152, 242, 245-246. *Also see: Blame.*
Vilaythong, Alexander P., 387.
Violence at work, 375. *Also see: Angry workers, Bullying, Civility, Conflict resolution, Harassment, Hostility, Workplace violence.*
Virtual assistant, 305-323. Visual perceptions, 105-111. *Also see: Illusions, Multisensory, Myths, Neurolinguistic programming, Perceptions.*
Visual modality. *See: Neurolinguistic programming.*
Volunteer, volunteering. *See: Contribute, Mentoring, Strengths, Talents.*
W
Waiting for reasons to be happy (as a joyblock), 69-71.
Ward, Yvette, 376.
Wardle, J., 377.
Weaknesses as strengths, 30.
Weaknesses, management of, 260-268, 292.
Weissberg, Peter, 377.
Weiten, Wayne, 377.
Well-being, relationship between employee well being and salary, 381-382.
Wenger, Win, 268, 381, 385, 387.
Whole-body, 90, 303-304. *Also see: Body, mind, & spirit, Mind-body, Whole-brain.*
Whole-brain, 90, 303-304. *Also see: Body, mind, & spirit, Mind-body, Whole-body.*
Willpower, 56. *Also see: Performance, Persistence, Self- actualization, Self-responsibility.*
Win-Win solutions, 27, 98, 136-138, 184, 367. *Also see: Connections, Relationships.*
Winfrey, Oprah, 21, 28.
Wolfe, Fred Alan, 384, 386.
Work in America Task Force report, 376-377.
Work and Family Connection, 374.
Work as play, 25-26.

Work environment—nonthreatening, healthy, ergonomic, shielded from negativity, enjoyable versus toxic, etc. 10, 15, 19, 21, 195. *Also see: Employee-centered organizations, Employee well-being, Equal treatment of employees, Ergonomics, Fair treatment of employees, Family-friendly organizations, Flexible schedule, Organizational health, Management Styles.*

Work-life balance, p 11-12, 19, 21, 52, 86, 88, 91, 127, 197, 374, 378, 380-382. *Also see: Employee-centered organizations, Employee well-being, Fair treatment of employees, Family-friendly organizations, Flexible schedule, Organizational health, Management Styles, Personal boundaries, Priorities.*

Work schedule. *Also see: Assignments, Priorities, Tasks, Workload.*

Workload, 7, 18-19, 21, 94, 112-113, 136, 372-381. *Also see: Assignments, Priorities, Tasks, Work-life balance, Work schedule.*

Workplace negativity and how to shield from it, 15, 36, 37, 42, 73, 372-382. *Also see: Bullying, Conflict resolution, Connections, Difficult people, Harassment, Misperceptions, Negativity at work, Policies, Professional support system, Reframing, Relationships, Support system, Toxic boss, Toxic organizational culture, Toxic workplace, Workplace violence.*

Workplace violence, 375. *Also see: Bullying, Harassment, Toxic boss, Toxic employees, Violence.*

Worry:

    As optional, 116, 231-236, 251. *Also see: Autonomic nervous system, Choice, Emotions, Situational optimist, Thoughts.*

    Constructive worry, 231-236. *Also see: Autonomic nervous system; Body, mind, & spirit; Control; Emotional balance; Emotions; Fear; Intelligent optimism; Neural networks; Obsessive, speculative worries.*

    Obsessive, speculative worries, 233-234. Also see: Emotions, Thoughts.

    The power of, 116. *Also see: Emotions, Fear, Priming experiments.*

Y

Yoga, 10, 124, 250.

Z

Zelcovitch, Morry, 296.

ABOUT THE AUTHOR

by Robin Lane
A proud *Joy on the Job Seminar* participant

Dr. Doris Helge is called *The Joy Coach* for very good reasons. As a participant in her *Joy on the Job Seminars*, I can verify that her audiences rave, "She's the speaker who adds sizzle to an average work day. Now our jobs feed our hunger for happiness instead of just putting food on the table."

Participants in Doris' keynotes and seminars discover their inner genius. She describes this as our innate ability to nurture our soul at work while we elevate our performance in ways that make us grin with delight. We convert tedious tasks into enjoyable activities. We develop a *Signature Style* that's great fun. Teamwork is easier because conflict is rare. Less stress = more productity. I love Doris' *Create Time* technique. Now I have more time and energy for my professional and my personal life.

I've seen massive positive changes in job satisfaction reported by burger flippers, corporate executives, and all kinds of positions in between. The results were dramatic and they continued from one seminar to the next.

In addition to being a visionary and an inspiring leader regarding happiness at work, Doris has a unique ability to entertain us while we're learning. We roar with laughter while we devour every gold nugget of wisdom she shares with us. Doris uses the most advanced multisensory teaching techniques I've ever seen. We don't have to endure ho-hum PowerPoint presentations! Doris' innovative style stimulates long-term memory. She jazzes us with her passion and enthusiasm, and we spontaneously make a powerful commitment to progressive change.

Doris is truly a master teacher and speaker. She has addressed thousands of employees and managers across the U.S. and Canada. Doris actively engages *everyone* in her audiences, even when thousands of people attend a single event. It's not surprising that she has won awards for her writing and speaking abilities.

Can she understand and identify with your unique challenges? You be the judge. I first met Doris after she gave a keynote address for a national conference for occupational health personnel. A spontaneous after-hours event made me decide to become a *Joy on the Job Seminar* participant.

Attendees from a variety of positions and industries quizzed Doris for two hours. We couldn't fathom why she seemed to understand our specific jobs since she had never performed them. She listened attentively to everyone. She wasn't "being nice." She sincerely wanted to help us gain more job satisfaction.

I was so amazed when she described the types and dates of her previous work experience that I scribbled down her answers. Unless you're a fighter pilot or an astronaut, Doris has walked paths similar to yours. She has been a retail clerk, secretary, fundraiser, educator, and a customer service troubleshooter. She's been a coach, grantwriter, caseworker, volunteer, and parent. She's even been downsized! She directed a nonprofit organization. She sold ads for a journal, worked for a temporary services agency, coordinated national conferences, and has been a professor at three different universities. She's been a researcher, counselor, editor, freelance writer, and executive director of two national membership associations. Whew!

This incredibly diverse background prepared Doris to be the awesome author and speaker she is today as well as a consultant to all sizes of organizations.

Can you trust Doris' statements that meaningful, fulfilling work can be more important than a steady paycheck? Her associates once gasped in disbelief when she made an extraordinarily difficult decision that resulted in temporary unemployment while she built a new career. Doris turned down a grant funded at over $500,000. It would have landed her a cushy job for three years. Why did she do this? "There was no challenge. If I had accepted the grant, I'd have been doing more of what I'd already done. I didn't want to grow stale floating on a raft that was secured to a sturdy dock in a stagnant pond. An occasional Class 5 whitewater kyak trip makes my Spirit soar. If I don't challenge myself, I'll never know who I could have been."

Like most of you, I've heard hundreds of speakers and read lots of books. Doris is different. She is a brilliant role model for her message. Her example inspires others like you and I to meet our full potential.

Doris is currently Executive Director of New Paradigm Seminars. She is also a frequent guest on television and radio programs such as CNN, The Today Show, and NPR. Some of her books have been printed in multiple languages with worldwide distribution.

Although Doris is now internationally known for her expertise, she overcame many very difficult personal and professional hurdles, some of which I wouldn't wish on my worst enemy. Doris has lived on both sides of the track. She has experienced both poverty and plenty.

Doris is absolutely convinced that the times she was forced to hobble up steep trails strewn with jagged rocks for days, weeks, and sometimes years were her most important training experiences. Each journey prepared her to help people like you and I gain more joy and fulfillment.

Serving humanity as an author and speaker is Doris' bliss. She genuinely cares about our well-being. You should see how radiant her face is when the "Aha's" and smiles illuminate her audiences. Doris was born for this job, and you and I get to benefit from her date with destiny.

She specializes in no-cost ways to boost employee satisfaction, performance, and creativity, so you don't have to wait until your organization becomes as concerned with your happiness as you are. You owe it to yourself to discover your bliss. Your journey to joy can be much faster and easier than you may think. Use Doris' techniques on your own today. You will immediately have more fun at work.

Check out some of her other books and e-books. Unlike some authors who recycle the same message, each of Doris' books contributes to your well-being in a unique way.

Take full advantage of the opportunity you gave yourself when you bought *Joy on the Job*. When the original seminar participants, including myself, tested Doris' materials, we envisioned the http://www.JoyontheJob.info web site as a resource for decades to come. Visit the site often. Download scads of free, helpful articles. Topics are frequently updated, and the articles are filled with wonderful content and strategies that will help you call in the happiness at work you deserve. While you're at the web site, sign up for Doris' popular, free e-zine, *Joy on the Job.*

You are now part of a very special global community of employees and managers. We are all helping each other experience more joy at work. There are thousands of us, so you're never alone when times are tough. Share your successes and request solutions to your dilemmas.

I look forward to meeting you at the web site.

BRING DORIS HELGE, PH.D.
TO YOUR ORGANIZATION!

Doris Helge, Ph.D., has delivered thousands of presentations and training seminars to employees and managers at organizations as diverse as Regence BlueShield, the American College of Occupational and Environmental Health, Royal Bounty International, Bristol-Myers Squibb, Exxon-Mobil, the National Athletic Trainers Association, the University of Texas, the American Association of Occupational Health Nurses, and Vanderbilt University.

Doris' dynamic presentations are packed with proven strategies based on over ten years of research that included interviews with managers and employees of 21 diverse companies and associations.

Her work is guaranteed to enhance leadership and elevate productivity, employee morale, and motivation. Because Doris is a master trainer, her audiences laugh while they learn the latest ways to improve performance and job satisfaction. Participants immediately use the new tools she teaches because she uses accelerated multisensory learning strategies that generate excitement and follow through.

Managers and employees explore innovative methods to easily resolve conflicts and improve communication. Doris prepares them to thrive during times of intense challenge and change. Leaders discover bold new ways to unlock their own peak potential, so they spontaneously motivate employees. Thorny diversity issues transform into organizational strengths. Harmony replaces the dysfunctional "difficult people syndrome," so customer service improves remarkably. Work becomes much more fun and fulfilling for everyone.

If you want remarkable results from a professional speaker you will love to work with, contact Dr. Helge about a keynote speech, *Joy on the Job Seminar*, or consulting.

E-mail: Doris@joyonthejob.info or visit her website at http://www.joyonthejob.info and download her printer-friendly brochure. You can also view a sample video of a presentation on the website and download lots of great articles you'll immediately use to create a more enjoyable work site and work force.

FOR INDIVIDUAL OR GROUP COACHING

Individual or group coaching kicks in where *Joy on the Job* leaves off. To apply for coaching regarding happiness at work, e-mail Doris@joyonthejob.info

SIGN UP FOR YOUR FREE E-ZINE!

Would you like to receive a steady supply of the latest and greatest ways to increase happiness at work?

Subscribe to Doris' free e-zine, *Joy on the Job,* by visiting http://www.joyonthejob.info. Just click on the *Free Joy on the Job Newsletter* link. Enjoy fresh new ideas every month that you'll easily use to substantially increase your happiness.

You were born
with the right
to be happy!

The following books will help you discover peace, joy, and personal fulfillment. Order your copies today!

Joy on the Job
Over 365 Ways to Create
the Joy and Fulfillment You Deserve

Transforming Pain Into Power
Making the Most of Your Emotions

TO ORDER ONLINE, go to:
http://www.amazon.com
or
http://www.joyonthejob.info

For additional information concerning these books or the author's availability for speaking engagements, contact shimodapub@ mindspring.com or Doris@joyonthejob.info

DISTRIBUTOR INQUIRIES AND BULK ORDERS

Discounts are available for bulk purchases of these books for resale, educational purposes, gifts, or fund raising. For information, please contact our Special Sales Department by e-mail:

shimodapub@mindspring.com